Posthuman Space in Samuel Beckett's Short Prose

Other Becketts

Published
Creative Involution: Bergson, Beckett, Deleuze
S. E. Gontarski

Beckett's Thing: Painting and Theatre
David Lloyd

Samuel Beckett and the Terror of Literature
Christopher Langlois

Samuel Beckett's How It Is: *Philosophy in Translation*
Anthony Cordingley

Posthuman Space in Samuel Beckett's Short Prose
Jonathan Boulter

www.edinburghuniversitypress.com/series/ORBT

Posthuman Space in Samuel Beckett's Short Prose

Jonathan Boulter

EDINBURGH
University Press

Edinburgh University Press is one of the leading university presses in the UK. We publish academic books and journals in our selected subject areas across the humanities and social sciences, combining cutting-edge scholarship with high editorial and production values to produce academic works of lasting importance. For more information visit our website: edinburghuniversitypress.com

© Jonathan Boulter, 2019, 2020

Edinburgh University Press Ltd
The Tun – Holyrood Road
12(2f) Jackson's Entry
Edinburgh EH8 8PJ

First published in hardback by Edinburgh University Press 2019

Typeset in 11/13 Adobe Sabon by
IDSUK (DataConnection) Ltd

A CIP record for this book is available from the British Library

ISBN 978 1 4744 3025 8 (hardback)
ISBN 9781474430265 (paperback)
ISBN 978 1 4744 3027 2 (webready PDF)
ISBN 978 1 4744 3028 9 (epub)

The right of Jonathan Boulter to be identified as the author of this work has been asserted in accordance with the Copyright, Designs and Patents Act 1988, and the Copyright and Related Rights Regulations 2003 (SI No. 2498).

Contents

	Series Editor's Preface	vi
	Acknowledgements	vii
	List of Abbreviations	viii
	Introduction: Beckett, Heidegger, the World	1
1	Homelessness: *The Expelled, The Calmative, The End*	38
2	The Poverty of World: *Texts for Nothing*	67
3	Spaces of Ruin: *All Strange Away, Imagination Dead Imagine, The Lost Ones, Ping, Lessness*	96
4	Space and Trauma: *Fizzles*	129
5	Fables of Posthuman Space: *Company, Ill Seen Ill Said, Worstward Ho*	155
	Conclusion: 'neither'	197
	References	208
	Index	217

Series Editor's Preface

In 1997 Apple computers launched an advertising campaign (in print and on television) that entreated us to 'Think Different', and Samuel Beckett was one of Apple's icons. Avoiding Apple's solecism, we might modify the appeal to say that *Other Becketts* is a call to think differently as well, in this case about Beckett's work, to question, that is, even the questions we ask about it. *Other Becketts*, then, is a series of monographs focused on alternative, unexplored, or under-explored approaches to the work of Samuel Beckett, not a call for novelty per se, but a call to examine afresh those of Beckett's interests that were more arcane than mainstream, interests that might be deemed quirky or strange, and those of his works less thoroughly explored critically and theoretically, the late prose and drama, say, or even the poetry or criticism. Volumes might cover (but are not restricted to) any of the following: unusual illnesses or neurological disorders (the 'duck foot, goose foot' of *First Love*, akathisia or the invented duck's disease or panpygoptosis of Miss Dew in *Murphy*, proprioception, or its disturbance, in *Not I*, perhaps, or other unusual neurological lapses among Beckett's creatures, from Watt to the Listener of *That Time*); mathematical peculiarities (irrational numbers, factorials, Fibonacci numbers or sequences, or non-Euclidian approaches to geometry); linguistic failures (from Nominalism to Mauthner, say); citations of or allusions to contrarian aesthetic philosophers working in a more or less irrationalist tradition (Nietzsche, Bergson, or Deleuze, among others), or in general 'the simple games that time plays with space'. Alternative approaches would be of interest as well, with foci on objects, animals, cognitive or memory issues, and the like.

S. E. Gontarski, Florida State University

Acknowledgements

This book would not have been written without the support of Stanley Gontarski. I thank him for his interest in this particular project and for his own indispensable work on Samuel Beckett, both critical and editorial.

I dedicate this book, as always, to Mitra Foroutan.

Abbreviations

Works by Samuel Beckett

CSP   *The Complete Short Prose: 1929–1989*, ed. S. E. Gontarski, New York: Grove Press, 1995.

F   *Fizzles*, New York: Grove Press, 1976.

NO   *Nohow On: Company, Ill Seen Ill Said, Worstward Ho*, New York: Grove Press, 1996.

Works by Martin Heidegger

AWP   'The Age of the World Picture', trans. Jerome Veith, Bloomington: Indiana University Press, 2009.

BDT   'Building Dwelling Thinking', in *Martin Heidegger: Basic Writings*, ed. David Farrell Krell, San Francisco: Harper, 1977, 319–39.

BT   *Being and Time*, trans. John Macquarrie and Edward Robinson, New York: Harper, 1962.

FCM   *The Fundamental Concepts of Metaphysics: World, Finitude, Solitude*, trans. William McNeill and Nicholas Walker, Bloomington: Indiana University Press, 1995.

LOH   'Letter on Humanism', in *Martin Heidegger: Basic Writings*, ed. David Farrell Krell, San Francisco: Harper, 1977, 189–242.

OWA   'The Origin of the Work of Art', in *Martin Heidegger: Basic Writings*, ed. David Farrell Krell, San Francisco: Harper, 1977, 149–87.

Introduction: Beckett, Heidegger, the World

What counts is to be in the world, the posture is immaterial, so long as one is on earth.

(Texts for Nothing 4)

Long live all our phantoms.

(Texts for Nothing 5)

Overview

The term 'posthumanism' has only relatively recently come to be deployed in readings of Samuel Beckett's work.[1] In retrospect this fact is curious given that Beckett's worlds – in his prose and drama – are replete with signs of the human subject having passed over to other planes of existence, or non-existence, being, or non-being. Critics and readers of Beckett have, of course, noticed the presence of the spectre and the ghost in the work, have had to grapple with finding a way to make sense of what Beckett is offering in these images of haunting. But it is only recently that critics and readers have begun to think about the spectre or the ghost in specific relation to the idea of the posthuman, a category that moves our understanding of Beckett's subject beyond what are assimilable, because still metaphysical, categories (the afterlife, limbo, hell). The category of the posthuman, for my purposes in this analysis, is one that allows me to think about Beckett's subject in relation to a plurality of philosophical ideas: being, ontology, community, ecology, space, and spatiality. That is to say, the posthuman is a concept that demands that we view the subject, first and foremost, as an emerging complexity, an event of being that challenges our conception of what, in fact, it means to be. Beckett's subject, I will argue, thematises the event of being, thematises the emergence of states of subjectivity not easily comprehensible but utterly crucial for our conception of the relation between being and space, between the human and his world. Moreover, to understand Beckett's posthuman subject is not to understand a theoretical subject position (the posthuman as future event) but to acknowledge that the posthuman is always already present in the human, *as* the human (or even, as we will discover, that the human persists in the posthuman, haunting it, if only as a trace). Beckett is not, thus, dismantling the subject, transforming or killing it, in his prose. His work, rather, is a *critique* of the subject in the true sense of the term: an analysis of the component elements of the human, an attempt to understand its context (ecological or social), an attempt to come to terms with the complexities of the subject's place in the world.[2] What is remarkable about this critique are its implications. The subject, for Beckett, is always already post-catastrophic, already inhabits spaces of ruin, always is in search of impossible sites of refuge; the subject, in other words, bears the marks of disaster even as the world he inhabits itself is disastrous. To understand Beckett's subject means therefore that we need to trace the dimensions of a critique that itself begins by positing the intimate and catastrophic relation between subject and space, between self and world: 'what counts is to be in the world, the posture is immaterial, so long as one is on earth'.

Part of my purpose here in *Posthuman Space* is to give an account of the genealogy of the posthuman in Beckett's short prose. I will be analysing the short prose that Beckett produced prior to and after his monumental *The Unnamable* (1953), a text that initiated Beckett's deconstruction of the human subject. *The Unnamable* is narrated by a subject without a fully realised body, who inhabits no identifiable space or time, who is, perhaps, dead. My argument is that Beckett, in his short prose, is continuing his exploration of the idea of the *posthuman subject*: the subject who is beyond the category of the human (the human understood as embodied, as historically and spatially located, as possessing some degree of subjective continuity). What we find in the short prose (my analysis begins with three novellas Beckett produced in 1945–6, *The Expelled, The Calmative, The End*) is Beckett's sustained fascination with the idea of the possibility of being *beyond* the human. We will encounter characters who can claim to be dead

(*The Calmative*, *Texts for Nothing*); who inhabit uncanny, perhaps even post-apocalyptic spaces (*All Strange Away* [1963–4], *Imagination Dead Imagine* [1965], *Lessness* [1969], *Fizzles* [1973–5]); who are unaccountably trapped in what appears to be some kind of afterlife (*The Lost Ones* [1966, 1970]); who, in fact, may even defy even the philosophical category of the *post*human (*Ill Seen Ill Said* [1981], *Worstward Ho* [1983]).

And yet despite the radical dismantling of the idea of the human, as such, the being that emerges in these texts is still – perhaps even insistently – spatially, geographically, even ecologically located: the posthuman subject still finds itself placed within material, phenomenological spaces. I am attempting here to come to some understanding of what it means for the posthuman to *be* in the world, and, as a general point of departure, what I will need to account for is the way in which the posthuman subject emerges within space, is perhaps *defined* by its relation to space, 'on earth'. For the Beckettian posthuman subject, *to be* means to be located, to be on earth, to exist (if this is indeed the term) within an ecological network of connections to spectral, perhaps post-apocalyptic spaces, spaces that uncannily, and impossibly, maintain the discontinuous traces of what may, or may not, be life.

Beckett's Posthuman

I wish in what follows to offer a set of ideas and a series of images that will operate as entry points into the various spaces of Beckett's posthuman world. I wish to offer an image of the posthuman, and a set of ideas that this image carries with it, in order to suggest ways in which Beckett's posthuman subject is a continuation of and departure from ideas of the posthuman developed in his prose prior to and contemporaneously with the short prose. My approach here is necessarily idiosyncratic and the image of the posthuman I wish to offer is, perhaps, an eccentric one. But we must admit, at the outset, that determining an image of the posthuman or devising a definition of what it means to be posthuman, in a general sense, is a difficult one, given the variety of approaches, theoretical and philosophical, to the concept itself. Despite this difficulty, it is, I think, safe to offer this idea to begin: posthumanism operates as a critique of the idea of the traditionally conceived humanist subject, the subject as transparent to itself, as self-aware, as possessed of a knowing and knowable mind, as being an ontological as well as a physically bounded unity. Theories of the posthuman may, and will, vary; there are indeed differences between the conception(s) of the posthuman in the work of, for instance, Haraway, Hayles, Wolfe, Latour, Deleuze and Guattari, Blanchot, and Derrida. But we can see that every theory of the posthuman shares a basic ground: the idea of the human has changed. It is not my intention here to provide a totalising genealogy of the posthuman; nor indeed is it my intention to review and rehearse all available theories of the posthuman; these would be tasks beyond the scope and possibility of this project. My intention here, rather, is to place Beckett's posthuman – that is, my understanding of what I am calling Beckett's posthuman – in relation to those theories of the posthuman with which his idea harmonises and diverges. Specifically, I am interested in placing Beckett's conception of the posthuman in dialogue with Hayles, Haraway, Blanchot, and Derrida, in order to tease out what I believe is an immanent and thus not fully acknowledged aspect of the theory of the posthuman: the posthuman, as Beckett instantiates it, and as these major thinkers may, or may not, theorise it, is what I will call *a spatially oriented emergent entity*. The posthuman in Beckett emerges – becomes itself – within space and is conceived as having an intimate relation to real space; space, in other words, defines the limits and boundaries of the Beckettian posthuman. Space, to be more precise, is the definitional threshold of and for the posthuman, whether it is the open space of fields or the closed space of the grave in *Texts for Nothing*; the uncanny interiorising spaces of enclosure in *Imagination Dead Imagine*, *All Strange Away*, or *The Lost Ones*; the ruined, traumatised landscapes of *Lessness* or *Fizzles*; or the spectral trajectories through what can be called the non-spaces of the late trilogy. Beckett's posthuman emerges from and is defined within space, within a spatially instantiated world, that provides a threshold and a limit to itself as a body, to itself as a trajective being, to that which defines itself in relation to a *here* and a *there*: to be an entity in this world, in other words, is to emerge as a localisable and located being.

What can we learn from the major theorists of the posthuman that will enable us to understand Beckett's figure of the posthuman? As I have said, all begin with the idea that the posthuman is a challenge to, if not a critique of, the idea of the liberal humanist subject. Katherine Hayles is explicit about this in *How We Became Posthuman*; here she rehearses what is essentially the orthodox reading of the posthuman:

First, the posthuman view privileges informational pattern over material instantiation, so that embodiment in a biological substrate is seen as an accident of history rather than an inevitability of life. Second, the posthuman view considers consciousness, regarded as the seat of human identity in the Western tradition long before Descartes thought he was a mind thinking, as an epiphenomenon, as an evolutionary upstart trying to claim that it is the whole show when in actuality it is only a minor sideshow. Third, the posthuman view thinks of the body as the original prosthesis we all learn to manipulate, so that extending or replacing the body with other prostheses becomes a continuation of a process that began before we were born. Fourth, and most important, by these and other means, the posthuman view configures human being so that it can be seamlessly articulated with intelligent machines. (2)

What Hayles offers here is crucial for an understanding of the posthuman as it emerges from cybernetics and informational and systems theory: the posthuman subject is what she calls 'an informational-material entity' (11) whose consciousness, or subjectivity, is no longer confined to a single location. Hayles' major contribution to the understanding of the posthuman, and an idea that influences my reading of Beckett's posthuman, is the notion of 'distributed cognition' (ix). Cognition (we might call this consciousness or subjectivity) is distributed in the sense that, for the posthuman in its cyborged and cybernetic instantiation, cognition may come from elsewhere and may find itself placed anywhere. Hayles asks us to consider the figure of the cyborg in popular culture to illustrate her point:

> Consider the six-million-dollar man, a paradigmatic citizen of the posthuman regime. As his name implies, the parts of the self are indeed owned, but they are owned precisely because they were purchased, not because ownership is a natural condition preexisting market relations. Similarly, the presumption that there is an agency, desire, or will belonging to the self and clearly distinguished from the 'wills of others'[3] is undercut in the posthuman, for the posthuman's collective heterogeneous quality implies a distributed cognition located in disparate parts that may be in only tenuous communication with one another. We have only to recall Robocop's memory flashes that interfere with his programmed directives to understand how the distributed cognition of the posthuman complicates individual agency. If 'human essence is freedom from the wills of others', the posthuman is 'post' not because it is necessarily unfree but because there is no a priori way to identity a self-will that can be clearly distinguished from an other-will. (3–4)

It is clear that Beckett's version of the posthuman is not the cybernetic/cyborg version that Hayles explores in her own work. The Beckettian posthuman is not a confluence of body and machine, and is not precisely an informational-material entity. Indeed, the Beckettian posthuman seems, at one level at least, to have done away with the body entirely. In *Texts for Nothing*, for instance, the narrator asks:

> What can have become then of the tissues I was, I can see them no more, feel them no more, flaunting and fluttering all about and inside me, pah they must be still on their old prowl somewhere, passing themselves off as me. (*CSP* 124)

However, while it is clear that the narrator is not a cyborg, his sense of his self is, perhaps, not far removed from Hayles' understanding of Robocop: the narrator here has lost touch with his body, his tissues, but they still haunt him, as he says of his eyes: 'The eyes, yes, if these memories are mine, I must have believed in them an instant, believed it was me I saw there dimly in the depths of their glades' (*CSP* 124). And indeed it is the question of the narrator's memory, whether it is his or not, that links him most explicitly to Hayles' model of the posthuman: his memory has been distributed, placed elsewhere, or, as in Text 8, disappeared entirely: 'till suddenly I was here, all memory gone' (*CSP* 132). With Beckett's posthuman it is always a question of the subject's essential condition changing, altering, or allowing itself to be read otherwise; if the posthuman subject still retains the body (without memory), that body is elsewhere, distributed to another consciousness, another being, as in Text 11: 'no, I'm not in the open, I'm under the ground, or in my body somewhere, or in another body' (*CSP* 144–5). But the narrator will offer this image only soon to retract it – 'Vile words to make me believe I'm here, and that I have a head' (*CSP* 145) – making it impossible for the reader to locate the being of the posthuman subject. If, in other words, Hayles offers an image of distributed cognition, that cognition is refracted from and to an identifiable entity: the material body of the cyborg, Robocop, or the Six Million Dollar Man. In Beckett, the body, as such, is not locatable as a body; or, perhaps most accurately – and here we anticipate Derrida's notion of the hauntological subject – the body is there and not there, simultaneously.

Beckett's posthuman, as we have seen and as we will see further, is constructed as a confusion of boundaries: body/not body; present consciousness/absent consciousness; located mind/dislocated mind. And again, while Beckett's posthuman is not a cyborg, is not the informational-material subject of Hayles, it still retains a genealogical filiation to that cyborg. What links Hayles' model of the cyborg/cybernetic posthuman to Beckett's figure of the dislocated posthuman is, of course, this idea of location. While Hayles never fully interrogates her own idea of distribution as a spatial metaphor, it is critical to notice how her model of consciousness is an explicitly spatialised one.[4] What defines the cybernetic posthuman, what *grounds* the cybernetic posthuman, is the distance between what we may call its nodes of consciousness or subjectivity: distributed cognition means that cognition itself, though perhaps directed by a governing authority (the police state in *Robocop*; the military-industrial complex in *The Six Million Dollar Man*), defies the authority of single spaces: to be a cybernetic consciousness, in other words, requires that consciousness to blur boundaries of space (and not of course to speak of time): consciousness *is*, in other words, insofar as it extends spatial boundaries.[5] And while Beckett's texts may not work overtly to define what cognition, consciousness, or subjectivity are (he is, as he will himself claim, not a philosopher), his work performs the idea – and thus perhaps we can call this idea an a priori – that subjectivity emerges insofar as it extends into space, insofar as it itself is distributed across space.

As I say, Beckett's posthuman is not explicitly a cybernetic entity, is not a cyborg, but it does share a genealogical or homological relation to these entities. And as we turn to the (still) most important reading of the figure of the cyborg – Donna Haraway's 'A Manifesto for Cyborgs' – we should attend to how Haraway's cyborg is, again, defined in specific and precise relation to an idea of space, real or, in this case, radically and politically idealised. Haraway's 'A Manifesto for Cyborgs', certainly one of the most well-known expressions of posthuman thought, is, in essence, an ecstatic celebration of the possibility of the cyborg. The cyborg (and I am suggesting we read the cyborg as a version of the posthuman even though the term 'posthuman' is not used in the essay) is for Haraway a figure of possibility; specifically, the cyborg is a utopian figure of the collapse of normative and restrictive regimes of power.[6] Haraway's cyborg, specifically, is a figure of liberation from patriarchal discourse which has sought to limit the possibility of the feminine; as such, given that the regimes of patriarchal power have not been, nor perhaps ever will be, overthrown, the figure of the cyborg is by definition a figure of imaginative possibility: 'A cyborg is a cybernetic organism, a hybrid of machine and organism, a creature of social reality as well as a creature of fiction' ('A Cyborg Manifesto' 149). The cyborg, in other words, in this real world *now*, is always already a figure for that which is *to come*: it is to come in every act of imagination that posits a space of resistance. This resistance is effected, or performed, by a radical confusion of boundaries; the cyborg instantiates itself as a deconstruction of the boundaries between nature and culture, between flesh and machine, between the human and the non-human animal. What emerges in the cyborg, and *for* the cyborg, is the possibility of what Haraway calls 'permanently partial identities and contradictory standpoints' (154). Given that the cyborg deliberately, consciously, perhaps even perversely (151) dismantles traditional binaries and hierarchies, what is left for the cyborg – and again we must keep in mind that Haraway insists that the cyborg is a utopian creature – is a field, or space, of becoming: the identity, the subject position, of the cyborg is partial and contradictory.[7]

Two aspects of Haraway's thought here fascinate me and lead into a link to Beckett's version of the posthuman. The first is Haraway's insistence that the cyborg is both real and imaginary, a social reality and a creature of fiction; the cyborg shimmers, almost spectrally, between the real and the non-real, the real and the imaginary, between absence and presence. I say 'almost' spectrally because the cyborg, insofar as it has yet to come into being, has had no ontology to pass off, or through, no ontology to cast away: the cyborg never lives and thus cannot assert a full claim to spectrality. Yet, the spectre, as Derrida reminds us, is always already a figure of that which is to come; the cyborg, the posthuman, as it is a figure of the imagination, emerges in Haraway as a work of messianic fantasy, a futural fantasy of non-humanist being. It is not only my intention to suggest that Haraway's cyborg and Beckett's posthuman subject are structurally analogous because they are both spectral; what is more important to me is the possibility of reading Haraway's and Beckett's posthuman both as expressions of a kind of fantasy. Haraway offers her cyborg as a figure of hope for a future beyond humanism; the question for a reading of Beckett's posthuman becomes: what is the fantasy at work in his figure of the posthuman? When, for instance, Hugh Kenner describes *Texts for Nothing* as thirteen 'fantasies of non-being' (*A Reader's Guide* 119), what fantasy is being enacted? What fantasy, Kenner should be asking more exactly, is being enacted if the subject is both of the world and removed from it? Both alive and dead?

I will, of course, offer an extended answer to this question in Chapter 2, but we might, just at the outset, suggest that Beckett's posthuman, like Haraway's cyborg, operates as a fantasy of moving beyond limitations and boundaries, limits and boundaries both material and purely conceptual. This is to say that both Beckett's posthuman and Haraway's cyborg instantiate themselves (or are instantiated) as figures of a necessary *spatiality*. I have suggested that one critical term in Haraway's fantasy is 'utopia': she uses the word 'utopian' twice in the early pages of her work, indicating that the cyborg is an act of imagination. The myth of the cyborg, she writes,

> is an effort to contribute to socialist-feminist culture and theory in a postmodernist, non-naturalist mode and in the utopian tradition of imagining a world without gender, which is perhaps a world without genesis, but maybe also a world without end. The cyborg incarnation is outside salvation history. ('A Cyborg Manifesto' 150)

Haraway is insistent that her task is to imagine a world; this is a utopian project, one that takes place nowhere, because it cannot yet be instantiated. But the figure of the cyborg is still granted a world, is granted a space: this is the space of margins (176) and boundaries (161), but it is still a space. Beckett's spaces too are utopian: if they exist for the narrator (say of *Texts for Nothing*), they can be easily read as only ever projected fantasies of space; if they exist for the reader – and we are called upon by the narrator to imagine these worlds as being real enough to support the narrator in his compromised being – these spaces are difficult to locate. The narrators of these texts will, for instance, offer a space only immediately to retract its viability: 'deep in this place which is not one' (*CSP* 147); the narrator, further, exists in an 'infinite here' (*CSP* 123), an idea which defies conventional comprehension. Beckett's spaces, thus, like Haraway's utopian spaces, are ones that cannot be located, cannot be realised or understood; and as such, as expressions of fantasy, these spaces emerge as spaces of a kind of endless possibility, of endless becoming, where the imagination can dictate, within limits, the possibilities of its own existence or non-existence, can itself define what is meant 'by here, and me, and being' (*CSP* 101).

Hayles and Haraway offer us two critical ideas with which to begin to make sense of Beckett's figure of the posthuman. The first is Hayles' notion of distributed cognition: the subjectivity of the subject, as Blanchot will put it (and to whom I will turn presently), is not locatable in a unique space or single entity; from Haraway we are offered the idea of the posthuman, the cyborg, as a creature of fiction, fantasy, and imagination, a creature who has yet to arrive, who inhabits the space of utopia, even as she emerges into a kind of hard, material reality. I am fascinated by how useful Haraway's notion of the cyborg utopia is for an understanding of Beckett's posthuman: she offers us a way of beginning to comprehend the strange temporal-spatial nature of the posthuman, the fact of its being *here*, inhabiting space, and its being *yet to come*. As I suggested above, the cyborg, as it unfolds in Haraway's thought, takes on a critical spectral quality given its status as a thing of fiction. I wonder thus if it is possible to place Haraway's model of the cyborg alongside Derrida's revenant in *Specters of Marx* in order to tease out some further elements in Beckett's image of the posthuman. Because Derrida surely does offer an image of the spectre that immediately resonates with the Beckettian posthuman's uncannily *present* spectrality. Here I am drawing on Derrida's insistence, in his reading of Marx's thought, that the spectre is never only pure spirit, pure ephemerality. Derrida insists that the spectre has an uncannily bodily quality:

> the specter is a paradoxical incorporation, the becoming-body, a certain phenomenal and carnal form of the spirit. It becomes, rather, some 'thing' that remains difficult to name: neither soul nor body, and both one and the other. For it is flesh and phenomenality that give to the spirit its spectral apparition, but which disappear right away in the apparition, in the very coming of the *revenant* or the return of the specter. (*Specters of Marx* 6)

> For there is no ghost, there is never any becoming-specter of the spirit without at least an appearance of flesh, in the space of invisible visibility, like the dis-appearing of an apparition. For there to be ghost, there must be a return to the body, but to a body that is more abstract than ever. (126)

Derrida's reading of the phenomenology of the spectre is very useful for our reading of the quality of the posthuman's being in Beckett's work, both early (as, for instance, *Texts for Nothing*) and late (as, for instance, *Worstward Ho*). For surely what defines the spectral quality of the posthuman in these texts is its paradoxical quality of being there and not being there; of being alive and not-alive; of being in the world and not in the world. The narrator of Text 1 can speak of giving himself 'up for dead all over the place' (*CSP* 103) but still seemingly move within the phenomenal world, just as he can speak, as we have seen, of there being 'no flesh anywhere, nor any way to die' (*CSP* 113); he can speak of being 'dead and kicking above, somewhere in Europe' (*CSP* 133), just as he can say 'I am dead, but I never lived' (*CSP* 147). In works following *Texts for Nothing* there is a strange return to bodies, of bodies that now seem to reside in, or inhabit, or haunt – perhaps this can be the only correct term – spaces of ruin; but these spaces, like Derrida's revenants, are spaces at once spectral and material. We have the uncanny container of *The Lost Ones*, the confining space of the rotunda in *Imagination Dead Imagine*: these are spaces that seem real, seem material, yet seem to threaten to slide inexorably into the economy of allegory. These are spaces, therefore, that compel critical questions: are these spaces in fact real? If so, what are the conditions of their existence? How did they come into being? And yet in these spaces of confinement and ruin, as, for instance, in the 'true refuge' of the ruins in *Lessness*, we are, again, given bodies, but bodies as close to being 'corpsed' (to use Clov's word in *Endgame*) as possible: 'Grey face two pale blue little body heart beating only upright' (*Lessness* 197). If the Derridean spectre contains, or is contained by, a paradoxical quality of presence and absence – 'this non-object, this non-present present, this *being-there* of an absent or departed one' (*Specters of Marx* 6, emphasis mine), as Derrida writes – then the Beckettian spectre, the Beckettian posthuman, is also defined by this essential condition of self-present effacement. The spectre is situated as body, and not as body; the spectre is situated in a place, but not in place; the spectre is of the world, even as its very presence seems to call that world into absolute question, *as world*: 'Say a body. Where none. No mind. Where none. That at least. A place. Where none. For the body. To be in' (*Worstward Ho* 89).

It is of course the nature of this *being-there* that I am concerned with in this analysis. Derrida's deployment of this phrase, a translation of Heidegger's notion of Dasein – being-there – draws attention, again, to the particularly spatial quality of the spectre, to the posthuman. The posthuman is located, even in its non-locality; it is 'in the world', as Beckett puts it, even as it stands outside of the world; it is a body (in the world) even as it is not a body. How are we to make sense of this distributed thing? Of this thing that resides in space and does not? That is and is not? While I am comfortable with characterising Beckett's posthuman as a species of the spectre – in *Worstward Ho* Beckett will refer to the posthuman subject as a 'shade with the other shades' (*NO* 97) – I am not completely convinced that this figure can be thought of as *only* a spectre, as only a partial remainder or partial object of the human that once was. My disquiet here has to do with the immanent metaphysics of the idea of the spectre, its link to the idea of spirit, of afterlives, of what is, essentially, a tradition of humanist spirituality, a tradition that, as a whole, Beckett's work would seem to critique strongly.[8] Perhaps it is simplest for me to say this: the Beckettian posthuman shares the structure of the spectre – absent presences, immaterial bodies – but without the metaphysics. Beckett is not, I would suggest, asking us to read his short prose as allegories of limbo or hell (or heaven); he is not asking us to fold his image of the spectre into some ultimately comforting, because comprehensible and assimilable, notion of the ghost as trace of the human. Beckett's *pos*t*human* is a radical critique of the very *idea* of the integrated, metaphysical subject as it has been figured within philosophy and theology. Beckett's posthuman asks us, ultimately, to consider the idea of *spectre without spirit*.

To ease us into this image – spectre without spirit – I want to take a turn into Blanchot and to examine a phrase that occurs in *The Writing of the Disaster*: '*subjectivity without any subject*' (30). I have measured the resonances of this phrase in relation to Beckett's posthumanism in previous work, specifically in my reading of the figure of the unnamable.[9] I find myself returning to the phrase because it offers a way of understanding the separation of self from affect in the Beckettian posthuman subject (and in this way, perhaps, Blanchot's phrase anticipates Hayles' notion of distributed cognition); it offers us a way of understanding the posthuman subject as a post-catastrophic, or post-traumatised, subject (a crucial idea for our reading of especially *Lessness* and *Fizzles*); finally, it offers us a way of grounding the posthuman

Introduction   13

subject within the *spatialised* terrain of catastrophe. I am drawn to Blanchot's idea, thus, because in it we find a conflation of all of the ideas that we have encountered to this point. Let me quote the passage in full:

> Levinas speaks of the subjectivity of the subject. If one wishes to use this word – why? but why not? – one ought perhaps to speak of a *subjectivity without any subject*: the wounded space, the hurt of the dying, the already dead body which no one could ever own, or ever say of it, *I, my body*. This is the body animated solely by mortal desire: the desire of dying – desire that dies and does not thereby subside. (*The Writing of the Disaster* 30)

Blanchot situates his idea in relation to Levinas whose work, as we know, requires a subject against which self can define itself. Levinas' notion of ethics – itself spatialised in the sense that the encounter between self and other is always a situated one, always takes place in space – is grounded on the idea that subjectivity, the capacity to recognise the self in specific relation to the Other, the capacity that is, to recognise a regime in which concepts of 'self' and 'other', still obtains.[10] Blanchot, as is clear, is interested in pursuing the idea that subjectivity, the capacity to recognise the self as self, may yet operate without a grounding in a localisable subject, or self. My reading of this phrase, *subjectivity without any subject*, begins with the idea that we have here the component elements of the self (these have yet to be eradicated) but these elements, for reasons we may intuit, have been *dislocated*: the subject, once the anchor, habitat, or refuge (to use Beckett's word) for the self's sense of itself, has been lost, has vanished, has been erased; or, more exactly, the viability of subjectivity *as a refuge of self* has been lost. What remains, thus, are exactly that: the remains of the self without its body, the habitat. This is a space where there is a disjunction between some version of the agential self and the I, which Blanchot, as we see, equates with the body: '*I, my body*'. But this is a body that, although dead, is still animated by desire. And we can already perhaps see how this idea resonates with the idea of the spectre: because Blanchot's notion of subjectivity without any subject is not one that, yet, entirely does away with the body (and we recall Derrida's insistence that the spectre has an uncannily bodily presence). Blanchot's notion of subjectivity without any subject, like the posthuman figure that emerges in Beckett, is a strangely bodily spectre and one, as we see especially in *Texts for Nothing*, that is still animated by desire and compulsion. And yet, these desires play out within what Blanchot calls a 'wounded space'; or, perhaps more exactly, this complex, this affect, this conjunction of subjectivity without any subject, *itself* emerges as a kind of traumatised space (the word trauma – *blessée* in the original French – means 'wound', of course). My interest here is in Blanchot's suggestion that this emergence of subjectivity without any subject – which for me is a way of naming the posthuman – is an emergence of a spatialised ontology: when the subject loses its subjectivity, when the self is dispersed, distributed (in Hayles' terms) into various competing regimes (of space, of memory), when the self is separated from itself to the point that only an affect of the self remains with no absolute grounding in the singularity of the body, then we enter into the space of the wound. That is to say, the idea of subjectivity without any body, as I read it, names a spatial, or spatialising, affect: this is an affect produced not necessarily only when a distinction between subjectivity and subject is announced. Subjectivity conjoined (impossibly?) with a lost subject can, it seems – for Blanchot, for Beckett – only emerge within a *space* of loss, a *space* of trauma, a *space* of catastrophe.

The Beckettian posthuman, as I argue throughout this study, is one that emerges in specific relation to space, material or imagined; space, at some profoundly paradoxical level, is the ground upon which the Beckettian posthuman is instantiated. Perhaps another way of saying this, and a way of introducing an entry into Heidegger, is to suggest that the Beckettian subject is *spatialised*, is realised in relation to its space, its place, its geography. We may, after Derrida in *Specters of Marx*, refer to the being of the Beckettian spatialised posthuman as an *ontopology*: 'By ontopology we mean an axiomatics linking indissociably the ontological value of present-being [*on*] to its *situation*, to the stable and presentable determination of a locality, the *topos* of territory, native soil, city, body in general' (82).[11] Of course our task here, if we read the Beckettian subject ontopologically, is made profoundly complicated by ascribing any 'stability' to its sense of locality as such: 'say ground', the narrator of *Worstward Ho* will put it, 'No ground but say ground' (*NO* 90). Beckett's posthuman may emerge ontopologically, but that being – that sense of being compelled 'on' – is immediately and unavoidably called into question as the ground for that being recedes or vanishes altogether. And yet we return, and more than once, to the uncanny persistence of space and thus being: ground *is* said, the ground for spectral being *is* announced, despite being retracted as a possibility; world *is* posited as a *topos*, a place where being, however compromised, however *disastrously compromised*, is given: 'what counts is to be in the world, the posture is immaterial, so long as one is one earth' (*CSP* 116).

Posthuman Space/the World: Beckett and Heidegger

Ce qui compte c'est d'etre au monde, peu importe la posture, du moment qu'on est sur terre.

What counts is to be in the world, the posture is immaterial, so long as one is on earth.

(*Texts for Nothing* 4)

This book is an extended meditation on the various resonances of this sentence from *Texts for Nothing* 4. It is an attempt to make sense of what the narrator here means by being in the world (*d'etre au monde*). What exactly does *world* mean here? What does *posture* mean here? Is the idea of *posture* a metaphor?[12] A philosophical position? (Should the word 'posture' remind us of the phenomenological question 'how does it stand towards me?'?) Should the word *immaterial* be taken as a literal reference to the immateriality of the body and its posture? Or is it simply a word meaning 'not important', as the French original suggests: 'peu importe la posture'? Most important for me are the questions and fascinating complications that arise when we gauge the idea of being in the world with the ontological, perhaps ontopological, reality of the Beckettian subject in the short prose. How are we to make sense of the relation between a subject that seems, at the very least, to be deeply compromised as an ontological entity – he is here/not here; alive/dead; singular/distributed; exists in time/and in an 'infinite here' – and the idea of world? How, in short, can a subject as deeply compromised as the Beckettian posthuman assert the reality of a world, the reality of an earth, the reality of *being* itself? What can the idea of 'world' mean to a subject who appears to have moved into a material, even ecological, space that is, simply, beyond categories of life and death, being and world?[13]

My philosophical inspiration for thinking through the ideas of world, space, earth, and even place here is the work of Martin

Heidegger, especially *Being and Time*, *The Fundamental Concepts of Metaphysics*, 'The Origin of the Work of Art', and 'Building Dwelling Thinking'.[14] I am drawing inspiration from Heidegger's early and later work because, as Jeff Malpas and others have argued, Heidegger's thinking about space, place, world, and earth unfolds and complicates itself over the course of his career.[15] My own reading of Beckett is indebted to the variety of ideas that Heidegger offers to us, from his early thinking about the spatiality of being in *Being and Time*; to the central assertion in *The Fundamental Concepts of Metaphysics* that man is world-making, the animal is poor in world, and the stone is worldless (an idea that grounds my reading of *Texts for Nothing*); to his idea that world is defined as a sheltering agent to the subject; and to his idea in 'Building Dwelling Thinking' that space, as such, is a boundary against which the subject emerges to itself, *as* a self. Perhaps it is simplest to say, at the outset, that what drives my interest here is the commonality of thinking that I see between Beckett and Heidegger: for both, being emerges as an experience of space, of spatiality. In Beckett, being 'in' the world and being 'on' the earth are phrases that assert the positionality of the subject, the positionality of the subject in space; Heidegger's version of this idea, in compressed form, is an even more urgent assertion of the relation between being and space: 'the "subject" (Dasein), if well understood ontologically, is spatial' (*BT* 146).

While I will argue here that Heidegger's notions of being, world, space, and even animality are useful frames through which to begin a reading of Beckett, it is clear that a pairing of Beckett and Heidegger is, at times, uncomfortable; but, as I will attempt to demonstrate throughout the book, this pairing is *critically* uncomfortable. In addition to examining the commonalities that exist between the philosophy of Heidegger and the narrative practice of Beckett, what I hope will emerge over the course of *Posthuman Space* is a reading of Beckett's figure of the posthuman that, importantly, is also a strong critique of Heidegger's understanding of being in relation to the human subject. And while I am convinced that a reading of Beckett with, or against, Heidegger is useful, on its own, as a way of making sense of both writers – and this is a task having an a priori value – there is, crucially, also some evidence that Beckett had more than a passing familiarity with Heidegger's work, as both Shane Weller and Rodney Sharkey have recently argued.[16] Indeed

Beckett's work may have been informed by a nascent phenomenology, if not Heideggerianism, via his important relationship with Jean Beaufret, a student and scholar of Heidegger. But the pairing of Beckett and Heidegger, as I say, is a critically *uncomfortable* one, for obvious reasons. It may strike some as odd that the philosopher who embraced the figure of the Führer and (some) tenets of National Socialism is used to read Beckett, an author whose work, however ruthless in its tracing of a diminished humanity, can be read at one level as a (compromised) celebration of the persistence of the human even into its posthumanity (a posthumanity that is read often as a figure of nostalgia for a lost, and true, humanism). While it is not my intention here to speak about Heidegger's Nazism,[17] I do wish to suggest that Beckett's work can, indeed should, be read as a critique of the full implications of Nazi thought. In one sense, and in brief, the figure of the homeless and dispossessed that appears in Beckett (in this study, especially in *The Expelled*, *The Calmative*, *The End*, and *Texts for Nothing*), as it moves into the world and as it assumes a position of posthuman animality – that figure, according to Heidegger himself, who 'both has and does not have world' (*FCM* 199) – stands, *even and especially in its liminality*, as a defiant *claimant* of the world.[18] As a species of what Agamben calls bare life, or the *homo sacer*, the Beckettian posthuman claims the world, and its immovable place within the world, even as it is dispossessed. The Beckettian posthuman, in other words, is always already a figure enmeshed in the world, whose presence (however compromised) is an insistent one. And it is this insistent, defiant presence that stands, if only weakly, opposed to National Socialist fetishisations of absolute strength and quasi-metaphysical links to blood, soil, and world. Heidegger embraces the diseased logic of National Socialist thought, but his own work, as I will demonstrate via a reading of Beckett's (which now becomes uncannily politicised), plants the seeds of a critique of that logic with one image: the compromised human, now linked to the animal who is poor in world but still inevitably *of* the world, who cannot, will not, be effaced.

In what follows I will be speaking of the relation between the posthuman subject and space. This discussion, of course, presupposes some conception of the idea of space as such and thus I need to take a few moments at the outset to stake out my territory. I draw my primary inspiration here from the work of geographer David Harvey, who has spent his career thinking through the implications of a seemingly very simple question: what is space? As Harvey suggests, and as anyone who has ever tried seriously to answer this question knows, defining space is no easy task. We all, I think, intuitively know what we mean by the term, but as we attempt clearly to theorise and conceptualise the idea things get complex. Is space material? Is space simply that emptiness bound by, say, walls, floors, ceiling? Does space have an absolute and fixed value or ontology?

In *Cosmopolitanism and the Geographies of Freedom* Harvey provides a useful outline of the various possible conceptions of space, all of which pertain to what follows in my analysis of the experience (and event) of space in Beckett. As Harvey sees it there are three traditional views and definitions of space that operate interchangeably and at times simultaneously in any theorisation (or experience) of space: absolute, relative, and relational. Inspired by Henri Lefebvre's work (primarily from *The Production of Space*) Harvey suggests we need to attend to space as it is 'materially sensed, conceptualized and lived' (*Cosmopolitanism* 134). Here then are the traditional views. *Absolute space*, as Harvey writes,

> is fixed and immovable. This is the space of Newton and Descartes. Space is understood as a preexisting, immovable, continuous, and unchanging framework (most easily visualized as a grid) within which distinctive objects can be clearly identified, and events and processes easily described . . . It is amenable to standardized measurement and open to calculation. (134)

This view of space, one that is perhaps the most commonly if only intuitively held, certainly obtains in terms of how the subject may perceive the economic management of distance, extension, and depth in space. Harvey suggests that absolute space is most easily visualised as a grid: any map operates along the line of a grid, showing where the subject 'is' 'in' space, what direction to go, what objects – usually landmarks – are to be found (or have already been found) and consequently mapped: 'Distinctive places, for example, can be identified named by their unique location on a map' (134). *Relative space*, as its name implies, finds its fullest conceptualisation in the work of Einstein, as Harvey suggests; here we are concerned with '*processes and motion*' (135). Harvey means that the idea of space cannot be thought of as distinct from the idea of time; to experience space in relative terms, in other words, is to experience the relation between movement through space and the time this movement takes. I will, borrowing from Paul Virilio, term this 'trajective movement'.[19] For my purposes here, relative space – Harvey suggests we should be using the term 'spacetime' to describe the idea of relative space – will refer to the experiential aspect of being the traject, that figure in Beckett we encounter especially in *Fizzles*. Harvey's third category is *relational space*, a concept that is as elusive as it is crucial for Harvey's socio-political readings of space (or spacetime). Harvey begins his discussion with a quotation from Alfred North Whitehead, who in *The Concept of Nature*, writes the following: 'the fundamental order of ideas is first a world of things in relation, then the space whose fundamental entities are defined by means of those relations and whose properties are deduced from the nature of these relations' (*Cosmopolitanism* 137). This would seem to imply that a definition of space, or even an experience of space, is secondary to ideas about space, ideas that seem, a priori, to have given us a sense that space, as a concept, only exists or emerges out of a network or relation of multiple concepts. Space thus is not an absolute notion or even an individually experienced relative notion; space emerges out of a network of connections which, in turn, suggests that there are many notions as to what constitutes an experience of space at a given time. Harvey is useful here because he moves from Whitehead to speak, if only tentatively, of conceptions of space that do not begin (or end) in an experience of a concrete relation to the world, but could, for instance, emerge from the experience of space in memory, in dreams, in the economy of desire:

> In relational spacetime, direct measurement is problematic, if not impossible. But why should we believe that spacetime only exists if it is quantifiable and measurable? Dreams and memories cannot be dismissed as irrelevant because we cannot quantify and measure their spacetime ... Relational conceptions bring us to the point where mathematics, poetry, and music merge, where dreams, daydreams, memories, and fantasies flourish. (139)

Harvey's categorisation of the three kinds of space experience are, I would argue, useful entry points into thinking about how space emerges in Beckett's work. Certainly there is an appeal in some texts to the commonality of experience that is absolute space: there is, for instance, no sense that space, as such, does not exist in the wilderness space in *Fizzles*; there is no necessary sense that space, as such, is not operational in its absolute mode in, for instance, *Ill Seen Ill Said*. And certainly we can see in certain texts, I think here primarily of *The Lost Ones* and *All Strange Away*, Harvey's sense that space, in its absolute sense, can be mapped and placed on a grid: the mathematical precision of the delineation of space in these texts speaks to a view of space as a kind of absolute grounding principle. I am also convinced that Harvey's notion of relational space will be useful, if only inversely, when we encounter what may be called the *negative spatiality* or *negative worldliness* of the narrator of especially *Texts for Nothing*. If, as Heidegger tells us in *The Fundamental Concepts of Metaphysics*, man is world-forming; if, that is, he is capable of conceiving of the world as an idea or picture (world, for Heidegger, is not the material place on which we move, but an idea of the spaces we inhabit), then part of that world involves the realisation that the self inhabits space in relation to others. As he writes, 'we understand world as the accessibility of beings' (*FCM* 198); 'world initially signifies the sum total of beings accessible to man or animals alike, variable as it is in range and depth of penetrability' (*FCM* 193). In 'The Age of the World Picture' Heidegger offers a clear, and useful, definition of world: 'World serves here as a name for beings in their entirety' (*AWP* 217). World, for Heidegger, is an ideal, almost ideational, structure within which a conception of relations between self and other is allowed to emerge. As I will argue in my reading of *Texts for Nothing*, Heidegger's conception of world does not necessarily harmonise with the Beckettian narrator's reality: to be, for Heidegger, is to be in space within which the idea of world (self or other) can emerge. Heidegger, in other words, is offering an ethic: world is the possibility of ethical relations. What I will argue in my reading of *Texts for Nothing* is that the narrator here is, unlike Heidegger's conception of man as world-forming, more closely aligned with Heidegger's conception of the animal who is poor in world. The narrator may assert that what counts is to be in the world, but what we come to realise is that the posthuman's being is circumscribed and radically solitary. World, for Heidegger, is the name for the emergence of ethical relations, or at least, world is the name for the possibility of the self in relation to the other; Beckett's posthuman, poor in world, cannot fully conceive of the possibility of being for others. And even if the Beckettian posthuman does exist in 'company' – I think here of *Worstward Ho* – that company, that world of 'shades', seems deeply compromised as a world, and as a space supporting the possibility of that world emerging. And this perhaps is the main point to emphasise here: for both Heidegger and Beckett, space is the ground(s) of being. Allow me to be formulaic: (1) Space is (where being emerges as) being; (2) World is a name for beings in relation to other beings; that is, world is an idea, or picture. Our task, as we read Beckett alongside Heidegger, with Heidegger, or against Heidegger, is to allow each version of world to enter into dialogue with the other. My task here, in other words, is to harmonise the Beckettian world with the Heideggerian; my task here is to see if there emerges some useful complications when aligning the ideas of world in both writers.[20]

And so, if we have noted a difference between the Heideggerian notion of world – as it works for the human being – and Beckett's notion of being in the world as a spectral posthuman, we should be fascinated to note the similarity in each writer's vision of being and space. As I have stated above, both Beckett and Heidegger would seem to conceive of being as being spatial. Heidegger is explicit about this in *Being and Time*:

> *Space is not in the subject, nor is the world in space.* Space is rather 'in' the world in so far as space has been disclosed by that Being-in-the-world which is constitutive for Dasein. Space is not to be found in the subject, nor does the subject observe the world 'as if' that world were in a space; but the 'subject' (Dasein), if well understood ontologically, is spatial. And because Dasein is spatial in the way we have described, space shows itself as *a priori*. (*BT* 146)

I will extract several ideas from Heidegger here, ideas that will be useful in making sense of what the posthuman subject *does* and *is* when he inhabits space. I understand Heidegger to be suggesting here that space (not being in the subject, not being only a perception of the subject), or a *sense* of space, comes about or is produced when the subject comes to consciousness of being in the world. Being aware, or even merely being – and the word Heidegger uses to describe this state is Dasein – is spatial insofar as the subject understands himself to be defined by the limits and parameters of the space he inhabits and perceives. My sense of Heidegger's reading of space is that space needs to be understood as an experience of something that is simultaneously inhabited and perceived, lived in and produced as one lives in it, as one inhabits it. Space, in other words, is experiential rather than an a priori given fact, or ontological ground (this is what Heidegger means when, in his later essay 'Being Dwelling Thinking', he writes: 'Space is not something that faces man. It is neither an external object nor an inner experience' [BDT 334]). Space is produced as one moves, as one gauges length and breadth, as one perceives the various economies of extension. Heidegger's notion that the subject is spatial – an idea that Paul Virilio will pick up on – will prove crucial to me later, but I do wish to suggest here that in this reading of the subject – the subject as space; the subject as experience of space – Heidegger moves into thinking about subjectivity in terms that complicate a traditional humanist conception of experience; it is here that Heidegger may have given us the terms by which we can begin to think of the posthuman subject as that which is defined by space, by an exteriority rather than an interiority imagined to be proper to the human subject, as such.

Merleau-Ponty continues to unravel the complexities of Heidegger's analysis of the curious ontology of space in *Phenomenology of Perception*. And it is surely Heidegger's notion, expressed in *Being and Time*, that space is neither subject nor object that inspires Merleau-Ponty to write:

> [Space] is neither an object, nor an act of unification on the subject's part; it can neither be observed, since it is presupposed in every observation, nor seen to emerge from a constituting operation, since it is of its essence that it be already constituted, for thus it can, by its magic, confer its own spatial particularizations upon the landscape without ever appearing itself. (*Phenomenology of Perception* 254)

I am drawn to Merleau-Ponty's specific language here because it does begin to unravel the complexities of the subject's experience of space: space cannot be observed, as an external reality, because space, its protocols and logics, determines and conditions the way space itself is perceived. Space, in this sense, is the ground from which space itself is perceived. Space thus emerges, in Merleau-Ponty's thinking, as a kind of 'magical' idea (the word is his). Space, perhaps to put this discussion into more familiar terms, emerges as a kind of uncanny field or site: neither appearing, nor not appearing; neither there nor not there; not in the subject but determining the subject's perception of it.

What I would posit here, after Heidegger, is the idea that being in space means to be directed, to find oneself – in all senses of the term 'find' – at the limits and boundaries of the idea of directionality itself. I derive this idea from Henri Lefebvre who, in *The Production of Space*, suggests that to be in space is to encounter directions and instructions: space directs our movements and our trajectories; space offers 'directions – multifarious and overlapping instructions' (142); space 'commands bodies, prescribing or proscribing gestures, routes and distances to be covered' (143). In one simple sense to be in space is to find the freedom and limitations of movement itself: being is, essentially, movement. What I am interested in unfolding here, in my analysis of Beckett's posthuman subject, is the relation between the philosophical thematisation of space in Lefebvre and Heidegger and the mode of being-as-space in the narrative itself. My argument will be that the posthuman subject, inhabiting space that is neither subject nor object, becomes something other than subject and object himself. To anticipate, I am interested in unravelling the idea, or series of ideas, that follow from Heidegger's grounding analysis: the subject is movement, is what Heidegger will call *directionality*; the subject, in relation to space, but also in specific relation to Heidegger's notion of 'world', becomes, again, something other than (human) subject or (human) object: being in the world means, to put it quite simply, to have become oriented in space that moves the subject beyond the human.

In Division One, Part III of *Being and Time* Heidegger offers two ideas that will prove crucial for my reading of the experience of space in Beckett: de-severance and directionality. These terms are linked in Heidegger's thinking by their relation to the idea that being itself, as we have discussed above, is spatial: being finds itself as revealed within space. The actual, pragmatic experience of space as such, however, is only revealed within the twinned experiences of de-severance and directionality. De-severance is Heidegger's term for the way in which being closes the distance between itself and the world:

> 'De-severing' amounts to making the farness vanish – that is, making the remoteness of something disappear, bringing it close. Dasein is essentially de-severant: it lets any entity be encountered close by as the

entity which it is. De-severance discovers remoteness; and remoteness, like distance, is a determinate categorical characteristic of entities whose nature is not that of Dasein ... Only to the extent that entities are revealed for Dasein in their deseveredness do 'remotenesses' and distances with regard to other things become accessible in entities within-the-world themselves. (*BT* 139)

Heidegger's general philosophical-ethical point about de-severance and Dasein is that Dasein, being in the world (which does and can mean being in the world with others), is defined by its relation to proximity to the Other. Being in the world is essentially spatial-ethical insofar as Dasein would seek to be striving for closeness as a means to overcome an essential distance between itself and the world. My intention here is not necessarily to read Heidegger's implicit ethic into Beckett's narratives. I am only wishing to emphasise how Heidegger's analysis of the ontology of Dasein – what it means to be human in the world as such – is grounded on a spatial category: de-severance means movement to close distance, in the general sense of being. Thus Heidegger: '*Dasein is essentially de-severance – that is, it is spatial* ... Dasein is spatial in that it discovers space circumspectively' (*BT* 143). For Heidegger this circumspective discovery is initiated within a mode of being that in its turn defines what de-severance is: *directionality*:

As de-severant Being-in, Dasein has likewise the character of *directionality*. Every bringing-close has already taken in advance a direction towards a region out of which what is de-severed brings itself close, so that one can come across it with regard to its place. Circumspective concern is de-severing which gives directionality. In this concern – that is, in the Being-in-the-world of Dasein itself – a supply of 'signs' is presented. Signs, as equipment, take over the giving of directions in a way which is explicit and easily manipulable. (*BT* 143)

I am interested in what Heidegger says about being in the world being defined by 'concern'. Concern, somewhat tautologically defined as being in the world, really does only mean that we find the world, and ourselves within the world, through an experience of space, an experience that is given to us from without – it is signposted, as he says – but one that depends fully on our response.[21] 'Dasein is spatial', Heidegger exactly states. This means that to comprehend being in a careful, concerned way means to take account of what it mean to be within space, what it means to allow oneself to be directed by signs, which for Heidegger seems to mean the sense of one's body as it orients itself within space: 'Dasein's spatialization in its "bodily nature" is likewise marked out in accordance with these directions' (*BT* 143).

Heidegger's thought here, in this twinned conception of de-severance and directionality, is a way of thinking about the subject as being more than the traditional humanistic subject, that entity transparent to itself, responsible for itself and its interiority; that entity defining itself as an active thing. Heidegger allows us to begin seeing that if the subject's essential being is defined by his response to directions that seem to precede and exceed him – directionality here begins to look like the spatial equivalent of a Freudian drive – then the subject is exactly that: subject to forces, stratagems, instructions, which precede him to define him. Moreover, if, as Merleau-Ponty and Heidegger argue, space itself is an unknowable philosophical category – a category which defines the human – then the human becomes itself enmeshed in unknowability: if space is neither subject nor object and yet seems to define the human, can we still rely on the categories of subjectivity and objectivity to think about the human, as such?[22]

The analysis that follows in the various chapters to come may simply demonstrate something at once obvious and uncanny, uncanny indeed because obvious. Beckett's representation of his subject in the world, in its various spaces, a subject defined by its compulsive directionality, its unfolding of itself at and as a series of boundaries and limits, seems in fact all *too* human inasmuch as its manner of being would seem to conform to that of Heidegger's representation of human being (Dasein). Unless we wish to suggest that Heidegger's subject is a crypto-posthuman we must acknowledge the resonance of this idea: Beckett's spatial posthuman when read in relation to Heidegger's analysis of the human as spatial is uncannily familiar. But of course this is not the entire picture. First, despite my suggestion that Heidegger's reading of the relation between subjectivity and space, that is, subjectivity as a kind of exteriority, I do not believe that his purpose is radically to undermine the idea of the human, as such. Indeed, Heidegger's project is singularly dedicated to understanding what *human* being means. His work may decentre the subject, it may serve as the grounds for a later deconstruction of subjectivity (say, for instance, in Derrida); but taken on its own, Heidegger's work is not, I believe, a blueprint for the posthuman (I will return to this crucial idea at the conclusion of this Introduction). Second, Beckett's posthuman subject, as we have seen (and will see), especially in our reading of *Texts for Nothing*, emerges as something *less* than human, and more closely aligned with Heidegger's conception of the animal. Here, the posthuman cannot claim to be in full hermeneutic relation to his space, his environment; the posthuman, in Beckett, cannot claim to exist in critical relation to others (he is generally a solitary figure). The posthuman, in other words, emerges here as more closely resembling a being bereft of world, who, perhaps like the animal, is 'poor in world'. The posthuman, therefore, stands as a radical critique of Heidegger's incipient humanism insofar as his (the posthuman's) being in the world falters and trembles before the reality of absolute solitude and what I will ultimately call the 'poverty of world'. Third, and crucially, the Beckettian posthuman still is – whatever, indeed, *is* means here – *spectral*, still is neither living nor dead: its location in space, its configuration *as* space, does not efface its spectrality. If anything perhaps we can argue that the spectrality of Beckett's posthuman *ironises* its worldliness; its spatiality becomes purely and radically ironic as it loses its humanness. And I mean to use the term irony here with an eye to the spatial quality of the term. Irony denotes distance, the distance, to put it simply, between expectation and reality: Beckett's spectral posthuman ironises the distance between the familiarity of its spatial configuration (the human being as spatial) and its uncanny and perhaps unknowable ontology or ontopology (the posthuman 'being' as spectral).

Posthuman Space in the World: Beckett against Heidegger

I wish in the final section of this Introduction to recapitulate the essential aspects of the argument that unfolds in my reading of Beckett's short texts. I wish, also, to offer my sense of the fundamental difficulties that arise when reading Beckett alongside Heidegger. These difficulties, ones that arise as we gauge the nuances of each writer's figuration of the subject, as such, mark Beckett's work, I wish to argue, as a critique of Heidegger's recalcitrant humanism. My fundamental point of departure, as I have noted several times, is the statement from *Texts for Nothing* 4: *what counts is to be in the world*. This idea then, of world, of being in the world, is what is crucial; this is an idea that Gadamer, in *Philosophical Hermeneutics*, would call 'questionable', an idea that demands and sustains questions, demands and sustains active hermeneutical engagement.[23] My supposition here is that Beckett, like Heidegger, offers the idea of world, of being in the world, as an experience that emerges from a grounding experience of space. Space, as Heidegger tells us in *Being and Time*, is an a priori. The subject's experience of being is always already a spatialised one; we orient ourselves, as bodies within space; we transect space via the event of directionality and de-severance; space, in other words – experiential and relational, in Harvey's terms – determines our initial experience of being, of being placed, of being thrown into existence: 'Dasein always has space presented as already discovered', as Heidegger writes in *Being and Time* (*BT* 147); or, as he states most emphatically, in 'Art and Space': 'before space there is no retreat to something else' (4). Space, the experience of space, the event of being-in-space, determines *how it is*, where 'it' is the experience of being, as such. My point of departure here thus is simple: can we take Heidegger's notion of the a priori nature of space – as determinate of being – as speaking to Beckett's representation of space (we have not yet spoken of world), of making sense of how space emerges in Beckett?

I wish, if only as a point of departure, to suggest that space, for Beckett's subject, is too an a priori: the Beckett character often comes to consciousness in space, within a deliberately delimited geography or even geometry (this is true for all of *Texts for Nothing, Fizzles, Lessness, The Lost Ones, Imagination Dead Imagine*). And it is from within the confines of these various spaces that some idea of world must emerge. And again I wish, if only as a point of departure, to suggest that Beckett's conception of world, at least initially, may seem to harmonise with Heidegger's. For Heidegger, world is distinct from space: space, our experience of it, is how we understand world, as such. Space, we might say, is the trellis, the skeletal structure, the bones, of world: space reveals the limits and boundaries of world, as world. In Heideggerian terms, space is the unique instantiation of subjectivity, through which, in that local moment, world – a totality beyond and before the individual – is made known: 'space', he writes in *Being and Time*, 'is constitutive for the world' (*BT* 135). What then is world? In a word, world is a totality: 'worlds serves', Heidegger writes in 'The Age of the World Picture', 'as a name for beings in their entirety' (*AWP* 217); in *The Fundamental Concepts of Metaphysics*, he writes: 'World is the manifestation of being as such as a whole' (*FCM* 284). It is within world that an individual instantiation of Dasein – the subject's subjectivity – is known by and comes to know others; world in one sense is the ecological promise of connection between subjects. Grounding this sense of ecological connection between subjects – Heidegger will define this connection as one subject having 'access to beings as beings' (*FCM* 197) – is the sense that world is where the subject emerges as a *concern* for itself. The world is where being is concerned, where a concern for being emerges: space instantiates the grounds for the emergence of world, which in turn instantiates a concern for being. Concern here – and I will unravel this idea more fully in Chapter 5 in my reading of *Worstward Ho* – means an anxious awareness of the weight of being in the world. Beckett uses the word 'count' in his critical phrase, *what counts is to be in the world*. Concern and this idea of counting are identical structures of anxious awareness of the implications of locality, of being placed, of being thrown into being. Heidegger uses the term concern to mean 'apprehensiveness' (*BT* 83) and links it explicitly to an existential affect; concern designates a way of being in the world, a way of comporting oneself to what lies before the self as a possibility. Concern speaks to the subject's awareness of itself as enmeshed in space as well as its sense of a need to respond to that facticity – 'What am I doing now, I'm trying to see where I am, so as to be able to go elsewhere, should occasion arise' (*CSP* 139) – even as that very response is grounded by an essential anxiety: 'I felt ill at ease with all this air about me, lost before the confusion of innumerable prospects' (*CSP* 49). Heidegger speaks of concern thusly: 'attending to something and looking after it, making use of something, giving something up and letting it go, understanding, accomplishing, evincing, interrogating, considering, discussing, determining . . . All these ways of Being-in have *concern* as their kind of Being' (*BT* 83). And although Heidegger does not use the term concern in the following definition of world, his notion of the response to 'essential decisions' is what he means by concern. In 'The Origin of the Work of Art' he writes:

> The *world worlds*, and is more fully in being than the tangible and perceptible realm in which we believe ourselves to be at home. World is never an object that stands before us and can be seen. World is the ever-nonobjective to which we are subject as long as the paths of birth

and death, blessing and curse keep us transported into Being. Wherever those decisions of our history that relate to our essential being are made, are taken up and abandoned by us, go unrecognized and are rediscovered by new inquiry, there the world worlds. (*OWA* 170)

I have argued thus far that there is a harmony between Beckett's figuration of space and world and Heidegger's philosophical unfolding of these same concepts. But we need, of course, to acknowledge several critical points of departure and difference. First, the *quality* of Beckett's space and subsequent world is not the one presupposed as an a priori by Heidegger. At a very basic level we must foreground this idea: Beckett's space, and his world, is a catastrophic one; his world is a world that is, to use his own words, ruined or corpsed; his world is, at least, always already a displaced projection of a ruined posthuman subjectivity. Heidegger, as far as I can gather, never posits a world or a subject in ruin; he may speak of 'the darkening of the world, the flight of the gods' (*Introduction to Metaphysics* 40); he may assert, as he does in 'The Letter on Humanism' and *The Fundamental Concepts of Metaphysics*, that man's condition is one of essential 'homelessness', of a separation from being that drives the human to find his home 'everywhere'.[24] And of course Heidegger will crucially delineate the experience of being in the world as being essentially anxious, of producing within the subject an uncanniness that, he suggests, looking to the etymology of the word, means 'not-being-at-home' (*BT* 233). It is not difficult to link the ideas of homelessness to not-being-at-home; and it is perhaps tempting to read Heidegger's essential assertion of the condition of thrownness and uncanniness as a figuration of the human subject as fundamentally displaced; that is, we might be tempted to see Heidegger as defining the subject as always already a refuge from world, from home, from Being, and thus as a model of a catastrophic subject. But this would be to ignore Heidegger's implicit faith in the subject's ability, by care, by concern, to find himself within the world. It is, he argues, philosophy's task to delineate the path to overcoming this homelessness, this separation from being; homesickness requires that the subject actively, through reason, carve out his home 'everywhere': 'to be at home everywhere means to be at once and at all times within the whole. We name this *"within the whole"* and its character of wholeness the *world*' (*FCM* 5).

It is my suggestion that in Beckett's prose from *Texts for Nothing* and on into the late texts of the 1970s and 1980s there is no such possibility of achieving some kind of reconciliation between a post-catastrophic subjectivity and a catastrophic world, a world realised through what can only be a deeply compromised negotiation with space. This impossibility emerges for several reasons. First, Beckett's subject, thrown into the space of the after, that space that defines the subject as what I call 'spectre without spirit', is far removed from Heidegger's talk of 'Man'. Heidegger, to speak bluntly, assumes a subject-who-knows: a subject who is able to gauge the economy of not-being-at-home, of his homelessness: he is able, hermeneutically, to make sense of his condition of thrownness. When Heidegger asserts that man is world-forming he is doing many things, but at the very base he is asserting that man has the ability to fashion a world within which to locate himself: as world becomes world, as space becomes place, it becomes knowable, readable, negotiable. But let us attend to this statement: *Man is world-forming*. Man. The subject of Heidegger's critical grounding a priori is the subject, as such. The world that follows from this a priori thus is a projection of imminent possibility given that the *subject* is never under erasure or lost as a possibility. Even as he critiques the notions of a traditional humanist model of the self as being still locked into a metaphysical model of subjectivity – 'every humanism remains metaphysical' (*LOH* 202) – he still maintains the idea of the human subject as a field through which Dasein fulfils itself even as it fulfils man: 'The Dasein in man forms world: it brings it forth; it gives an image or view of the world, it sets it forth; it constitutes the world, contains and embraces it' (*FCM* 285). Heidegger here may offer us an image of the subject as subject to forces that seem to precede and exceed it – Dasein here begins to sound like a Freudian drive or compulsion; and perhaps here there is a subterranean glimmering that the subject is never himself entirely – but he does not ever let the subject fall away: his Man must be in place in order for Dasein to fulfil itself. Even, that is, if Man is not the centre of Dasein's destiny, he is absolutely critical to its unfolding: 'Dasein may choose a hero' (*BT* 437).

Perhaps the clearest expression of the centrality of man as man, the human as subject-who-knows, comes from 'The Age of the World Picture'. It is clear that Heidegger, mapping out as he does a genealogy of the emergence of the humanist model of the subject, is offering a critique of the modern conception of the human. That is, I am not suggesting that the model of the human that emerges in the following is one that Heidegger wishes were necessarily in place. What I am fascinated by is, however, the fact the model he does offer here bears a striking resemblance to the model that grounds his analysis of world and world-formation in, for instance, *The Fundamental Concepts of Metaphysics*, a series of lectures given ten years before the publication of 'The Age of the World Picture' (1938). In 'The Age of the World Picture' Heidegger draws a distinction between his view of the Greek subject as apprehension – being is apprehended by Being, just as the subject 'opens himself to what is present by apprehending it' (*AWP* 219); the Greek subject, it seems, 'exists as a receiver of beings' (*AWP* 219), a somewhat passive participant in the field of being; and because of its essential passivity before the field of being, the Greek subject, again according to Heidegger, is not capable of forming what he calls a world picture, that is, the ability to see the world before us and place the world, *as world*, before him. This is what he will in *The Fundamental Concepts of Metaphysics* call world-forming. Now, as opposed to the Greek subject, modern man is capable of standing before the world, 'to keep it permanently before one as so placed' (*AWP* 218). The modern subject is not one who merely, passively apprehends the world; the modern subject presents it:

> Modern presentation, whose significance is best expressed by the word *repraesentatio*, means something different from Greek apprehension. Presentation here means: to bring the present-at-hand before one as something standing over-and-against; to relate it to oneself, the presenter; and in this relation, to force it back to oneself as the decisive domain. Where this happens, the human puts himself in the picture concerning beings. Yet when he does this in this way he places himself in the scene, i.e., into the open horizon of what is generally and publicly presented. Through this, the human situates himself as the scene in which beings must thenceforth place themselves, present themselves, be a picture . . . However, what is new in this occurrence is not at all that the position of the human in the midst of beings is simply other than it was for ancient or medieval humans. What is decisive is that the human specifically takes up this position as one constituted by himself, intentionally maintains it as that taken up by himself, and secures it as the basis for a possible development of humanity. Now for the first time there exists such a thing as the position of the human. (*AWP* 219–20)

This is not, I believe, merely Heidegger offering a genealogy of the emergence of the humanist subject, as such; what is crucial here is his conception of the human who is not a passive apprehension, a subject receiving the world that stands in some ways out of reach because it is not yet a projection of the human's own agency. It strikes me as crucial to acknowledge how, for Heidegger, to be human is to assert agency: 'the human specifically takes up this position as one constituted by himself' (*AWP* 219);[25] as the human 'intentionally maintains' that position a clear view of the human subject as a subject who knows – and who projects, and who understands – the world emerges. Beckett's subject will say 'what counts is to be in the world'; Heidegger's subject might say, 'what counts is to constitute the world'. For Heidegger, the subject, the human, is the 'decisive domain', 'the domain of measuring and accomplishing the mastery of beings as a whole' (*AWP* 220). And while, as I say, Heidegger seems to be attempting to critique this model of the human subject, there is a deep concurrence between the ideas of the human who 'situates himself in the scene of the world' (*AWP* 219) (and we note, again, the appeal to spatial metaphors to describe this situating) and Man as world-forming, responsible for situating himself in the world for Others.

And thus we come, finally, to my critical question: what are we to make of the relation between Beckett's conception of the subject that at once deeply resonates with Heidegger's own understanding of the subject as spatialised entity (with all that this entails: (trajectivity, de-severance, homelessness) and yet stands so far removed from Heidegger's resolute humanism? How, in other words, are we to understand the dissonance between Heidegger and Beckett when Beckett's posthuman subject, the spectre without spirit, enters his world? We may be tempted, perhaps, to offer this idea: Beckett's model of the subject as that which comes after being, the subject placed within the interstices of space and world, the subject who emerges within and is defined by the economy of this interstitiality, offers itself as a posthumanising of Heidegger. That is, Beckett's model of the posthuman subject, resonating at several levels with Heidegger's own models of space, world, and subject, suggests a latent posthumanism in Heidegger, that Heidegger's emphasis on the subject as directed by Dasein, as an expression of Dasein, as emerging from within a world, suggests a subject not exactly at the centre of things, not exactly, as he puts it in 'The Age of the World Picture', 'constituted by himself'. This is, I say, a temptation: but it must remain only that. Because Heidegger never offers the radical critique of the human subject that Beckett does, he never offers the possibility of imagining the subject as ruin emerging from within the space and world of ruin. Heidegger's subject, in other words, is never one that emerges from the space and time of the after-effect; Heidegger's subject is always already one that looks forward to what is to come: the possibility of world, the possibility of care, of concern, of being-towards-death. And this, perhaps, is the very crux of the matter: if Heidegger's subject looks towards death as an event that fashions the subject's disposition towards his world, Beckett's looks back on death – if we can even call it death – as an event that has passed, as an event that has fashioned the subject as what I am calling a 'spectre without spirit': 'I am dead, but I never lived' (*CSP* 147). Heidegger's subject must retain the metaphysical possibility of the future, of the economy of the being-towards; Beckett's subject, the after-human, the post-human, is never vouchsafed this possibility. But still there are these uncanny parallels between Heidegger's resolute humanism and Beckett's ruined posthuman. There is still the fact, or facticity, of both thinkers offering the image of subjectivity emerging from within world and space. And it is because of these parallels that I arrive at my final, fundamental thesis: Beckett's posthuman, linked in so many ways to Heidegger's human, can be read as a critique of that very humanism. Beckett's insistence on the possibility of the spectre without spirit, the possibility of being in the after-effect, of being in ruined worlds and ruined spaces – *and comprehending what this kind of being looks like* – is a way of approaching the limit of what philosophy can offer us in terms of imagined spaces of *being otherwise*. Beckett's posthuman, as it stands at the limits of subjectivity, as it stands at the limit of what can be known and said about the subject and its world, compels us to witness the instantiated limits of the human, the limits that Heidegger's philosophy cannot, perhaps, even imagine.

Notes

1. For important recent readings of Beckett and the idea of the posthuman, see David Houston Jones' *Samuel Beckett and Testimony*; Liz Effinger's 'The Ontopology of *The Unnamable*'; Jean-Michel

Rabate's *Think Pig!*; Peter Boxall's 'Science, Technology, and the Posthuman'; Gabriele Schwab's *Imaginary Ethnographies*; Alys Moody's 'A Machine for Feeling'; Karalyn Kendall-Morwick's 'Dogging the Subject'; and Paul Sheehan's 'Posthuman Bodies'. And although the idea of the posthuman is not central in his work, Yoshiki Tajiri's work on the economy of the prosthesis in Beckett's work allows us to begin thinking about the possibility of posthuman *extension* operating within the Beckettian world (*Samuel Beckett and the Prosthetic Body*).

2. This Beckettian critique is similar to the Heideggerian process of *destruction*, as characterised by Derrida: destruction, he writes, is 'a deconstruction, a destructuration, the shaking that is necessary to bring out the structures, the strata, the system of deposits' (*Heidegger: The Question of Being and History* 9).

3. Hayles is quoting C. B. Macpherson's *The Political Theory of Possessive Individualism*.

4. Bruno Latour's idea of the 'quasi-objects, quasi-subjects' (*We Have Never Been Modern* 136) that make up his theory of a networked, or systematised, posthuman is similarly spatial. Describing his theory of what he calls the actor-network (the human as enmeshed within human and non-human systems of social and informational exchange and relation), Latour suggests that we begin to think of networks not only as systems of connections but as a 'topology' ('On Actor-Network Theory' 3). For further elaborations on Latour and his systems-information vision of the posthuman, see Bruce Clarke's *Posthuman Metamorphosis* and Pyyhtinen and Tamminen's 'We Have Never Been Only Human'.

5. Paul Virilio's notion of the '*citizen-terminal*' enmeshed within prosthetic technologies that allow for action at a distance is another image of the posthuman instantiated within (a now deeply catastrophic) space (*Open Sky* 20).

6. Indeed Haraway seems to repudiate the term 'posthumanism': 'I never wanted to be posthuman, or posthumanist', she writes at one point in *When Species Meet* (17); and yet at another she allows that there is a posthumanist voice 'whispering in her ear' (73) when she contemplates, for instance, the status of animals.

7. Haraway figures cyborg critique as itself working towards contradiction and the confusion of borders: 'Cyborg anthropology attempts to reconfigure provocatively the border relations among specific humans, other organisms, and machines' (*Modest_Witness* 52).

8. Derrida, in his reading of Heidegger in *Of Spirit*, announces a similar anxiety around Heidegger's use of the word *spirit* which, like other central terms in his work, particularly *Dasein*, 'leaves intact, sheltered in obscurity, the axioms of the profoundest metaphysical humanism'

(*Of Spirit* 12). I turn to a brief consideration of Heidegger's humanism at the close of this Introduction.
9. Boulter, *Beckett: A Guide for the Perplexed* (123–9).
10. See Levinas' *Totality and Infinity* and *Otherwise Than Being*.
11. For a superb reading of Beckett and Derrida's ontopology, see Liz Effinger's 'Beckett's Posthuman'.
12. There are variations of this sentence throughout the short prose (*All Strange Away*: 'A place, then someone in it, that again' [169]; *Lessness*: 'flatness endless little body only upright same grey all sides earth sky body ruins' [198]; *Worstward Ho*: 'A place. Where none. For the body. To be in' [89]).
13. Readers of Heidegger, and of course Beckett, will note that I have elided the question of the 'earth' in this sentence. Beckett's narrators, when they do use the words 'world' and 'earth', tend to do so interchangeably. Beckett's use of the word 'earth' has no correlation to Heidegger's use of the same term, in contrast to the word 'world' which means something similar in both writers' work. For Heidegger, 'earth', especially and most importantly in his later work, comes to signify nothing we may associate with the common sense of the term. Heidegger's 'earth' emerges in 'The Origin of the Work of Art' as a term meaning something like the physical placement of the artwork in the world, as such, what Jeff Malpas calls 'the material objectivity of the artwork into which the art is set' (*Heidegger and the Thinking of Place* 243). In a more mystical register 'earth' is something like a metaphor for the essential hiddenness of things; earth is, Heidegger writes, 'continually self-secluding and to that extent sheltering and concealing' (*OWA* 172). World, as I will argue, is a space, perhaps material, perhaps imaginary, which allows itself to be mapped, traversed, and known: the world, in other words, is spatial, just as is Being, according to both Beckett and Heidegger. On the question of Heidegger's opposition of earth and world, see chapter 15 of Agamben's *The Open*, 'World and Earth', where Agamben, ingeniously, links Heidegger's understanding of the earth to the ontology of the animal, to that which remains hidden, yet immanent, in the human.
14. I am not, of course, the first to read Beckett with, or against, Heidegger. My own thinking here is strongly indebted to Lance St. John Butler (*Samuel Beckett and the Meaning of Being*), David Hesla (*The Shape of Chaos*), and Carla Locatelli (*Unwording the World*).
15. See Jeff Malpas' *Heidegger and the Thinking of Place*, especially chapter 2, 'The Turning to/of Place'; see also chapter 4, 'The Turning of Thought: Truth and World', of *Heidegger's Topology: Being, Place, World*.
16. On Beckett's possible familiarity with Heidegger's work, see Rodney Sharkey's 'Beaufret, Beckett, and Heidegger: The Questions of

Influence'. This important article argues that Beckett may have come into contact with Heidegger's writing through his friendship with Jean Beaufret. (It was, crucially, Beaufret's series of questions to Heidegger that prompted Heidegger's 'Letter on Humanism'.) Sharkey also suggests that Beckett was given a pamphlet on Heidegger by the painter Karl Ballmer in 1937 and that Beckett pored 'eagerly over Ballmer's interpretation of Heidegger' (415). Shane Weller, in his reading of the historical evidence, comes to similar conclusions in 'Phenomenologies of the Nothing: Democritus, Heidegger, Beckett', arguing for a 'close textual proximity of Beckett, Beaufret and Beckett' (46). On the question of Beckett's reading of the Ballmer pamphlet, see also Eric Tonning's 'Beckett, Modernism and Christianity'. Tonning, however, unlike Weller, concludes that Heidegger's work had little to no influence on Beckett.

17. George Steiner's Introduction to *Martin Heidegger*, 'Heidegger: In 1991', is still, to my mind, the best, the most capaciously nuanced justification of his reading, in all senses of this term, of Heidegger. Steiner's argument is that Heidegger has set the grounds for thinking about what is, for him, the crucial questions of the contemporary moment: the tragic vision, the immanence of Greek thought, the nature of human language. Steiner finds himself, perhaps uncomfortably, 'compelled to enter into the world of Heidegger's discourse' (*Martin Heidegger* 15).

18. In 'The Human in a Post-Humanist Landscape', Haraway speaks of her interest in the figure of the suffering subject, 'the figure of a broken and suffering humanity, signifying – in ambiguity, contradiction, stolen symbolism, and unending chains of noninnocent translation – a possible hope' (48). Beckett's dispossessed subject is, perhaps, a similar posthuman figure.

19. Virilio uses this word in *Politics of the Very Worst*: 'I do not work on the subject and object – that is the work of the philosopher – but rather on the "traject". I have proposed to inscribe the trajectory between the subject and the object to create the neologism "trajective", in addition to "subjective" and "objective"' (39–40).

20. On this question of the relation between Beckettian and Heideggerian worlds, see Stephen Barker's '*Qu'est-ce que c'est d'après* in Beckettian Time', which argues that Beckett actively '*deconstructs* the Heideggerian world' (104–5).

21. On this question of concern in Heidegger and Beckett, see St. John Butler's *Samuel Beckett and the Meaning of Being*. Butler's reading of Heidegger's notion of world in Beckett is also a useful intervention in reading Beckett phenomenologically.

22. In *The Production of Space*, Lefebvre writes, 'In philosophical terms, space is neither subject nor object. How can it be effectively grasped?' (92).

23. Gadamer writes, 'the real power of hermeneutical consciousness is our ability to see what is questionable' (*Philosophical Hermeneutics* 12).
24. Man is homeless in the sense that his being has fallen away from Being, as such: this, as Heidegger writes, is a 'homelessness in which not only man but the essence of man stumbles aimlessly about' ('Letter on Humanism' 242). To overcome this homelessness, which seems at least in part to originate in the essential condition of thrownness – or of continually being in the throw (*BT* 223) – requires Man to overcome an essential nostalgia for origins, what Heidegger calls homesickness, and to discover, or uncover, 'beings as a whole' (*FCM* 5).
25. In his gloss on Heidegger's 'The Age of the World Picture' in *Not Saved: Essays after Heidegger*, Peter Sloterdijk speaks about how Christian and post-Christian modernity 'shifted the accent from the human being's createdness to his own creative power' (175).

I

Homelessness: *The Expelled, The Calmative, The End*

I don't know when I died.

(*The Calmative*)

This chapter offers an analysis of three novellas, *The Expelled*, *The Calmative*, and *The End*, written in 1945–6, immediately before the first trilogy of major novels (*Molloy, Malone Dies, The Unnamable*). Beckett published these novellas with *Texts for Nothing* in 1955 as *Stories and Texts for Nothing*. It is clear that despite a four- or five-year gap between composition (*Texts for Nothing* was written in 1950), Beckett sees a link between the novellas and the texts that immediately follow the great decomposition of the human subject in *The Unnamable*. My argument here is that the novellas, in their thematisation of a radical state of homelessness, begin to analyse the precondition for the entry into the posthuman condition that is fully embraced in *Texts for Nothing*. Indeed, at first glance these texts would seem to be almost perfect allegories of the condition of the human subject that Heidegger defines in *Being and Time*. Striving to articulate what it means initially to find oneself in the world, Heidegger deploys the term *Geworfenheit*, or thrownness, to define that sense of being in the world without guidance, support, or, indeed, meaning. Finding itself in the world, as such, the subject is forced, in that purely existential moment, to find its own path, its own trajectory towards significance. And it is here, in this condition of thrownness, that each protagonist of the novellas finds himself. *The Expelled* begins with the protagonist literally thrown out of his refuge into the street; the protagonist of *The Calmative* is always already expelled into what he calls, critically, the 'nightmare thingness' (*CSP* 69) of the world; *The End* traces the trajectory of the protagonist from a charity institution to a basement, a sea cave, a cabin, and finally to a shed: his is an increasingly desperate discovery that being in the world means never finding refuge; his is the discovery, in other words, of being nowhere: 'Strictly speaking I wasn't there. Strictly speaking I believe I've never been anywhere' (*CSP* 94). It is, I will argue, as the subject finds himself without refuge, without location, without home, that the question of the subject's essential humanness arises: the narrator of *The End* quotes a union organiser who refers to the protagonist as a 'leftover' (*CSP* 94), a 'living corpse' (*CSP* 94); the speaker of *The Calmative* seems to imagine himself as a posthumous subject: 'I don't know when I died' (*CSP* 61); and while the speaker of *The Expelled* refers to himself as being among 'living souls' (*CSP* 60), the trajectory of his narrative makes clear that living in the world without home or refuge is to live without that which makes him truly recognisable as a human subject. Homelessness and expulsion from community thus are givens here. And yet, the subject still is in the world, even in its 'nightmare thingness'. In other words, community and home may be lost, but the world persists: as the speaker of *The Calmative* puts it: 'it was always from the earth . . . that my help came in time of trouble' (*CSP* 66). My interest here will be to read the subject here in these novellas as always already in a state of nostalgia for what has been lost (refuge/home) even as it comes to negotiate, if not quite understand, its place 'in' the world.[1] Unlike the subject in the later prose who has no real, and perhaps only spectral, connection to the human spaces of community (churches, homes, cabins), the subject in these three novellas must read the space of the world – the earth, as such – always in relation to the lost spaces of community. And it is here, in the space between loss and the world, between community and absolute solitude, that the transformation into the posthuman begins. The posthuman subject is always already a subject in mourning, a subject compelled to mourn – perhaps beyond his own capacity – not only his place within community but the *spaces* in which community becomes possible.

The Expelled

We may, perhaps, take Beckett at his word when he seems to suggest that philosophical discussions of being and existence, as for instance undertaken by Heidegger, are somehow beyond his expertise.[2] As I say, we may wish to take Beckett at his word, but any reader of Heidegger will be struck by how uncannily the opening of *The Expelled*, and indeed a great number of thematic developments that follow, resonate with Heidegger's thinking on, for instance, thrownness, fallenness, dwelling, and being. Indeed we may be tempted to read *The Expelled* almost as an allegory of what Heidegger understands to be the general condition of the human: cast into the world without guidance; compelled to find direction and purpose; forced to confront the need, what Heidegger would call the 'concern', for dwelling, for home.[3] If I read *The Expelled* closely with Heidegger, I will also wish to suggest that what makes Beckett's text so fascinating, even as it is read with Heidegger, is how the text departs from certain Heideggerian preconditions: if Beckett's narrative is, at one level, an exploration of thrownness and fallenness, we will discover that Beckett's subject – the narrator of the story – while at one level a perfect allegory for Heidegger's human, finds himself in a state of being that at times comes to more closely resemble something other than the model of the human that Heidegger offers. Because Beckett's subject is, I wish to argue, a subject without home, without refuge, without dwelling (and this is true for *The Calmative* and *The End*), he stands as a negative image of Heideggerian man. Beckett's subject, perhaps more accurately, forces us to ask the difficult question: what is man without refuge? In more Heideggerian terms the question must become: what is being without dwelling? If, as Heidegger tells us in *Being and Time*, a room is 'equipment for residing' (*BT* 98), what happens to the human when that equipment is stripped away? What happens when the human is cast out of his room?

And this casting out, of course, is where *The Expelled* begins. The first five extraordinary paragraphs of this story trace the narrator's expulsion from his room. The pace of these paragraphs, slowed down so as to allow the narrator to recall the memory of counting the very steps he is passing over as he falls from the house from which he is being cast out, play out in the uncanny time of trauma and accident. This expulsion, these paragraphs suggest, is a critical one; it is an important fall. And while the seeming nonchalance of the speaker suggests a certain comedy, the narrative time of the fall tells us that this fall into the world beyond the room is not quite a laughing matter. The slow time of these opening paragraphs thus is at odds with the narrator's own assessment of the importance of the expulsion and yet his own reading of the event suggests that if this particular expulsion was not crucial to him,

Homelessness 41

its resemblance to other expulsions from community – expulsions that have come to define his existential situation – necessitates its recollection:

> I got up and set off. I forget how old I can have been. In what just happened to me there was nothing in the least memorable. It was neither the cradle nor the grave of anything whatever. Or rather it resembled so many other cradles, so many other graves, that I'm lost. (*CSP* 48)

The narrator's word, 'lost', is crucial, for this is the uncanny space of thrownness; this is the awakening into the prospect of being in a world beyond knowledge; this is, or indeed should be, the space of anxiety before the possibility of being. And indeed the narrator returns to this word, lost, once more:

> I did not know the town very well, scene of my birth and of my first steps in this world, and then of all the others, so many that I thought all trace of me was lost, but I was wrong. I went out so little! Now and then I would go to the window, part the curtains and look out. But then I hastened back to the depths of the room, where the bed was. I felt ill at ease with all this air about me, lost before the confusion of innumerable prospects. (*CSP* 49)

The narrator's feeling of being lost, we notice, pre-dates his expulsion into the world, now. And while his looking back on the many expulsions imparts a feeling of being lost within memory in the now of the narration, the narrator does not indicate that this expulsion necessarily is the cause of any real anxiety. His feeling of being ill at ease arises while in his room: the expulsion from the room into the world, this loss of what Heidegger refers to as his 'equipment for residing', curiously does not produce the anxiety we might expect. This is to say that the narrator, while having been thrust into the world, having lost his refuge, having entered into a condition of homelessness, does not exhibit what for Heidegger is the primordial condition of the human: anxiety in the face of the world. For Heidegger, anxiety reveals a kind of truth about being in the world: that one is, fundamentally, alone in one's place on the earth. If in everyday being the self, the human, lives in what he calls a 'tranquility' (*BT* 233), a feeling of comfort and familiarity that arises while in relation to others, with what he calls the 'they', anxiety arises when the absorption into the they falls away. I do not necessarily wish to suggest that Beckett's narrator, as he is expelled from this house at the outset of the narrative, is undergoing a process of removal from the tranquillity of being with others, given that he seems to have always already been solitary in his room; and I do not necessarily wish to suggest that his entry into the world beyond the room is an entry into what Heidegger calls the uncanniness of anxiety because, I have said, the narrator seems not to exhibit any of the symptoms of the anxiety of being forced into the world. Heidegger calls the feeling of anxiety that arises from the removal of the tranquillity of being with the they *unheimlich*, uncanny, and draws particular attention to the metaphor of home that underpins the term: 'as Dasein falls, anxiety brings it back from the absorption in the "world". Everyday familiarity collapses ... Being-in enters into the existential "mode" of the *"not-at-home"*' (*BT* 189). Beckett's narrator is, or should be, the perfect emblem of the uncanny, the not-being-at-home. And it is because he is not anxious, not ill at ease in the condition of thrownness, that his lack of uncanniness becomes uncanny.

What does this mean? The uncanny lack of uncanniness? Heidegger suggests that anxiety, what we might parse as a radical self-consciousness of one's solitary place within the world, defines the human, as such; anxiety is, he writes, 'a basic state of mind' that 'belongs to Dasein's essential state of Being-in-the-World' (*BT* 234); the uncanniness of anxiety, the sense of displacement from familiarity, the feeling of not being at home within oneself, or others, is, for Heidegger, a 'primordial phenomenon' (*BT* 234); and critically, as a primordial phenomenon, anxiety serves what appears to be a purely hermeneutical function in that it locates the subject, as subject, in the world: anxiety reveals the world, *as* world:

> Being-anxious discloses, primordially and directly, the world as world. It is not the case, say, that the world first gets thought of by deliberating about it, just by itself, without regard for the entities within-the-world, and that, in the face of this world, anxiety then arises; what is rather the case is that the *world as world* is disclosed first and foremost by anxiety, as a mode of state-of-mind. (*BT* 232)

What I wish to emphasise here is that anxiety, as both a primordial state of mind and a means by which one knows the world, is, for Heidegger, what makes the human human. Anxiety defines the human and allows it to locate itself within the world. If, as Beckett's narrator in *Texts for Nothing* will say, 'what counts is to be in the world', it is anxiety that allows that world to emerge as such. Beckett's subject here in *The Expelled*, now removed from his equipment for residing, now moving away from his refuge, should, from a Heideggerian-existentialist position, stand as the perfect emblem of the human, as such. But what marks his discourse and his state of mind, it seems, is what I am calling an uncanny lack of anxiety, an uncanny lack of angst, of even fear, of being now thrust into the world. And this lack of anxiety – which is not quite the same thing as a lack of self-consciousness: the narrator is aware of himself – emerges as perhaps the affective symptom of the subject's distance from the community of humans he is now thrust, unwillingly, into. That is to say, the reader is allowed a glimpse of the narrator's interiority with its uncanny dispassion. But the narrator's own community, the people on the streets, the policemen (or is it only one policeman?) that he encounters, have already marked the narrator as something other than reducible to familiar categories.

Let us follow the narrator as he begins his perambulations. Given his curious walking gait – 'with the legs stiff and wide apart, and this desperate rolling of the bust' (*CSP* 51) – the narrator walks not on the sidewalk but in the street; a policeman forces him back up onto the sidewalk and the narrator promptly throws himself to the ground to avoid crushing a child ('I loathe children' [*CSP* 51]) but brings down with him 'an old lady covered with spangles and lace' (*CSP* 52). As he begins to move on once more he is stopped by another policeman:

> similar to in all respects to the first, so much so that I wondered whether it was not the same one. He pointed out to me that the sidewalk was for every one, as if it was quite obvious that I could not be assimilated to that category. Would you like me, I said, without thinking for a single moment about Heraclitus, to get down in the gutter? Get down wherever you want, he said, but leave some room for others. If you can't bloody well get about like every one else, he said, you'd do better to stay at home. It was exactly my feeling. And that he should attribute to me a home was no small satisfaction. (*CSP* 52)

It is this phrase – 'as if it was quite obvious that I could not be assimilated to that category' – that is crucial here; and indeed, it is the critical line in the entire story, given our concern here with the subject, his world, his status within the community of humans. The policemen's gesture, a priori authoritative, perhaps even definitional, suggests that he, the policeman, views the narrator as not part of the community of the 'every one'. The gesture marginalises the narrator, fixes him as other to what Heidegger would call the 'they', the community of familiarity. And as the policeman speaks, and thus confirms what the narrator has to this point only surmised – that he is not like the every one – the idea of exclusion and home emerges: 'if you can't bloody well get about like every one else . . . you'd do better to stay at home'. The narrator's response is telling: he feels a satisfaction that the idea of home should be 'attributed' to him; the idea of home offers satisfaction, but no real comfort: home, now, is a spectralised because lost ideal. I am interested to notice how carefully Beckett pairs the idea of the lost home and exclusion from community here; I am especially interested to notice how these ideas are placed within the frame, ideological, authoritative, of the figure of the policeman who at once defines the narrator as other and, unwittingly, raises the major theme of the lost refuge. It is not my argument that Beckett is framing his narrator as an emblem of the posthuman; but I am interested to note how Beckett here, in *The Expelled*, anticipates the idea of the marginalised subject without home, without, in some sense, those things that mark the human subject as human. That is to say, our narrator is denied that equipment for residing; if man is, as Heidegger says, that which 'dwells', we are compelled here to return to my initial question: what exactly is the subject who cannot dwell, who is denied refuge?

The remainder of the story offers one response: the thing that cannot dwell becomes the thing who attempts, and fails, to find dwelling. For this is the trajectory of the narrative: the narrator finds himself befriended by a cabman – though this term, befriended, is perhaps too strong – who brings him to his home; aware that the narrator has 'lost his room' (*CSP* 56), the cabman seems strangely insistent on finding him a replacement: 'he had taken it unto his head, whence nothing could ever dislodge it, that I was looking for a furnished room' (*CSP* 56). Failing to find a room the cabman takes the narrator to his own home and installs him in the stable. The narrator settles instead inside the cabman's cab until morning, when he leaves, awkwardly, through the stable window: 'It wasn't easy. But what is easy? I went out head first, my hands were flat on the ground of the yard while my legs were still thrashing to get clear of the frame' (*CSP* 59). This concluding image thus echoes the opening image of *The Expelled*. Here, however, the narrator is responsible for his departure, but even so, the result is that he finds himself in the same condition of thrownness, of fallenness, with which the story begins: this is a position of absolute loss. And the final lines of *The Expelled* are crucial: they offer us perhaps the first real glimpse of the fully dispossessed, fully thrown subject in the short fiction. Here we are offered an image of the subject, excluded, or self-excluded, from community, now fully enmeshed, though once again 'lost', in the world:

> Dawn was breaking. I did not know where I was. I made towards the rising sun, towards where I thought it should rise, the quicker to come into the light. I would have liked a sea horizon, or a desert one. When I am abroad in the morning I go to meet the sun, and in the evening, when I am abroad, I follow it, till I am down among the dead. (*CSP* 60)

With these images of loss and of movement into the space of death, symbolic or ontological, Beckett prepares the way for thinking about the radically dispossessed subject in texts to come; and while, as I have argued, it is too early to read the narrator of *The Expelled* as a posthuman subject, we will notice how Beckett will intensify the ideas of the lost subject, of the possibly dead subject, in the texts that immediately follow, *The Calmative* and *The End*. *The Expelled*, in other words, lays the ground for thinking about the preconditions of what will eventually constitute the posthuman: loss of home, loss of humanity, loss, finally, of Being.

The Calmative

And certainly *The Calmative*, even from its opening sentence, intensifies the issue of Being, its relation to space, its possible loss: 'I don't know when I died' (*CSP* 61). *The Calmative* thus becomes our first short text explicitly to situate its subject in what can be called a posthuman ontology. The posthuman, in Beckett, must be understood as an entity that explicitly challenges categories of conventional being: it will be explicitly spectral, as in *Texts for Nothing*; it will, as in *Imagination Dead Imagine*, emerge as a consciousness only prosthetically conjoined to the subject; it will, as in *Worstward Ho*, instantiate itself, or be instantiated, as an effect (or affect) of a discourse that precedes and exceeds it. The posthuman, further, emerges in Beckett as an explicitly, though aporetically, spatialised entity: it haunts space, or is, in turn, haunted by it. The facticity of the spatialised posthuman – orienting itself in space, traversing space, mapping space – emerges, as I argue, as something of a philosophical aporia given, as Heidegger argues, that human Being, as such, is a priori spatial. In other words, the posthuman's placement within spaces, in Beckett, in some sense threatens to reconstitute the subject, as such: space threatens to make the posthuman human. This is, perhaps, all to say that as the subject seems to pass into alternate categories of being – 'I don't know when I died' – space, the world, seems to assert itself with uncanny insistence. And this tension, between a subject who has died and his uncanny placement within the world, defines the narrative trajectory of *The Calmative*.

Certainly the image of the subject that emerges in the first paragraphs of *The Calmative* challenges conventional ontologies: the subject claims to have died, yet remains – if this is the word – corporeal enough, still, to be in 'his icy bed' (*CSP* 61). The subject, indeed, is corporeal enough to fear the experience of the body's decay and so, like Malone, will tell himself a story in order, perhaps, to distract himself from the material reality of his present situation. And so we are forced to ask: is this truly a spectral voice? Or is death being offered to us merely as a metaphor for a state of being – perhaps one of absolute immobility – that follows a life of 'stumblings upon the earth' (*CSP* 61)? How are we to gauge the value of the claims of the narrator? What is the status of the *word* in this text? If this question is essentially unanswerable, and we can only allow ourselves to be guided by the claims of this narrator, we must allow this observation: narrative – the word – is the space within which this subject comes into being; this, in other words, is what Blanchot would call the space of literature, a space where the subject exists only as he speaks; a space in which the subject traverses only the space of suspect memory; this is the space where the subject comes into being only as a trace, perhaps a disfiguration, of itself. I will follow Blanchot's line of thinking about the status of the writing subject more aggressively in my reading of the space of disaster in *Worstward Ho*, but *The Calmative*, again as an anticipation of thematics to come, does offer us an early version of what I will come to call the *discursive posthuman*: the subject as trace, as disfiguration. Beckett of course radicalises the idea of the relation between writing/narrative and subject: in order to argue that writing in some sense is a displacement of ontology, is a disfiguration of what *is* (as De Man will argue), we must assume an a priori, a state of being that precedes the entry into writing. Beckett's subject, I would argue – and, I will argue again, in *Ill Seen Ill Said* and *Worstward Ho* – is always already discursive: he is an effect of a discourse that precedes and exceeds him. In some senses there is no prior material state of being; writing is not a dangerous supplement to being: writing *is* that state of being. Beckett's narrator makes this point in the first paragraph, narrating, we must notice, the insertion into the narrative: 'So I'll tell myself a story, I'll try to tell myself another story, to try to calm myself, and it's there I feel I'll be old, old, even older than the day I fell, calling for help, and it came' (*CSP* 61). Narrative is the space of feeling, of affect; it is *there* that feeling comes into being. Moreover, and crucially, the space of narrative becomes the *time* of being: 'I speak as though it all happened yesterday. Yesterday indeed is recent, but not enough. For what I tell this evening is passing this evening, at this passing hour' (*CSP* 62). Here, in this sentence – 'what I tell this evening is passing this evening' – the narrator conflates temporalities: the time of narrative becomes the time of being and in this manner history, or time, is effaced. This conflation of temporalities perhaps is merely the expression of a desire to escape the manifold pains of the present moment – 'I'm no longer with these assassins, in this bed of terror, but in my distant refuge' (*CSP* 62) – and he does revert to narrating in the past tense 'as though it were a myth, or an old fable' (*CSP* 62) in order to see the trajectory of his life – 'I need another age, that age to become another age in which I became what I was' (*CSP* 62) – but the claim that the time of narrative and the time of being are identical remains.

I am intrigued by this conflation of temporalities and the discourse of spatialisation that marks the narrator's desire essentially to escape the weight of history; narrative becomes the *there*, the space, where affect resides ('it's there I'll feel I'm old'). It is within the space of narrative that other spaces of respite are visited, as if for the first, and only, time: 'I'm no longer with these assassins, in this bed of terror, but in my distant refuge'. If the claim of having died is merely a metaphor for the present state of immobility, in the icy bed, or is, in fact, real – perhaps the narrator is indeed dead – narrative, as it is spatialised, becomes the means to revisit space *and thus being*. By this I mean that the subject makes use of narrative not merely as a means to escape the agonies of the present moment – 'the great red lapses of the heart, the tearings at the caecal walls . . . the slow killings to finish in my skull' (*CSP* 61) – but as a means to enter into an entirely new state of being, an entirely new ontology.[4] The space of narrative, in some sense, thus acts as a prosthesis, an extension of the possibilities of the always already compromised human.[5] What then defines the posthuman in *The Calmative* is not only the paradoxical ontology of the subject – perhaps dead; perhaps still alive – but the relation between a compromised ontology and the prosthetic narrative that always already functions as a space of profound melancholy. The subject, here in *The Calmative* (but also in later texts such as *Texts for Nothing* or *Imagination Dead Imagine* and *All Strange Away*, where the subject is instantiated as an expression of a prosthetic discourse), emerges as what Katherine Hayles, in her discussion of the material posthuman, would call a 'distributed consciousness': subjectivity inheres not merely in a single location but is spatially distributed across a variety of sites and locations; consciousness and subjectivity are, for Hayles, always already in a state of becoming rather than being fixed and stabilised. My own sense of posthuman subjectivity in Beckett is that it operates in a similar manner: the subject, in *The Calmative*, is not merely in his icy bed; he is not merely in the space of imagination. The subject emerges as, or in, the spatial relation between these spaces, real and imaginary. Consciousness thus is emergent and concurrent with both narrative – the time of narration – and being – the time of illness and immobility; the narrator makes this idea clear in his appeal to myth and fable: 'I need another age, that age to become another age in which I became what I was' (*CSP* 62).

Beckett's narrator signals the intimate connection between the narrative he tells – and the narrative is more than a mere story, or myth; it appears to be an episode from his own life, perhaps – and the present moment by insisting that the narrative, which is both distant and close – 'what I tell this evening is passing this evening' – effects his self, now.[6] After recounting an episode of a man telling a story to a group of women, the narrator relays the following:

> But it's to me this evening something has to happen, to my body as in myth and metamorphosis, this old body to which nothing ever happened, or so little, which never met with anything, loved anything, wished for anything, in its tarnished universe, except for mirrors to

shatter, the plane, the curved, the magnifying, the minifying, and to vanish in the havoc of its images. (*CSP* 63)

Still later, after telling us about his father who in turn tells him the story of 'one Joe Breem, or Breen, the son of a lighthouse-keeper' (*CSP* 64), the narrator says the following: 'For me now the setting forth, the struggle and perhaps the return, for the old man I am this evening, older than my father ever was, older than I shall ever be' (*CSP* 64). It is unclear if this 'setting forth, the struggle and perhaps the return' (the classic pattern of heroic narrative) refers to the subject's own 'mythic' life; it is unclear how we are to parse the notion that the subject is older than he will ever be. What is, however, critical in this line is the temporal deictic, *now*. The word *now* functions as the discursive link between states of being; it is the discursive ecological link between the world of myth and the world of the body in the real. The word *now* signals that, for the narrator, what has happened is happening, that the entry into narrative is the entry into a sort of eternal present. This is, however, not a conflation of worlds, not a superpositioning of one world on another: this *now* signals a kind of essential simultaneity.

We see another example of what I am calling emergent simultaneity as the narrator relates his climbing of a cathedral tower. Prior to entering the church the narrator has encountered a young goatherder; this encounter, this contact with a human, spurs thoughts of the relation between the time of the encounter and the time of its narration. He recalls the goat's dung:

> I was nearly going to have the goat dung, then pick up a handful of the pellets so soon cold and hard, sniff and even taste them, no, that would not help me this evening. I say this evening as if it were always the same evening, but are there two evenings? I went, intending to get back as fast as I could, but it would not be quite empty-handed, repeating, I'll never come back here. (*CSP* 67–8)

It is this idea of not returning empty-handed that is critical here. The phrase is repeated after the narrator's climbing of the cathedral tower and his encounter with a man at the top. The description is important:

> He gazed at me wild-eyed for a moment and then, not daring to pass me on the parapet side and surmising correctly that I would

not relinquish the wall just to oblige him, abruptly turned his back on me, his head rather, for his back remained glued to the wall, and went back the way he had come so that soon there was nothing left of him but a left hand. It lingered a moment, then slid out of sight. All that remained to me was the vision of two burning eyes starting out of their sockets under a check cap. Into what nightmare of thingness am I fallen? (*CSP* 69)

I will return to this final line – 'Into what nightmare of thingness am I fallen?' – but let me quote the phrase that the narrator uses to round off this episode. After descending the stairs and entering into the streets once again, he says: 'I wasn't returning empty-handed, not quite, I was taking back with me the virtual certainty that I was still of this world, of that world too, in a way' (*CSP* 69–70). What the narrator claims to take back with him – but take back where, exactly? – is what he calls a 'virtual certainty' of the world, that he is of *this* world and of *that* world. I wonder if the echo of the phrase 'empty-handed' is intended to suggest that his encounter with the goat-herder, also an encounter with a human, is another reminder of his placement within the world, as such? That is to say, the narrative we are presented with here, more than merely a retracing of a trajectory through space, is a retracing of a series of encounters with humans within the world. And these encounters, with the goat-herder, the man on the top of the tower, the man who bestows a kiss on the narrator's forehead, are reminders of the world and of a kind of community. But two ideas should detain us here. First is the narrator's qualification: 'I was still of this world, of that world too, in a way'; the second is the notion of nightmare thingness. Both ideas in fact serve a similar purpose: they suggest that the narrator inhabits two states of being, two locations, two spaces: this world and that.[7] The phrase 'Into what nightmare of thingness am I fallen?' occurs after he encounters the man in the tower, but the tense of the phrase seems to speak, or could be heard to speak, to the time of the encounter as well as to the time of its narration. And so our question now becomes: what does this idea of *thingness* mean here? How does the idea of thingness, and its nightmare quality, relate to the idea of the plurality of spaces, of worlds?

As I begin to unfold my reading of thingness and world(s), I will return to my opening remarks regarding Beckett and Heidegger. Despite what Beckett may claim, there is a definitive feeling of Heidegger in these texts; it is impossible to read a phrase like 'nightmare thingness' and its critical relation to the idea of 'world' without thinking about Heidegger; it is hard not to think of Heidegger when, to cite another example, the narrator, looking down at his feet, says 'It was always from the earth . . . that my help came in time of trouble' (*CSP* 66). I am not necessarily arguing that Beckett intentionally cites (parodically or otherwise) Heidegger here, or that he is even reflecting a certain philosophical temper current at the time of writing. What I am interested in pursuing is the consonance between the *ideas* of Heidegger and Beckett, to observe, perhaps even simply, that both writers are concerned with similar issues: the place of man in the world; the weight of things on him; the intimate connection between the subject and space. But part of my suggestion is, however, that despite these similarities, Beckett departs from Heidegger in critical ways. Heidegger's project is to define the place of *man* within the world; his concern is in a way to define the essence of what makes the human. Beckett, as I will argue more fully in the texts to follow, presents a vision of the subject that is not quite human in Heidegger's sense. Beckett's subject, a remainder of a man, is not quite human, in the philosophical sense, but he still is haunted by those elements that define the human, as such: space, thingness, others. In some critical fashion, Beckett's mobilisation of the posthuman, his placement of his posthuman subject within those elements that define the human proper, has the effect of estranging those elements, making them seem uncanny, unfamiliar, and, perhaps, new to us. It is perhaps in this way that Beckett's texts rise to the level of a kind of philosophy: the strangeness of his subject, and his strange relation to his world, compels us to ask questions about the ground of that subject's experience. Moreover, our question about what *world* means to the posthuman becomes a general, but now uncannily pressing, question: what does world mean, as a whole? What, exactly, does thingness mean?

I want to draw from Heidegger here, primarily from two sources, 'The Origin of the Work of Art' and 'The Thing'. While these essays are separated by a space of fourteen years and clearly Heidegger's theorisation about thingness has altered in the interim, there is a commonality of thinking about the thing and its relation to the world that is critical. 'The Origin of the Work of Art' is manifestly an exploratory piece of writing: here he attempts to come to some understanding of what the thingly quality of the work of art is; to do so he must think through what the thing, as such, is. The question is, as Heidegger suggests, perhaps unanswerable: the thing, he concludes, is a 'bearer of traits', 'the unity of a manifold of sensations', and presents itself as 'formed matter' (*OWA* 160). Heidegger, unsatisfied with these ideas and the way thinking about things is always already an inescapable combination of these ideas, suggests we move away from this line of thought and allow the thing, simply, to be, 'to rest in its own self ... in its thing-being' (*OWA* 161). The thing comes, thus, to be read as a kind of shard of being, of Dasein: the thing is where being, as such, is felt, affectively; the thing is that which affects the subject in his materiality, in his body. And while Heidegger will wish to move beyond the idea of the thing as that which awakens sensation, his thought here is absolutely pertinent to the way the thingly quality of the world affects the subject, specifically Beckett's subject. Heidegger speaks of the necessity of allowing the thing to emerge unmediated to the subject:

> Everything that might interpose itself between the thing and us in apprehending and talking about it must first be set aside. Only then do we yield ourselves to the undistorted presencing of the thing. But we do not need first to call or arrange for this situation in which we let things encounter us without mediation. The situation always prevails. In what the senses of sight, hearing, and touch convey, in the sensations of color, sound, roughness, hardness, things move us bodily, in the literal meaning of the word. The thing is the *aistheton*, that which is perceptible by sensations in the senses belonging to sensibility. (*OWA* 155–6)

I wish to keep the above idea in play and look to a moment in Heidegger's 1965 lecture 'The Thing'. Here, in thinking about how the world is a conjoining and presencing of what he calls the fourfold – earth, sky, divinities, and humans – Heidegger suggests that the thing is that space, that entity, through which the fourfold is known; the thing, in some senses, is the manifestation of the world, or makes possible the understanding of what constitutes the world. The thing orients the subject by allowing the world to be seen and felt. The crucial sentences in Heidegger's essay are the following: 'The thing stays – gathers and unites – the fourfold. The thing things world' ('The Thing' 178). The thing things world. The thing is what makes the world a thing; in other words, the thing is what allows the world to be perceived as a sensation-affect, without mediation. The thing is what allows the world to emerge for the subject and be perceivable and felt. We may radicalise Heidegger here and suggest, as we read these ideas emerging in Beckett's texts, that the thing is what forces the subject into relation to a world that assaults the subject; the thing is a reminder of this world, its messiness; the thing is what enmeshes the subject in the stickiness of the world; the thing, invariably in Beckett's early texts, is what compels the subject into relation with others. We notice, for instance, that the narrator of *The Calmative* says 'Into what nightmare of thingness am I fallen?' after his encounter with the man in the cathedral tower. What immediately precedes this sentence is a description of the man's eyes: 'All that remained to me was the vision of two burning eyes starting out of their sockets'. The thing here is not merely the man, not merely his eyes, both of which affect the narrator as the *aistheton*; the thing here is the encounter as an event that reminds the narrator of his placement within the world, as such: 'I wasn't returning empty-handed, not quite, I was taking back with me the virtual certainty that I was still of this world, of that world too, in a way' (*CSP* 69–70).

Thingness is a reminder of world, is an imposition of world: the thing things the world. For the Beckett narrator – and this will be true for *Texts for Nothing* as well – the inevitability of the world means, as it will mean for Heidegger, contact with the other.[8] Indeed, for Heidegger being in the world means that Dasein, as such, emerges out of its connection to others: 'world is rather the *manifestness of beings as such as a whole*' (*FCM* 284). For Heidegger this manifestness of beings is an a priori, an inevitability: being is a being there, but also a being with. For Beckett, I wish to suggest, and by means of concluding this reading of *The Calmative*, this encounter may also be an inevitability, but it is a nightmare, and one that may precipitate a retreat into an order of being – real or imaginary; material or discursive – that, at the very least, speaks to a desire to evade the claims of the world, the thingness of things. Immediately after the narrator says that he is part of this world, and part of that world, he adds: 'But I was paying the price' (*CSP* 70). What is the price of still being part of this world and of that? Is it that he, by still being part of this world and that, is compelled into the thingness of things, a thingness that, by a ruthless logic, in its turn enmeshes the subject into an intensification of the nightmare materiality of things? Immediately following this mention of paying the price, he suggests that he would have been better to remain alone in the top of the cathedral, but, despite his desires, 'suddenly I was descending a wide street' (*CSP* 70). It is as if the subject now is compelled by forces that exceed his own control: this external compulsion takes him into this encounter with the man who bestows a kiss on his forehead; it takes him to the moment when he falls, 'first to my knees, as cattle do, then on my face, I was in a throng' (*CSP* 76). As the throng departs, we read:

> I said, Stay where you are, down on the friendly stone, or least indifferent, don't open your eyes, wait for morning. But up with me again and back on your way that was not mine, on uphill along the boulevard. (*CSP* 76)

While Beckett's text does not makes explicit the relation between having fallen into a nightmare thingness and this final fall among the throng, we do notice that immediately following each fall there is a sense that the subject has lost some of its agency, its control over its own desire. The fall into the world of things, of others, it seems, precipitates the transformation of self, perhaps even, we might say, a loss of self, or, at least, agency. The world, in other words, is not, as for Heidegger, that which orients the subject, defines the subject as subject in the world; the world, in Beckett, seems to *deprive* the subject of his subjectivity. Is it this loss of agency that leads the narrator to declare his own death, if only discursively, at the outset of the narrative? 'I don't know when I died' (*CSP* 61). This is a question which is perhaps unanswerable. But we have circled back to the beginning of our analysis and we should note, of course, the obvious aporia: the world has deprived the subject of his agency; the deprived subject announces his own death. This is to say that the subject here still is vouchsafed what Beckett will call the 'mere minimum' of agency that will allow him to announce his own disappearance. The discursive posthuman is the subject that emerges, and can only emerge, within the extreme limitations of an extreme narrative of deprivation and depletion. This is all to say that this remainder of agency, this ghost of subjectivity, flickering between the here and the there, fading out of existence and fading in to announce that vanishing, is the site, the *thingly* site, perhaps, of the persistence of the trace, the trace that announces the end of the human even in its persistence.

The End

The question that guides my reading of *The End* looks back to that which oriented my reading of *The Expelled*: what is a human without a dwelling? The similarity of question reminds us that both texts follow similar trajectories: a subject, made homeless, is cast into the world. I argued that *The Expelled*, while indeed tracing the implications of a radical thrownness, is more acutely interested in exploring the uncanniness of the subject's affective response to that state of (non-)being: the narrator's lack of anxiety about his state of homelessness marks him, or threatens to mark him, as a radicalised outsider to the community of humans. *The End* is not, I would argue, as much concerned with what I called the uncanny lack of uncanniness that arises in *The Expelled*. This story, *The End*, is explicitly concerned, perhaps even parodically so, with tracing a series of events of becoming homeless, a condition of incremental expulsion and thrownness. The narrator of *The End*, as we will see, is cast out of, or voluntarily leaves, a series of dwellings: a charity house, a basement, a sea cave; the story ends with the narrator, now sleeping within a boat in the shed, imagining his relation to the natural world: 'The sea, the sky, the mountains and the islands closed in and crushed me in a mighty systole, then scattered to the uttermost confines of space' (*CSP* 99). I wish to meditate on the narrator's trajectory here in *The End*, from expulsion to expulsion, from human community to critical relation to the natural world. This is a spatial trajectory, a trajectory that leads the subject from the limited interior spaces of human dwelling to the absolute boundary line, the confines, of outer space; my task here will be to offer a way of thinking about what it means to have been on this trajectory, to understand what it means to exist in this state of placelessness, of homelessness. Our narrator puts the situation perfectly: 'Strictly speaking I wasn't there. Strictly speaking I believe I've never been anywhere' (*CSP* 94).

I wish to use as my entry point an essay by Heidegger that will prove useful here and in our readings of subsequent texts. 'Building Dwelling Thinking' is a relatively late essay (1959) but it looks back to work such as *The Fundamental Concepts of Metaphysics* and

Being and Time in critical ways. The essay, like these earlier texts, addresses the relation between the human, his being, and his place within the world. In *Being and Time* Heidegger will assert that man is a spatialised entity, moving through trajectories and closing distances: being, here, is defined as a process by which space, neither intrinsic nor extrinsic to the subject, is mapped out and made known. Knowing the space and the place of the human in the world is, of course, central to *The Fundamental Concepts of Metaphysics*: here, as I will explore in much greater detail in Chapter 2, Heidegger argues that the human is that entity which can build worlds. The human is defined by its allowing of Dasein, a force within the human, to express the world: Dasein in man, Heidegger writes, 'constitutes the world, contains it and embraces it' (*FCM* 285). World, for Heidegger, is not an abstraction. For him it means, at least, two things: first, having a world – that is to say, allowing Dasein to express itself through the subject – means finding oneself located within a human community, what he calls the 'accessibility of beings' (*FCM* 269); second, world, somewhat tautologically, is the means by which the human finds himself within world, within community, within space. *World worlds*, to use Heidegger's own expression: and by this he means that world is found by the human, discovered as he moves within it, as, crucially, he dwells on it. World, in other words, allows the human subject, to discover how his being, his Dasein, retrospectively, but for the first time, has been expressed, how, that is, his nature is instantiated: 'The Dasein in man *forms* world; it beings it forth; it gives an image or view of the world, it sets it forth' (*FCM* 285). In 'Building Dwelling Thinking' Heidegger in some sense simplifies his argument about what constitutes world and being by asserting, after unpacking the etymologies of the German word *bauen*, that being is dwelling; that being is residing within space; that being means having the ability to create, to fashion a house, a room, a space, what he calls, in *Being and Time*, 'equipment for residing' (69). And while his language, in this later phase of his thinking, becomes somewhat metaphysical, even spiritual – he will here begin to speak of the fourfold unity of earth and sky, divinities and mortals – Heidegger grounds his thought in specific assertions of the materiality of this instantiation of the fourfold; the way, that is, the human finds himself within the fourfold, within the world. It is, he asserts, by dwelling that the human is: Dasein is expressed by dwelling. If Dasein expresses world – or world is vouchsafed to the human through Dasein – dwelling is what allows Dasein to express itself: without dwelling, in other words, Dasein cannot be expressed, world cannot be realised. In some critical ways then *The End*, even as it looks back on *The Expelled* and *The Calmative*, and even as it looks forward to *Texts for Nothing* or the traumatised spaces of *Fizzles*, asserts a fundamental truth: without a home, there is no world.

I wish to allow three sentences from Heidegger's 'Building Dwelling Thinking' to guide us in my reading of this trajectory of homelessness in *The End*:

> Dwelling is the manner in which mortals are on the earth. (*BDT* 326)
>
> To say that mortals *are* is to say that *in dwelling* they persist through spaces by virtue of their stay among things and locations. (*BDT* 335)
>
> Man's relation to locations, and through locations to spaces, inheres in his dwelling. The relationship between man and space is none other than dwelling, thought essentially. (*BDT* 335)

This second sentence – '*in dwelling* [mortals] persist though spaces by virtue of their stay among things and locations' – is, for me, crucial; it is here that Heidegger somewhat modifies his earlier thinking about being and space, or spatiality, in *Being and Time*. If in that previous text being was defined, almost theoretically, almost, that is, as a pure thought, as spatiality itself – 'the "subject" (Dasein), if well understood ontologically, is spatial' (*BT* 146) – here Heidegger begins to insist on the materiality of space. Another way of putting this is to suggest that by 'Building Dwelling Thinking' Heidegger begins to assert that *space* must become *place* if mortals are to be able to instantiate world, as such. I will unfold this idea in greater detail in Chapter 3, specifically through the ideas of Yi-Fu Tuan, who argues that space, an abstraction, becomes place, a material, *affective* reality, when the subject begins to invest it with what he terms 'value' (*Space and Place* 6), but for now let us allow these ideas to stand: dwelling allows space to become place. Dwelling, from Heidegger's perspective, is what allows space to become place even as it allows the human to become the human, as such: 'dwelling is the manner in which mortals are on the earth' (*BDT* 326). My argument about *The End* thus is quite simple: it follows a trajectory of homelessness to what may be called a terminal point of the subject, to the point, that is, where the subject is defined, via another, as less than human, ' a leftover ... a living corpse'

(*CSP* 94); to the point where he figures himself as somehow dispersed beyond the space of the human to become, perhaps, spatiality itself: 'the sea, the sky, the mountains and the islands closed in and crushed me in a mighty systole, then scattered to the uttermost confines of space' (*CSP* 99).

The End begins, like *The Expelled*, with the subject being compelled to leave his space of dwelling, in this case, a 'charitable institution' (*CSP* 80). 'Never come back', he is told, 'you would not be let back in. Don't go to any of our branches either, they would turn you away' (*CSP* 80). Cast into the world, the narrator is 'lost': 'I did not know where I was supposed to be going' (*CSP* 81). Despite this sense of displacement, despite, that is, his condition of thrownness, the narrator does perceive the need to find shelter: 'I longed to be under cover again, in an empty place, close and warm, with artificial light, an oil lamp for choice, with a pink shade for preference' (*CSP* 82). The narrator will, in fact, find a series of shelters. He is initially allowed to rent a basement from a woman who promises never to 'put me out in bad weather' (*CSP* 83); he is 'comfortable enough in this house' (*CSP* 84), despite, or because of, the rats for company, but he is eventually expelled from this dwelling because the owner needs the space for a pig; he then meets a man, a former acquaintance, who offers him a space in a cave by the sea and, ultimately, a cabin – more accurately 'a sort of wooden shed' (*CSP* 89) – in the mountains which he shares with a cow. He sleeps within an uprighted boat that he finds within the shed, the boat providing some protection from the water rats that also inhabit this space. Thus the trajectory of the narrator: from charitable institution to dilapidated shed, from space of what we assume to be some kind of community, to a space of community only with animals, all of which are hostile: as he says of the cow who resists the narrator's attempts to drink her milk, 'I didn't know our cows too could be so inhuman' (*CSP* 90).

This reference to the inhumanity of the cow, deeply humorous though it is, perhaps signals something of the narrator's relation to the world, to the world of humans and animals. I will unfold the Beckettian subject's relation to animality in much greater detail in my reading of *Texts for Nothing*, but I do wish to note how Beckett figures his subject in relation to the animal and the human here in *The End*. My reading of the posthuman subject in *Texts for Nothing* is indebted to Heidegger's reading of animality in *The Fundamental Concepts of Metaphysics*. In this text Heidegger defines his concept of world by teasing out what he perceives to be the difference between the human and the animal (and the stone). As he famously puts it, the stone is worldless; the animal is poor in world; man is world-forming (*FCM* 177). This thesis is grounded, or is eventually grounded, by the idea that world emerges out of the subject's self-conscious engagement with externality, with, ultimately, others, that is to say, community, what Heidegger calls the 'accessibility of beings' (*FCM* 198). Externality is an impossibility for the stone, argues Heidegger; only man is able to negotiate a relation between himself, as subject, and others as subjects; only man is possessed of the ability to negotiate a *self-conscious* relation to his environment. The animal is poor in world; poor here means a state of deprivation, of having been deprived of access to a conscious notion of externality; and yet the animal, argues Heidegger, is not completely unaware, like the stone, of his environment. The animal thus emerges 'as a being which both has and does not have world' (*FCM* 199). It is this phrase that will guide my reading of the subject in *Texts for Nothing*. It is this phrase that defines the Beckettian subject perfectly as it places him closer to the animal than the human. To both have and not have world: this means, for Heidegger, to have an awareness of externality, of the world of beings, and yet not have it; it means perhaps to have had that connection and to have lost it. Beckett's subject is one, like the narrator of *The End*, who exists in the space – and spaces – between the world of human community and its absence. Beckett's subject, in fact, is one that exists in the space – and spaces – between the human world and the animal, belonging fully to neither. Humans treat the narrator, for the most part – his friend in the caves is the exception that tests the rule – terribly; animals, if not actively hostile, like the rats wishing to feast on his flesh, treat him much as humans do: 'I didn't know our cows too could be so inhuman' (*CSP* 90).

I think, to speak plainly, that Beckett's real question is this: what is this being that belongs to neither one world nor the other? What is this being that is not fully human, not animal, but somehow neither? How are we to understand the subject – for our narrator has, at least, still a sense of subjectivity; he is not, yet, that subjectivity without any subject that we will see in the full expression of the posthuman in later Beckett texts – that emerges out of, or from within, this curious space of radical neutrality? Perhaps the externality that once defined the human as human will give us a clue. Perhaps, that is, if we turn to how the human other views the narrator we might be able to find a way of thinking about our subject. For my purposes here the most important encounter with others is not the narrator's initial ejection from his charity house; nor is it his ejection from the basement; nor, again, is it the kindness he receives from the cave-dwelling man whom he has known 'in former times' (*CSP* 87). We need, rather, to pause over the narrator's encounter with what appears to be a Marxist who is 'haranguing the passers-by' (*CSP* 94) with his political views. I am interested not only in how the Marxist figures the narrator here, but with how the narrator views himself: 'One day I witnessed a strange scene. Normally I didn't see a great deal. I didn't hear a great deal either. I didn't pay attention. Strictly speaking I wasn't there. Strictly speaking I believe I've never been anywhere' (*CSP* 94). This self-representation as absence is critical. It reminds me, for instance, of how Hamm will come to justify, weakly and self-servingly, his ethical failures, his moral absence from the world in *Endgame*: 'I was never there ... Absent always. It all happened without me' (74). But it is not necessarily the subject's moral absence that interests me here; it is, more precisely, how the subject understands himself as spatially absent and how this spatial absence – a spatial absence that is also a sensory or affective absence: I didn't *see*; I didn't *hear* – becomes an ontological one. Because not being there, or anywhere, means, and not only from a Heideggerian perspective, not *having been*. The subject does not, as it were, inhere in the world; if what counts is to be in the world, this subject does not count, and knows *himself* that he does not count: 'To say that mortals *are* is to say that *in dwelling* they persist through spaces by virtue of their stay among things and locations' (*BDT* 335). Persistence and staying: this is what defines the being of the human. To persist through a space means that some form of staying has occurred. There is an obvious way in which this idea applies to Beckett's narrator here in *The End*. He is defined, almost perfectly, as an entity that does not persist, does not stay. He moves, or is moved, from one location to another with some rapidity: from charity home to basement, to cave, to shed. Heidegger's point here, however, is that persistence and staying define the human, as such. That is, being is a staying; humanity is a persistence through spaces, locations, things. It is perhaps too easy to suggest via this Heideggerian formulation that one that is homeless, or transient, is not human; but perhaps it is accurate to suggest that one that is always already, and *only*, transient is hard to define, ontologically and philosophically. It is perhaps too much to suggest that Beckett's narrator, in his transience, rises to the level of what Paul Virilio calls the traject, that entity that is neither subject nor object; the thing that comes to be as an entity in motion.[9] I say it is perhaps too much given that Virilio is attempting to affix this new form of human, the traject, with an ontology: the traject is neither subject nor object, but it is still *defined* as motion. And while the idea of the traject dovetails nicely with Heidegger's idea of being as directionality and de-severance, we should notice again that Heidegger is defining the subject *as* subject. The subject *is* inasmuch as it traverses space: Dasein is spatial. I am interested, rather, in how one comes to understand this idea of *being* nowhere: 'Strictly speaking I wasn't there. Strictly speaking I believe I've never been anywhere'. This idea is not an assertion of a philosophical position; is not, necessarily, an assertion of a position for Dasein: this is an assertion of nullity, of absence, of not having been. This is a position, I would suggest, of the beginnings of an understanding of the subject – but perhaps this word is no longer viable – as posthuman: being nowhere means not being. And thus I return to my initial question: what is a being that does not dwell?

And perhaps the Marxist speech-maker provides us with an answer. What is fascinating is how the narrator's private self-understanding, his private self-presentation – strictly speaking I wasn't there – anticipates how the Marxist publicly figures him, publicly marks him:

> The car was drawn up against the kerb, just in front of me, I saw the orator from behind. All of a sudden he turned and pointed at me, as at an exhibit. Look at this down and out, he vociferated, this leftover. If he doesn't do down on all fours, it's for fear of being impounded. Old, lousy, rotten, ripe for the muckheap. And there are a thousand like him, worse than him, ten thousand, twenty thousand –. A voice, Thirty thousand. Every day you pass them by, resumed the orator, and when you have backed a winner you fling them a farthing. Do you ever think? The voice, God forbid. A penny, resumed the orator, tuppence –. The voice, Thruppence. It never enters your head, resumed the orator, that your charity is a crime, an incentive to slavery, stultification and organized murder. Take a good look at this living corpse. You may say it's his own fault. Ask him if it's his own fault. The voice, Ask him yourself. Then he bent forward and took me to task. (*CSP* 94)

Despite the narrator's seeming dismissal of the speaker – 'He must have been a religious fanatic . . . Perhaps he was an escaped lunatic. He had a nice face, a little on the red side' (*CSP* 95) – it is crucial that this is an encounter the narrator *chooses* to tell (we will return to the narrative's final sentence presently: 'The memory came faint and cold of the story I might have told in the likeness of my life' [*CSP* 99]). That is to say, this is an encounter with some resonance for the narrator. And no wonder: the Marxist figures the narrator in a variety of terms, all of which dehumanise, objectify, and nullify the narrator's humanity. The narrator is an 'exhibit', a 'leftover'; he is 'Old, lousy, rotten, ripe for the muckheap'. The speaker's final insult to the narrator is to call him a 'crucified bastard' (*CSP* 95), a phrase that perhaps evidences some kind of compassion as it likens him to a self-sacrificing god; but it is his phrase 'living corpse' that resonates most strongly here as it figures the narrator as beyond the pale of humanity (as does the allusion to Christ, perhaps). It strikes me as critical that Beckett places the narrator's self-description in such close proximity to the recounting of the encounter with the Marxist: taken together we get a clear image of a being without place, or space, an image of a being that privately views himself as absent from the world and who, now, is publicly figured as no longer part of any human community, as, more accurately, no longer human at all.[10]

The narrator seems to comprehend this trajectory of exclusion as his narrative comes to its end. As he recounts the various nights spent in his boat/shelter he feels himself in something approaching an ecological connection to the weather, to his environment:

> I heard the lapping of water against the slip and against the bank and the other sound, so different, of open wave, I heard it too. I too, when I moved, felt less boat than wave, or so it seemed to me, and my stillness was the stillness of eddies. (*CSP* 97)

And it is here that the narrator understands his final exclusion from the space of humanity; it is here that he understands his radical solitude:

> It seemed to me I had grown more independent of recent years. That no one came any more, that no one could come any more to ask me if I was all right and needed nothing, distressed me then but little. I was all right, yes, quite so, and the fear of getting worse was less

> with me. As for my needs, they had dwindled as it were to my dimensions and become, if I may say so, of so exquisite a quality as to exclude all thought of succour. To know I had a being, however faint and false, outside of me, had once had the power to stir my heart. You become unsociable, it's inevitable. It's enough to make you wonder sometimes if you're on the right planet. (*CSP* 97)

It is this sentence – 'to know I had a being, however faint and false, outside of me, had once had the power to stir my heart' – that is important here; and it is this word – being – that is crucial. Does it refer to another being? Does it refer to the narrator's own sense of his own being having once extended, perhaps like Hayles' notion of distributed cognition, into the world of others? The sentence that immediately precedes it offers an image of radical solitude, as his desires contract spatially to the boundaries of his own body: his body, in other words, has become his world. The sentence that immediately follows the idea of being outside again offers an image of radical solitude, even at a planetary level: 'it's enough to make you wonder if you're on the right planet'. And what follows this sense of spatial and bodily contraction is the narrator's final movement into what we need to call the space of the imagination or what the narrator himself calls 'vision'. As he rests in his boat he imagines being outside, on the water; he recalls scenes from his childhood, scenes that include his father. That is to say, we move from the absolute contraction of absolute solitary space to the space of imagination in which the narrator moves freely through the space of memory.

And then we come the narrative's final movement. The narrator shifts from remembering having set fires to the gorse as a child to what we may assume is a 'vision' of being out in his boat on the water; the scene and space then seem to shift and we are, perhaps, once again with the narrator in his boat in the shed. That is to say it becomes difficult to locate oneself, and indeed the narrator, spatially and temporally in these final moments. Is Beckett conferring a sense of locationlessness to the reader here in order to close the distance between text and reader?

> That night then, all aglow with distant fires, on sea, on land and in the sky, I drifted with the currents and the tides. I noticed that my hat was tied, with a string I suppose, to my buttonhole. I got up from my seat in the stern and a great clanking was heard. That was the chain.

> One end was fastened to the bow and the other round my waist. I must have pierced a hole beforehand in the floor-boards, for there I was down on my knees prying out the plug with my knife. The hold was small and the water rose slowly. It would take a good half hour, everything included, barring accidents. Back now in the stern-sheets, my legs stretched out, my back well propped against the sack stuffed with grass I used as a cushion, I swallowed my calmative. The sea, the sky, the mountains and the islands closed in and crushed me in a mighty systole, then scattered to the uttermost confines of space. The memory came faint and cold of the story I might have told, a story in the likeness of my life, I mean without the courage to end or the strength to go on. (*CSP* 99)

Do we move here from a memory of being on a boat, a memory that links the narrator to his childhood gorse-burning? We do move from 'that night then', a night in which, it seems, there is some fantasy of a suicide attempt. Or perhaps this vision of sinking with the boat has moved forward in time? What is clear is that from this movement of the boat sinking – that night then – we move to 'Back now in the stern-sheets'. Are we now with the narrator in his shed, in his boat? Is this still the space of fantasy, of vision, of memory? In either case, whether we are in the space of vision/memory or in the present moment, now, both spaces witness the narrator unfolding a fantasy of disappearance, either sinking in his boat or, having swallowed a tranquiliser, imagining his body crushed, perhaps dissolved, into nature: 'the sea, the sky, the mountains and the islands closed in and crushed me in a mighty systole, then scattered to the uttermost confines of space'.[11] I am fascinated to notice how the pronominal marker disappears in the latter half of this sentence: the sky and mountains crush him, then 'scatter', as if with him, as if the narrator has become absorbed in his environment, as if he has become the external world and has now, in fact, become the boundary of that world: the uttermost confines of space. And yet, even as this fantasy of dissolution unfolds – perhaps this is a complex description merely of falling asleep; perhaps, even, this is a description of the process of dying – a memory comes to the narrator. Like the memory of being that once existed outside of him, this memory is 'faint'; it is a memory of an alternative, hypothetical narrative; a narrative only perhaps tropologically related to the narrator – 'in the likeness of my life'. And in the final clause of this final sentence the narrator opens up a space, a systolic space perhaps, between ending and going on.

This is a space of absolute powerlessness, a space of *being* between the failure to end and the inability to move onwards. This space, entirely, it seems, hypothetical, coming into being in the space of fantasy, or imagination, or in the moment of dying, is, I want to suggest, finally, the space where posthuman being may emerge: this is a space, perhaps only discursive, but certainly affective, where the subject exists, or does not, only on the very margins of being. In the uttermost confines of space, being fades but it never disappears.

Notes

1. Marjorie Perloff's historical contextualisation of these texts is crucial; she reads these images of homelessness and anxiety as reflective of life in Vichy France and as 'perfectly consistent with Beckett's actual escape from Paris' ('In Love with Hiding: Samuel Beckett's War' 91).
2. In his interview with Tom Driver, Beckett says, 'When Heidegger and Sartre speak of a contrast between being and existence, they may be right, I don't know, but their language is too philosophical for me. I am not a philosopher' (219).
3. On the question of Heidegger, home, and homelessness, see Robert Mugerauer's *Heidegger and Homecoming*, especially chapter 3.
4. On the image of the skull in *The Calmative*, see Rubin Rabinovitz's *Innovation in Samuel Beckett's Fiction* (109).
5. Ulrike Maude's reading of technology, and specifically prosthetic technologies, in *The Calmative* (and other texts) is illuminating ('"whole body like gone": Beckett and Technology' 150).
6. David Weisberg's reading of the relation between narrative and the space of the city in *The Calmative* is revealing; making an explicit link between spatiality and the narrative drive, Weisberg writes, 'In "The Calmative", the dissolution of the city and the loss of narrative order is intertwined from the outset' (*Chronicles of Disorder* 68).
7. On the question of ontologies, being, and world, see Ulrike Maude's reading of the trope of vision on *The Calmative*; Maude suggests that the subject in Beckett's text locates himself, or is fixed into this world, via the logic and economy of sight and vision. In *The Calmative* 'vision may not, after all, constitute the space that guarantees the subject's detachment form the world, but rather, through the chaos of sensation, makes him part of that world' (*Beckett, Technology and the Body* 37).
8. In *Time and the Shared World*, Irene McMullin defines the relation between self and world thusly: 'To be a self is to occupy a way of

being characterized by relationality and responsiveness to the world and others' (15); further, McMullin defines 'world' as 'not merely the totality of objects but is instead the network of meaningful references in terms of which we understand ourselves' (15). Thomas Nenon defines Heidegger's notion of 'world' in similar terms in '*Umwelt* in Husserl and Heidegger': 'For Heidegger, the world is not the sum of the objects within the world, but rather the interconnected possibilities that we are aware of, that guide our actions, and determine the relevance of things within the world as useful or obstructive to our ends' (87).

9. Virilio uses this word in *Politics of the Very Worst*: 'I do not work on the subject and object – that is the work of the philosopher – but rather on the "traject". I have proposed to inscribe the trajectory between the subject and the object to create the neologism "trajective", in addition to "subjective" and "objective"' (39–40).

10. On the encounter with the Marxist, see Steven Matthews' 'Bodily Histories', in which he reads the protagonist as a figure of abjection and animality. Russell Smith reads the Marxist orator as a parody of a 'glorious Marxist tradition of vituperative hostility both to the "down and out" and to the complacent bourgeois charity that keeps them starving' ('Radical Sensibility in "The End"' 73).

11. Garin Dowd's reading of the economy of proxemics is perhaps useful here in making sense of this dispersal of the subject; his reading of proxemics allows the suggestion that, following Deleuze and Guattari, space in these texts (and the late prose) seems deliberately instantiated to dislocate the subject ('The Proxemics of "neither"').

2

The Poverty of World:
Texts for Nothing

> What counts is to be in the world, the posture is immaterial, so long as one is on earth.
>
> (*Texts for Nothing* 4)

My task here in *Posthuman Space* is to come to an understanding of what I am calling the posthuman subject as it is figured in the short and late prose. To do so I am situating the idea of the posthuman subject within a series of critical theoretical terms: space, world, ecology. My argument is that to understand the being of the subject in works like *Texts for Nothing*, *Lessness*, *Fizzles*, *Ill Seen Ill Said*, or *Worstward Ho* requires us to begin to understand what it means for the subject to 'be' in its world. As the speaker of *Texts for Nothing* 4 puts it: 'What counts is to be in the world, the posture is immaterial, so long as one is on earth' (*CSP* 116). My attempt, to speak in general terms, is to unfold how the subject comes to an understanding of its world, its place in its world, its place on earth. This process will involve the development of a phenomenology of the subject as it emerges in a critical ecological relation to its world. Ecology here will mean a variety of things, but fundamentally it requires us to see how the subject *situates* itself in space, in its world. Of course the subject, as it develops over this series of texts, stands in a variety of postures to its world: in *Texts for Nothing* the subject emerges from what I will call a positionless space, a space that defines the posthuman subject as grounded in a radically pluralised state of being. My fundamental interest here in my reading of *Texts for Nothing* is to begin to come to some understanding of how the world can claim a discontinuous and positionless subject; more precisely, I wish to understand how the posthuman subject can, in its turn, stake a claim on a world that seems fundamentally out of reach.

To begin to answer this central question – what does it mean to 'be in the world'? – we must first understand the condition of the subject in the texts that follow *The Unnamable* (1953). As I have argued elsewhere, perhaps the best way to begin thinking about the subject is as some sort of species of the posthuman. What does this mean for us? We can, I believe, trace the emergence of the posthuman in Beckett to the space between *Malone Dies* (1951) and *The Unnamable*. In *Malone Dies* the subject is still, as it were, locatable within some kind of recognisable world: he is in space (in a house of some sort); he has a body (albeit failing and soon to fail utterly); he has, albeit again in a limited sort of way, the discursive and linguistic means to present himself to himself in his work; thus while not entirely self-coincidental or absolutely continuous or transparent to himself, Malone is recognisably 'in' the world 'as' a subject. As we move into the space of *The Unnamable*, there is a shift to a different order of being entirely: the subject now is fully subject to the discourse and language of others; he is no longer in recognisable space (or time); his body, if there is one, is not recognisable as immediately human. Perhaps the best way to characterise the subject in *The Unnamable* is as a radical form of diminution or limit. In this way I am reminded, once again, of Iain Chambers' useful definition of the posthuman: 'To accept the idea of post-humanism means to register limits; limits that are inscribed in the locality of the body, of the history, the power and the knowledge, that speaks' (*Culture after Humanism* 26).[1] The posthuman, as I am characterising it here, is a form of transformation into a different order of being, one in which the body has become radically spectralised even as its language no longer emerges naturally from itself. The posthuman, in other words, is understood as a subject that is subject to forces of history, of language, and of desire that radically precede and exceed it:

> I'm in words, made of words, others' words, what others, the place too, the air, the walls, the floor, the ceiling, all words, the whole world is here with me . . . I'm all these words, all these strangers, this dust of words, with no ground for their settling. (*The Unnamable* 386)[2]

Texts for Nothing, the 'grisly afterbirth' of *The Unnamable*, as Beckett once called it, continues the exploration of the ontology of the posthuman, but we do notice something different about its world.[3] As we move away from *The Unnamable* the subject is still given to us as discontinuous, still at a radical limit, but his world has, or appears to have, a materiality, a reality, that marks a change from the world of *The Unnamable*. Where *The Unnamable* inhabits (if that is the word) a kind of non-space (a space without history, dimension, or extension), in *Texts for Nothing* the subject, as we discover him, is back in the world of nature. He is, in other words, back in the 'world':

> I'll describe the place, that's unimportant. The top, very flat, of a mountain, no, a hill, but so wild, so wild, enough. Quag, heath up to the knees, faint sheep-tracks, troughs scooped deep by the rains. It was far down in one of these I was lying, out of the wind. (*CSP* 100)

If we read *Texts for Nothing* in sequence with *The Unnamable* (and Beckett's afterbirth metaphor certainly invites us to do so), we can imagine the subject in *Texts for Nothing* as being, paradoxically, reborn into the world.

As I have said, my task here will be to understand what it does mean for the subject in *Texts for Nothing* to 'be' in the world. It is my sense that one valuable approach to this question will be through the thinking of Heidegger, specifically his phenomenological analysis of world and space. Ultimately my argument over the course of this chapter – and indeed *Posthuman Space* as a whole – is that Beckett is offering a phenomenology of posthuman being. Beckett's texts are concerned with those questions that haunt Heidegger (as well as Levinas, Lefebvre, even Bachelard): how does one enter into an understanding of one's place and placement within space, within the world? How does the world stand towards the subject? How does the world manifest itself to, and 'in', the subject? To frame my question in more specific terms: how does the subject find itself positioned, ecologically, in the fabric of the world? If it is a grounding supposition in ecology that the human finds itself woven into a space, perhaps even fabric, of interconnectedness, that one stands towards the world as an essential element within it, can this ecological subject position make sense of Beckett's posthuman positioning of the subject, who, perhaps like Heidegger's animal, is 'poor' in world?

To begin, let us recall what Heidegger calls his '*provisional delimitation of the concept of world*' (*FCM* 282). In his extended effort to determine how the animal, as opposed to the human, is poor in world, Heidegger offers the following:

> World is not the totality of beings, is not the accessibility of beings as such, not the manifestness of beings as such that lies at the basis of this accessibility – world is rather the *manifestness of beings as such as a whole*. (FCM 284)

As I will understand this, Heidegger is offering an image that suggests that being-in-the-world means, for the human, an awareness of a kind of total connection between beings, even to Being itself (Dasein); the human is that entity who by his world-forming ability is offered the possibility of seeing his place within a larger totality of relation: the world is an event of the manifestness of beings, meaning that the world appears for the human as a possibility for the perception of connection. The human is the only being that is able to perceive this connection between itself and what Tim Morton would call the 'strange stranger' that is the Other in the world, that is, in another fundamental sense, the *world itself*.[4] And what then of this idea of world-forming? Heidegger writes:

> Man as man is world-forming. This does not mean that the human being running around in the street as it were is world-forming, but that the *Da-sein in* man is world-forming . . . The Dasein in man *forms* world: it brings it forth; it gives an image or view of the world, it sets it forth; it constitutes the world, contains and embraces it. (FCM 285)

Heidegger's image of man as vessel or agent of forces that precede and exceed it (Dasein in man) offers, again, another image of a kind of essential ecological connection: Dasein is what would seem to bind all being; but, and this is crucial, it is only as Dasein finds itself in its agent, trajectively moving through the world, that world is revealed. The human, in other words, has world insofar as it is an agent of Dasein: the Dasein in man forms the world.

There is a critical kind of tautology at work here, one that Heidegger himself may acknowledge: being is given; world is given. Man has world only insofar as he has being; world has being only insofar as it is expressed through man (that is, through an essential act of being in the world). And what follow from this essential state of things are Heidegger's assumptions about what it does mean to be in this world, his assumptions about the phenomenal experience of being in this essential event of ecological connectedness. For my purposes here, in my reading of *Texts for Nothing*, it is crucial from the outset to emphasise that, for Heidegger, to be in the world implies that one comports oneself to it in an hermeneutical manner; that is, to be in the world comes with the unavoidable fact of having to interpret one's place in the world by grounding a kind of knowledge of that being: 'Knowing the world – or rather addressing oneself to the "world" and discussing it – thus functions as the primary mode of Being-in-the-world' (*BT* 85).[5] For Heidegger, being in the world seems to be a continual event of revelation of the subject's place within an unfolding connection to the environment, to space, to the surroundings. The world becomes 'world', as it were, not merely because it has an a priori ontological presence, not simply because it *is*. The world comes into being just as the human comes to understand itself in relation to the world. In Heidegger's words:

> The *world worlds*, and is more fully in being that the tangible and perceptible realm in which we believe ourselves to be at home. World is never an object that stands before us and can be seen. World is the ever-nonobjective to which we are subject as long as the paths of birth and death, blessing and curse keeps us transported into Being. Wherever those decisions of our history that relate to our essential being are made, are taken up and abandoned by us, go unrecognized and are rediscovered by new inquiry, there the world worlds. (*OWA* 170)

I will return to the assumptions made here by Heidegger – that the human's world, his relation to it, is dependent upon a knowing, a knowing which in turn would seem to suppose a subject with a history – but I should ask, if only by means of preparing the grounds for my inquiry: can the world world if the subject is not in possession of a history? Can the world 'be' if the subject itself is poor in world?

I wish to keep these questions in play as I move into my discussion of *Texts for Nothing*. But to begin, let me return to one of my opening observations: in *Texts for Nothing* the world has returned. Perhaps we need to refine this statement and suggest that in *Texts for Nothing*, space or spatiality – surely the condition for some sense of a possible ecology of connection – has returned, after being (seemingly) entirely vitiated in *The Unnamable*. Space, for Heidegger, is essential to the subject's locating of itself in the world. In *Being and Time* in fact Heidegger will argue that being itself is spatial. If Heidegger maintains that part of what it means to be in the world is to know the world, to know one's anxious placement within the world, he will also suggest that being is dictated by a specific relation to space and movement. Two key terms emerge here in Division Two of *Being and Time*: de-severance and directionality (terns of great importance for our understanding of especially *Fizzles* and the second trilogy of novels). De-severance is Heidegger's term for locating oneself within space in relation to what is seen or perceived and stands, as he writes, 'for a constitutive state of Dasein's Being' (*BT* 139); 'desevering amounts to making the farness banish – that is making the remoteness of something disappear, bringing it close' (*BT* 139).[6] Further, Heidegger writes:

> Proximally and for the most part, de-severing is a circumspective bringing-close – bringing something close by, in the sense of procuring it, putting it in readiness, having it at hand. But certain ways in which entities are discovered in a purely cognitive manner also have the character of bringing them close. *In Dasein there lies an essential tendency towards closeness* . . . When one is oriented beforehand towards 'Nature' and 'Objectively' measured distances of Things, one is inclined to pass off such estimates and interpretations of deseverance as 'subjective'. Yet this 'subjectivity' perhaps uncovers the 'Reality' of the world at its most Real; it has nothing to do with 'subjective' arbitrariness or subjectivistic 'ways of taking' an entity which 'in itself' is otherwise. *The circumspective de-severing of Dasein's everydayness reveals the Being-in-itself of the 'true world' – of that entity which Dasein, as something existing, is already alongside.* (*BT* 139–41)

De-severance, a process by which the world's distance is made close, the process by which the subject becomes a part of a larger totality, reveals both world and being to the subject: perhaps it would be more accurate to say that de-severance reveals the subject as world to itself. My interest here is to begin mobilising this term de-severance as a marker of an essential ecological connectedness between subject/human and its world. Without the ability to perceive one's position within the world, without one's ability to position oneself in the world and have one's essential being revealed – being in the world – the essential connectedness of things, what Heidegger calls 'closeness', cannot emerge.

But how does de-severance work, actually? Here Heidegger's second spatially inflected term comes into play: directionality. Heidegger suggests that '*Dasein is eventually de-severance – that is, it is spatial*' (*BT* 143); Dasein is spatial insofar as it comes to know itself as oriented within the world; being 'in' the world means, first, that one can locate oneself, orient oneself 'in' the world. One's essential condition of thrownness, which originally disorients the subject and marks his entry into the world as anxiously unfamiliar, is ameliorated as one begins, as it seems one must, to know the world (as Beckett might put it, one is 'on earth, there's no cure for that' [*Endgame* 68]). Being on earth means that one must begin to map out that world, to map out a trajectory. One begins this process as soon as one locates oneself in space, via what Heidegger calls directionality:

> As de-severant Being-in, Dasein has likewise the character of *directionality*. Every bringing-close has already taken in advance a direction towards a region out of which what is de-severed brings itself close, so that one can come across it with regard to its place. Circumspective concern is de-severing which gives directionality. In this concern – that is, in the Being-in-the world of Dasein itself – a supply of 'signs' is presented. Signs, as equipment, take over the giving of directions in a way which is explicit and easily manipulable . . . Out of this directionality arise the fixed directions of right and left. Dasein constantly takes these directions along with it, just as it does its de-severances. Dasein's spatialization in its 'bodily nature' is likewise marked out in accordance with these directions . . . De-severance and directionality, as constitutive characteristics of Being-in, are determinative for Dasein's spatiality – for its being concernfully and circumspectively in space, in a space discovered and within-the-world. (*BT* 143–4)

It is crucial to keep in mind that Heidegger is speaking here, in his discussion of de-severance and directionality about grounding, *essential* facts of being in the world; these terms are not metaphors for other relations; they are facts, primordial facts. To be in the world means to be able to locate oneself spatially, to fix oneself in space, to close distance, to know oneself as a marker of the facticity of distance, relation, and closeness. To locate oneself in space is to be given signs of oneself in space, to be able, fundamentally, to read these signs. Being thus is fundamentally interpretive and hermeneutical: to be in space is to know space. And because these terms, de-severance and directionality, are primordial facts of being, they would thus seem to be perfect for beginning to think about the fact of being in Beckett's *Texts for Nothing* where the subject, simply and essentially, is on earth: *what counts is to be in the world.*[7]

But perhaps our discussion of *Texts for Nothing* should begin with some simple questions: Can these terms – directionality, de-severance – work in *Texts for Nothing*? Do Beckett's texts pose a problem for thinking about these terms? How is Heidegger's notion of the fundamental facts of being in the world, of locating oneself in space, compromised, and perhaps ultimately critiqued, by Beckett's figuration of the posthuman subject?

And so, let us begin with an examination of the subject and his world in *Texts for Nothing*. Text 1 opens, it would seem, with an image of a kind of eviction. The speaker finds himself here, in nature, having being obliged to remove himself from his den: 'I could have stayed in my den, snug and dry, I couldn't' (*CSP* 100); the question for the speaker, as for us, is 'what possessed you to come?' (*CSP* 100); the answer, given a few lines later, would seem to be that his body acted according to its own propulsive, perhaps even de-severant, logic, and compelled him to move: 'one day the harm was done, the day my feet dragged me here, that's what possessed me to come' (*CSP* 102). I am interested in the seeming conflict between desire and body, perhaps between the desire of the mind and the drive of the body: if mind cannot understand why it moves, the body does; the body compels the speaker, perhaps against his own interests and desires, to move, to locate itself within a space beyond the seeming comfort of 'home' (the den). It is tempting to read this opening text as a kind of allegory of Heidegger's notion of thrownness (*Geworfenheit*): the subject is cast into the world initially without signposts, without guidance: he simply finds himself 'in' the world, compelled to make sense of himself within the space of being. But does Heidegger's notion of the subject in space, in the world as I have suggested, not presuppose a hermeneutical awareness of this condition of thrownness? As I mentioned above, Heidegger's presupposition of being in the world is that the human subject *knows* its condition: 'Knowing the world – or rather addressing oneself to the "world" and discussing it – thus functions as the primary mode of Being-in-the-world' (*BT* 85). But what kind of knowing is possible here? What kind of knowing is possible for a subject as far removed from knowing its own condition of being, let alone being in the world? The subject here, *subject to* the whims of a body beyond his own control, to the desires of others who seem to wish to dictate his being, cannot find himself in the world, or in the time of this world: 'How long have I been here, what a question, I've often wondered. And often I answer, An hour, an month, a year, a century, depending on what I meant by here, and me, and being' (*CSP* 101). And of course this is the precise question: what does he mean – or what could he have meant – by being? What can being mean to a subject who seems beyond life, beyond death, to inhabit a space between or beyond these rather too simple oppositions and categories? 'I've given myself up for dead all over the place, of hunger, of old age, murdered, drowned, and then for no reason, of tedium, nothing like breathing your last to put new life in you' (*CSP* 103). And yet he would seem to insist on being here, in a real space – or real enough for a subject beyond life and death – that seems refracted through a sense of time that has become unmoored: 'I am down in the hole the centuries have dug, centuries of filthy weather, flat on my face on the dark earth sodden with the creeping saffron waters it slowly drinks' (*CSP* 101).

It is of course this oscillation between a groundlessness within time and the precision of these earthly details (saffron waters, mist, sheep-tracks, sounds of curlews) that must detain us. I am tempted here to ask a series of blazingly naive questions, questions that are, I think, encouraged by the uncanniness of the presentation of the subject in *Texts for Nothing*: Is the subject real (that is, material)? Or is he merely – but what a word – a discursive effect of the condition of being past all categories of being? Is he real, or an effect of a language that precedes and exceeds him?[8] I ask this question, looking back, of course, to *The Unnamable*, and here will remind myself of what was observed earlier: in *Texts for Nothing* the world has made something of a return. If the subject is merely an effect of discourse, the ghostly or spectral traces of a language no longer attached, because no longer attachable, to a concrete subject/body, the world does seem to be here, insisting, in its way, on its presence. If the subject has breathed his last, all over the place, those places, if we take the speaker at his word – to do so is perilous, of course, but what other choice do we have? – are present. And thus we must come to some negotiation with *Texts for Nothing*'s presentation of its subject in the world. We must balance lines like the following, with their radical displacement of the subject in time and its bare suggestion of mind at work, but mind displaced perhaps into the space of another, ivory dungeon:

> And now here, what now here, one enormous second, as in Paradise, and the mind slow, slow, nearly stopped. And yet it's changing,

something is changing, it must be in the head, slowly in the head the ragdoll rotting, perhaps we're in a head, it's as dark as in a head before the worms get at it, ivory dungeon. (*CSP* 106)

Or these: 'I'm here, that's all I know, and that it's still not me, it's of that the best has to be made. There is no flesh anywhere, nor any way to die' (*CSP* 113); we must, as I say, balance these lines with those critical lines from Text 4: 'there is only me, this evening, here, on earth . . . What counts is to be in the world, the posture is immaterial, so long as one is on earth' (*CSP* 115–16).

But perhaps my sense that things oscillate here between a groundlessness and a specificity of real-world detail is incorrect, implying as it does a movement between sites of being; perhaps we must not read *Texts for Nothing* as offering two distinct positions of being: the bodiless, positionless posthuman and a more integrated instance of a kind of presence. Perhaps what is being offered here in these texts is an image of a *positionless world*, a world that deprives the subject of the ability to locate itself ('what now here?'), that deprives the subject of the ability to overcome its essential thrownness; a positionless world – and I will return to this critical concept – is one that casts the subject into a space of radical becoming, what Deleuze and Guattari term a 'no man's land' (*A Thousand Plateaus* 293), and thus threatens utterly to neutralise the idea of the subject or, at least, to transform the subject into an entity recognisable only as the objective correlative of that positionless space.

From a perspective that considers the Heideggerian understanding of being as unfolding in the event of de-severance and directionality, the Beckettian subject would seem to remove itself, in some fashion, from consideration *as* a subject. If movement, closing space and distance, defines the subject as it locates the subject as subject, what happens, we must ask, when the subject emerges in and as an essential immobility? And not merely immobility, but in a position of spectral irreality? Perhaps we need to question, again as we consider the possibility of an ecology of the Beckettian subject, an ecology that may, or may not, be grounded in a relation between self and world, of the world that seems at least here in *Texts for Nothing*, to be claimed as real for the subject; perhaps, I say, we need to question the very *possibility* of a phenomenology of the ecological subject. This phenomenology would, at least at the outset, demand that we consider how the world unfolds itself to the subject. Heidegger has given us the idea of the phenomenal subject framed *as* subject by its relation to distance, space, and de-severance. Merleau-Ponty, working from Heidegger's sense of the spatialisation of the subject in the world, too would seem to demand an acceptance of the image of the subject as bodily, as materially present, not merely as adjunct of a discourse that may or may not precede and exceed it. In *The Phenomenology of Perception* Merleau-Ponty makes clear that the body is the beginning of knowledge just as it fundamentally grounds and orients the subject in the world:

> For if it is true that I am conscious of my body *via* the world, that it is the unperceived term in the center of the world towards which all objects turn their face, it is true for the same reason that my body is the pivot of the world: I know that objects have several facets because I could make a tour of inspection of them, and in that sense I am conscious of the world through the medium of my body. (82)

The body becomes the means by which the world is revealed and in turn reveals the subject to itself; and Merleau-Ponty surely follows directly from Heidegger when he insists that knowing what 'world' is begins with understanding its orientation within space, as such. In Heideggerian terms the world is the totality of things that can only be known through the body as it negotiates the world's space; a knowledge, or experience, of space thus would seem, from a phenomenological perspective, a critical, even essential – perhaps unavoidably essential – first step into understanding world: understanding the human's critical ecological connection to world via space thus becomes the task. Here is Merleau-Ponty, building on Heidegger:

> Space is not the setting (real or logical) in which things are arranged, but the means whereby the position of things becomes possible. This means that instead of imagining it as a sort of ether in which all things float, or conceiving it abstractedly as a characteristic that they have in common, we must think of it as the universal power enabling them to be connected. Therefore, either I do not reflect, but live among things and vaguely regard space at one moment as the setting for things, at another as their common attribute – or else I do reflect: I catch space at its source, and now think the relationships which underlie this world, realizing then that they live only through the medium of a subject who traces out and sustains them. (243–4)

Crucial here is Merleau-Ponty's a priori assumption of the perceiving subject who locates himself within space, within the connections that arise in that perception of the spatiality of things:

> We have said that space is existential; we might just as well have said that existence is spatial, that is, that through an inner necessity it opens on to an 'outside', so that one can speak of a mental space and 'world of meanings and objects of thought which are constituted in terms of these meanings'. (294)

But what follows when one begins to think about the phenomenological model of space and its relation to the subject in Beckett? We should keep two essential ideas in place here as we begin to answer this question. From Heidegger we arrive at the notion that being in the world is from one perspective, a matter of locating oneself as a dynamic being: being is movement, de-severance, and directionality. Being, that is to say, is a fundamental effect of shifting oneself from position to position, of mapping out a relation between self and world; from Merleau-Ponty we have the sense that what accomplishes this task of dynamic motion is the body; a minimal level of material reality seems necessary in order that the body/self locate itself within the world. And of course, given Beckett's figuration of the subject in his work from at least *The Unnamable* onwards, the body seems to be disabled and movement increasingly, and radically, compromised (*Fizzles*, as we shall see, perhaps offers itself as an exception to the rule of disability and stasis). Beckett's subject in *Texts for Nothing* is not a subject in motion; it is a subject that has been radically stilled: 'flat on my face on the dark earth' (*CSP* 101); even if he observes himself in what appears to be some kind of dynamic motion of looking, the subject is motionless: 'I'm up there and I'm down here under my gaze, foundered' (*CSP* 102); the subject, in fact, looks back nostalgically to those times when motion was possible: 'Once, I mean in the days when I still could move' (*CSP* 127); and he looks forward, indeed, as *Texts for Nothing* concludes, to the possibility of movement, of directionality, of getting to 'where time passes and atoms assemble an instance . . . Yes, out of here' (*CSP* 153). Our task, it now appears, is to consider the Beckettian subject as a subject in the world but in only a part of that world; we must, in other words, understand what it means to be in the *here* the subject insistently, impossibly, agonisingly, inhabits.

The Poverty of World 79

And of course the subject himself provides the grounds for beginning to think through the logic of this question, as we have seen. I quote Text 1 once again:

> How long have I been here, what a question, I've often wondered. And often I could answer, An hour, a month, a year, a century, depending on what I meant by here, and me, and being, and there I never went looking for extravagant meanings, there I never much varied, only the here would sometimes seem to vary. (*CSP* 101)

Only the *here* sometimes varied. Varied in what sense? Does the here of *Texts for Nothing* refer to temporality or spatiality? As we have seen, the speaker often conflates the spatial and temporal condition of the here: 'And now here, what now here, one enormous second, as in Paradise' (*CSP* 106); the speaker will return to this understanding of the infinite stasis of being: 'Elsewhere perhaps, by all means, elsewhere, what elsewhere can there be to this infinite here?' (*CSP* 123); 'deep in this place which is not one, which is merely a moment for the time being eternal, which is called here and in this being which is called me' (*CSP* 147). These statements would seem to make it difficult to conceive of the speaker of these texts as conceiving of himself as claiming a hold on any material reality or presence; he inhabits a temporality that, given its effacement of the possibility of progression (there is only an eternal present), precludes, in one fundamental way, the possibility of being human in Heidegger's sense of the term. To be human, as Heidegger would have to argue, is to feel the absolute weight of temporality, the absolute weight of the future; it is the future, the radical *inevitability* of the future, that conditions the human's sense of what he is. Beckett's subject, here in *Texts for Nothing*, cast into a space and time with no futurity, can only be thought of as something beyond the claims of time. The speaker makes this condition clear in Text 8:

> Well I'm going to tell myself something (if I'm able), pregnant I hope with promise for the future, namely that I begin to have no very clear recollection of how things were before (I was!), and by before I mean elsewhere, time has turned into space and there will be no more time, till I get out of here. Yes, my past has thrown me out, its gates have slammed behind me, or I burrowed my way out alone, to linger a moment free in a dream of days and nights, dreaming of me moving,

season after season, towards the last, like the living, till suddenly I was here, all memory gone. Ever since nothing but fantasies and hope of a story for me somewhere, of having come from somewhere and of being able to go back, or on, somehow, some day, or without hope. (*CSP* 131–2)

And yet, for all the speaker's insistence on his condition of being without time – there will be no more time – and for all our sense that he inhabits a radical condition of posthumanity – beyond body, beyond memory, perhaps even beyond being – we cannot ignore the speaker's equal insistence that he is on 'earth', 'in the world'. The question that fundamentally must ground our reading of the subject in *Texts for Nothing*, as I have been suggesting, is this: what kind of being does the subject have? How does he inhabit the world? I wish to begin to unfold these questions by returning to an idea that I raised at the outset of this analysis, the idea of the *poverty of the world* of the subject. I wish, in a manoeuvre that may at first glance seem somewhat odd, to suggest that one way of understanding the subject here in *Texts for Nothing* – and perhaps the subjects in the totality of Beckett's prose post-*The Unnamable* – is by linking it back to Heidegger's question of the distinction between the stone, the animal, and the human, and each object's, or subject's, relation to the idea of world. Let us keep in mind that Heidegger's famous distinction between the worlds of the stone, the animal, and the human is entirely motivated by his desire to come to an understanding of the term 'world'. One step in his argument about what constitutes the understanding of world must be the comparison between the world available to the animal and that of the human: between the stone, which is worldless, and the man, who is 'world forming', is the animal who is 'poor in world' (*FCM* 184). My suggestion here, in my reading of *Texts for Nothing*, is that one way to think of the subject is that he more closely resembles Heidegger's conception of the animal than he does Heidegger's conception of the human. What follows from this observation for me are the quite serious, but rather difficult, questions: what are the implications of beginning to think about Beckett's subject as close, if only philosophically, to Heidegger's conception of the animal? Is Beckett's posthuman subject better understood as a species of animality? Is it possible, in fact, that Beckett's depiction of the posthuman subject demands that we return to Heidegger with an eye to reading his conception of the animal in new ways, ways that, perhaps, suggest that Heidegger has offered a reading of the posthuman *avant la lettre*? And what, finally, does our idea of the Beckettian subject as being closely aligned with the Heideggerian animal offer to us in our effort to think *ecologically* about Beckett's world?

To begin, we must understand what Heidegger means by the poverty of the animal's world. Two ideas are crucial as the ground for Heidegger's thinking. First, like that of the speaker in *Texts for Nothing*, the animal's world is limited spatially, geographically, and hermeneutically (even to use the word 'hermeneutically' here in the negative is absurd, from Heidegger's point of view; the animal is not capable of offering any knowledge of the world, as such); the animal's world is 'strictly circumscribed' (*FCM* 193), meaning that it can experience, insofar as an animal will *experience* anything in the true sense of that term, only what is immediately present to it:

> The animal is poor in world, it somehow possesses less. But less of what? Less in respect of what is accessible to it, of whatever as an animal it can deal with, of whatever it can be affected by as an animal, of whatever it can relate to as a living being. (*FCM* 193)

Moreover, what the animal does experience is not *known* in any fundamental sense of the term. And this is Heidegger's second, and crucial, point:

> The worker bee is familiar with the blossoms it frequents, along with their colour and scent, but it does not know the stamens of these blossoms *as* stamens, it knows nothing about the roots of the plant and it cannot know anything about the number of stamens or leaves, for example. (*FCM* 193)

The distinction here between the animal and the human, for Heidegger, is rather obvious: the animal's world is limited experientially and hermeneutically; it cannot penetrate into the true essence of things. This is not to say that the animal does not have, unlike the stone, some dim sense of the world as a world, merely that it cannot come to understand its placement within the world as such, cannot understand what the world is as a world. The animal is in the world, has an awareness of some aspect of the world, but cannot experience the world beyond its own radical limitations. The stone, as Heidegger says, is utterly worldless because it has no access to the being of the world: the stone lies on the path with no awareness of the path, of the sky, of the wind. Worldlessness is the absence of knowledge about the world. The animal, however, has some kind of relation to the world, but it is compromised:

> The animal's *way of being*, which we call 'life', is *not without access* to what is around it and about it, to that amongst which it appears as a living being. It is because of this that the claim arises that the animal has an environmental world of its own within which it moves. Throughout the course of its life the animal is confined to its environmental world, immured as it were within a fixed sphere that is incapable of further expansion or contraction. (*FCM* 198)

Heidegger is clear that despite being deprived of absolute knowledge of the world, the animal does 'have world'. The animal is not the stone; but the animal can never be the human: thus the animal 'reveals itself as a being which both *has and does not have world*' (*FCM* 199).[9] The human, on the other hand, does know the world as world; does realise the complexity of things; is able, in Heidegger's term, to *penetrate* into the true structure of things:

> As against this, the world of man is a rich one, greater in range, far more extensive in its penetrability, constantly extendable not only in its range (we can always bring more and more beings into consideration) but also in respect to the manner in which we can penetrate ever more deeply in this penetrability. Consequently we can characterize the relation man possesses to the world by referring to the extendibility of everything he relates to. This is why we speak of man as worldforming. (*FCM* 193)

What fascinates me, in thinking about Heidegger's representation of the animal as it relates to the Beckettian subject in *Texts for Nothing*, is Heidegger's idea that the animal 'reveals itself as a being which both *has and does not have world*'.[10] I am going to take this sentence as a kind of guide for my reading of the Beckettian subject in *Texts for Nothing* and beyond. I want to suggest, on a purely theoretical basis, that we can begin to think of the Beckettian subject as inhabiting this same, curiously liminal space

The Poverty of World   83

of being both in and out of the world, of having and not having world, of being, in Heidegger's terms, radically poor in world (deprivation here, being poor in world, in a fascinating way, is *fully dependent* upon possessing some aspect of the thing one does not fully have). This is not necessarily to say that Beckett's subject here is a species of the animal, but merely that Heidegger's distinction between the three orders of things – stone, animal, human – allows us to begin thinking about what kind of world is available to the subject in *Texts for Nothing*, and this – the question of world, of its essential poverty – is our primary question. It is this image – of the animal having and not having world – that must direct our understanding of the Beckettian posthuman and its space. It is this image of a kind of ecological distribution across states of being and non-being, world and not-having-world, being here and there, simultaneously, that emerges as the defining philosophical image of the subject in *Texts for Nothing*. The Beckettian subject, as we will see, like the animal, both has and does not have world, is both in the world and separated from it.[11] The critical task here is to begin to find ways of understanding what this movement between being and utter deprivation means. Is it possible to suggest that the Beckettian subject's world – its ecological understanding of itself as distributed between positions of being and deprivation – hinges exactly on the space between having and not having a world?[12] To refine my question: is the Beckettian posthuman subject's world, in a fundamental way, only ever the *space between* having and not having a world?[13]

I have mobilised the term ecology thus far rather loosely, using it merely to refer to the sense of interconnectedness that Heidegger suggests is central to being. As he writes in *The Fundamental Concepts of Metaphysics*:

> World is not the totality of beings, is not the accessibility of beings as such, not the manifestness of beings as such that lies at the basis of this accessibility – world is rather the *manifestness of beings as such as a whole*. (FCM 284)

For Heidegger, human being, the act or event of being human, is defined by the human's ability to direct itself to, to de-sever the distance between, itself and other being or beings: 'we can always bring more and more beings into consideration' (FCM 193). An ecology of being, for Heidegger, would mean a kind of inevitable, unavoidable fact of connection between human and human, human and environment, human and world. In ecological terms one might be tempted to suggest that Heidegger's phenomenology offers a 'deep ecology', a fundamental sense of the radical connectedness of all things. My speculation about the term ecology and its relation to Beckett does begin, can only begin, after we have come to some understanding of the peculiarities of the world in *Texts for Nothing*, the peculiarities of the subject that inhabits it. We have here a subject who may not be fully integrated as a subject; whose sense of time and space has radically diminished; whose world is radically circumscribed in terms of its ability to move, to close distance. What this adds up to is an image of a species of the posthuman whose defining ontological, and ecological, feature (ontology and ecology may be one and the same thing here) is a kind of positionlessness: the subject inhabits what I will presently call a *positionless world*.[14]

But I must pause and point out another level of complexity in *Texts for Nothing*. I have, up to this point, used the term 'world' in the singular, assuming, even for the sake of a kind of philosophical clarity, that the term makes sense of the positionless space that the subject inhabits: that is, even if the Beckettian subject inhabits a space and time beyond recognition as space and time; even if he does inhabit a positionless world and thus, in Heidegger's terms, is not really a candidate for human being at all, he still is in *one* world of positionlessness. But is not an essential element in the ontological and phenomenological structuring of the subject in *Texts for Nothing* the fact that he inhabits not one but at least two worlds? Is not one of the defining elements of the structuring of the subject's world – or worlds – in *Texts for Nothing* the fact that he inhabits what appears to be a present moment of the here but also seems to 'be' in a different space, perhaps different time? It is tempting to suggest that in *Texts for Nothing* we have, like in Beckett's *How It Is*, a division in the subject's world: he is in the present moment of radical diminution, haunted by memories of a time elsewhere where time and space functioned, where the subject interacted with other humans (in the manner of Heidegger's definition of what constitutes being and world, as such). But, as we will discover, the separation between the time of the now, this here, and the then that may or may not mark the space (and time) of memory is not clear: in *Texts for Nothing*, in fact, the subject inhabits both the space/time of the here *and* the then, somewhat equally. What therefore defines the Beckettian posthuman, and its crucial ecological relation to its world, is that (a) he is positionless, (b) he is poor in world, and (c) there is no ontological distinction, in his mind, between the present and the past, the 'here' and the 'there'. The ecology of the subject, therefore, is an ecology of poverty/deprivation and plurality, at once: the subject is positionless and poor in world but he is condemned to inhabit a plurality of worlds; the brutal irony of the Beckettian posthuman figure is that he has too many worlds within which his deprivation comes into being.[15]

The clearest figuration of the separation of states of being comes at the outset of Text 2, in a moment that prefigures the separation of memory and the present that will occur in *How It Is*:

> Above is the light, the elements, a kind of light, sufficient to see by, the living find their ways, without too much trouble, avoid one another, unite, avoid the obstacles, without too much trouble, seek with their eyes, close their eyes, halting, without halting, among the elements, the living. (*CSP* 105)

The spatial separation, the 'above' versus the 'pit of my inexistence' that marks the present moment of the 'here', suggests a division of the order of being, the implication being that the subject, now, has passed away from the above, the above where beings encounter each other, in the Heideggerian instantiation of being in the world for and with the human. The subject, now, is, as he says, in the 'here', 'under a different glass, not long habitable either' (*CSP* 105). Following this placement in the here he says, 'You are there, there it is, where you are will never long be habitable. Go then, no, better stay, for where would you go, now that you know? Back above? There are limits' (*CSP* 105). It would seem, given the articulation of what appears to be the impossibility of re-joining the living 'above', that the subject is cast into a permanent state of loss: he is 'here'; the above, there, is a state, an order of being, forever lost:

> Perhaps above it's summer, a summer Sunday, Mr. Joly is in the belfry, he has wound up the clock, now he's ringing the bells. Mr. Joly. He had only one leg and a half. Sunday. It was folly to be abroad. The roads were crawling with them, the same roads so often kind. Here at least none of that, no talk of a creator and nothing very definite in the way of creation. (*CSP* 107)

But, as I have said, this separation of orders of being is not, perhaps, a clear separation at all. Even from the first Text the subject suggests that the 'there', the above, is not necessarily an order of being permanently lost or left behind. He claims, in a passage we looked at previously, to be 'down in the hole the centuries have dug' (*CSP* 101), having entered a condition of being beyond the condition of the human; he looks up to see others looking at him 'above, all round me, as in a graveyard' (*CSP* 101). And then this crucial line: 'I'm up there and I'm down here, under my gaze, foundered' (*CSP* 102). And thus my question: what does it mean, what can it mean, to have given oneself 'up for dead all over the place' (*CSP* 103), and still maintain a perspective on that state of non-being? What does it mean, perhaps, to witness one's entry into a condition past the human, and into the posthuman? Because this line merely sounds the theme of consistent connection to the past, spatially separate, world. In Text 6, the subject addresses explicitly his condition of posthumanity, a condition that would seem to demand at least the possibility that the 'here' and the 'there' are not ontologically distinct orders of being:

> What can have become then of the tissues I was, I can see them no more, feel them no more, flaunting and fluttering all about and inside me, pah they must still be on their old prowl somewhere, passing themselves off as me. Did I ever believe in them, did I ever believe I was there, somewhere in that ragbag, that's more the line, of inquiry, perhaps I'm still there, as large as life, merely convinced I'm not. (*CSP* 124)

This final thought – perhaps I'm still there – arises once more in Text 7 where the subject plays out an elaborate fantasy (but what can this term *fantasy* mean here in *Texts for Nothing*?) of perhaps still being there, in the space of the past: 'And what if all this time I had not stirred hand or foot from the third-class waiting-room of the South-Eastern Railway Terminus' (*CSP* 128);

> is that me still waiting there, sitting up stiff and straight on the edge of the seat ... ticket between finger and thumb, in that great room dim with the platform gloom as dispersed by the quarter-glass self-closing door, locked up in those shadows, it's there, it's me. (*CSP* 129)

And while the subject may, in his ambivalent fashion, disavow this fantasy – 'And to search for me elsewhere, where life persists, and me there, when all life has withdrawn, except mine, if I'm alive, no, it would be a loss of time' (*CSP* 129–30) – the idea has been offered that the subject *is* there: *It's me*. And thus in Text 9 we read:

> I must be getting mixed, confusing here and there, now and then, just as I confused them then, the here of then, the then of there, with other spaces, other times, dimly discerned, but not more dimly than now, now that I'm here, if I'm here, and no longer there. Coming and going before the graveyard, perplexed. (*CSP* 139)

All hinges on this 'if': if I'm here, and no longer there. The suggestion of doubt about the passing through a past time (and space) into the present moment of deprivation and radical solitude offers us the possibility that the subject exists in two spaces, two times. And I will reiterate: the suggestion here is not necessarily that the subject exists in the now and has some connection to a past, that memory is in any real way a different state of being. The past, in *Texts for Nothing*, is a *present* state of being, not a historical state of mind. The subject here exists, if indeed 'exists' is the term, in two times and spaces. Now the question becomes, how are we to understand this distribution of being? How can we understand, now, the world(s) the subject inhabits? What kind of being is being offered to us here?

An answer to this question requires us to think carefully about what it might mean to be, or to *have being*, in these two states, times, spaces. One fruitful avenue of thinking here is to suggest that what Beckett has given us, in his figuration of the subject in *Texts for Nothing*, is a model of what might be called distributed cognition or, more accurately, *distributed being*. I am adapting the term 'distributed cognition' from Katherine Hayles who deploys it in her critical analysis of the posthuman. In *How We Became Posthuman* Hayles uses the term to account for the figure of the cyborg that emerges in science fiction, but she is clear that the posthuman is not only, or even primarily, an entity, or being, that emerges out of the technological manipulation of the body. Hayles argues that the posthuman is an event of emerging subjectivity, a subjectivity that challenges traditional conceptions of the integrated, unified, humanist subject. Critical to her conception of the posthuman is the idea that the posthuman's agency may in fact precede or even exceed the subject:

The presumption that there is an agency, desire, or will belonging to the self and clearly distinguished for the 'will of others' is undercut in the posthuman, for the posthuman's collective heterogeneous quality implies a distributed cognition located in disparate parts that may be in only tenuous communication with one another. (*How We Became Posthuman* 3–4)

In Hayles' words, the posthuman offers to us 'new models of subjectivity' (4) and it is my sense that thinking about Beckett's subject in *Texts for Nothing*, and indeed the subject that emerges in his short prose up to and including his final texts (especially *Ill Seen Ill Said* and *Worstward Ho*) is one of these new models of the subject. I am attracted to Hayles' notion of the distributed cognition, the idea that the posthuman subject's mind is located in a variety of spaces, because, as should be clear here, this is the model of thought that is offered to us in *Texts for Nothing*. I am adapting the phrase *distributed cognition* and deploying my own term *distributed being* because I am not certain, again looking back to Heidegger's notion that the human is that which can engage, cognitively and hermeneutically, with the world, that cognition is what the subject displays in *Texts for Nothing*. There is being here; there is indeed perhaps even consciousness, but I am uncertain that cognition, a term that suggests a kind of knowing, or knowledge, is operational here. Moreover, as I have been attempting to argue here, Beckett's subject here, this posthuman subject, is defined not by cognitive or hermeneutical processes, but by its positionality. By its placement in the world.

And thus we find ourselves with a more or less complete image of the Beckettian posthuman: poor in world and a model of distributed being. I have mobilised the term positionlessness to speak of the subject here in *Texts for Nothing* and it remains, finally, to understand what this term offers in terms of understanding Beckett's world. Positionlessness is a term I am deploying in an effort to understand the effect – and perhaps affect – of the state of being distributed, of inhabiting simultaneous states of being and mind. The term is not intended to imply that the subject does not inhabit space, but that he inhabits more than one space. I would, as suggested above, go as far as to argue – and here ultimately answer the central question of this chapter, What does it mean to be in the world? – that the term positionlessness is an attempt to locate the subject not here, or there, but in the space between. My wish, however, is not to suggest that the space between implies movement or any state of becoming. Positionlessness, for me, implies a kind of radical stillness: the subject in *Texts for Nothing*, as we have seen, inhabits 'one enormous second' (*CSP* 116), the 'infinite here' *CSP* (123) that precludes movement, directionality, becoming; this is a state of being poor in world that should remind us of Heidegger's characterisation of the animal as 'confined to its environmental world, immured as it were within a fixed sphere that is incapable of further expansion or contraction' (*CSP* 198). Or, if becoming is what indeed defines the Beckettian posthuman, it would have to be the aporetic understanding of becoming that Deleuze and Guattari offer in *A Thousand Plateaus*. '[B]ecoming', they write, 'cannot be conceptualized in terms of past and future' (292):

> A line of becoming has neither beginning nor end, departure nor arrival, origin, nor destination ... A line of becoming has only a middle ... A becoming is always in the middle ... A becoming is neither one nor two, nor the relation of the two; it is the in-between, the border or line of flight or descent running perpendicular to both. If becoming is a block (a line block), it is because it constitutes a zone of proximity and indiscernibility, a no-man's land, a non-localizable relation. (293)

Ultimately, positionlessness is a term that explains the uncanny affect the subject must feel when acknowledging a connection between states of being each without historical priority; indeed, positionlessness, like Deleuze and Guattari's becoming, is ahistorical because it annuls any claims to history; and even as it threatens the subject's claim to any world, historical or otherwise, the state of positionlessness truly does become what Deleuze and Guattari call a 'no man's land'. In Text 12, as the subject elaborates the notion that he is split across time and space – he begins to speak of himself, there, as 'he' – he details what Malone would call his 'present state': 'deep in this place which is not one, which is merely a moment for the time being eternal, which is called here, and in this being which is called me and is not one' (*CSP* 147). This, for me, is a perfect image of the positionless no-man's-land: being in a place that is not one; being a subject, which is not a subject at all. Positionlessness: a state of being and not being; inhabiting a space which is not space, a time which is not a time; being human and not human. And I use this final phrase carefully: being human and not human. Because, as mentioned, this position of distributed being, as even Hayles would say, is never one that fully leaves the human behind: the human in post*human* still haunts the present state of positionlessness.[16] The subject, as I have attempted to suggest, still is, in some sense, in the there that would seem not to have *preceded* this present state of the here, but is *simultaneous* with it.

And thus my metaphor of haunting needs to be refined. It is not the subject who haunts himself; that is, the subject now is not haunted by a past, because his past is with him in this distributed simultaneity. What haunts the here is not the subject, but the subject's *world*. The idea, as the narrator puts it in a crucial line in Text 13, of being itself haunting the subject requires the (now) obsolete idea of temporality, a history that demarcates the subject, now, as having had a past; this, as he puts it, is a 'dream', a fantasy 'of being past, passing and to be, end of lie' (*CSP* 154). No, it is not being that haunts the subject; it is not the idea of having lost a world of contact with others. What haunts is the idea that the world itself that has passed out of possibility.[17] Here, the everlasting now that the subject inhabits, is a world, a space, that is ecologically poor, to itself. And while the subject, as I have argued, is perhaps to be understood as himself being poor in world, what emerges in the final movement of *Texts for Nothing* is an image of the poverty of the world, as such: the subject persists in his positionless poverty; the subject persists in his posthuman position in the here: for the subject, there is no possibility of another place to be: 'Unfortunately it is not a question of elsewhere, but of here' (*CSP* 153). But the here, as again the narrator himself suggests, is void, spectral, perhaps not even recognisable as a world. I imagine the subject, as Text 13 opens, now fully positionless, now split between worlds, divided within himself and perhaps against himself, speaking of himself in a voice that perhaps could have functioned in a world of plenitude but is now divorced from its source and haunting the subject as both his own and not his own; I imagine the subject now coming to some deeply compromised understanding of what it means to be, now, in the world of the here, the world that *itself* is poor in world:

> Whose voice, no one's, there is no one, there's a voice without a mouth, and somewhere a hand, it calls that a hand, it wants to make a hand, or if not a hand something somewhere that can leave a trace,

of what is made, of what is said, you can't do with less, no, that's romancing, more romancing, there is nothing but a voice leaving a trace. A trace, it wants to leave a trace, yes, like air leaves among the leaves, among the grass, among the sand, it's with that it would make a life, but soon it will be the end, it won't be long now, there won't be any life, there won't have been any life, there will be silence, the air quite still that trembled once an instant, the tiny flurry of dust quite settled. Air, dust, there is no air here, nor anything to make dust, and to speak of instants, to speak of once, is to speak of nothing, but there it is, those are the expressions it employs. (*CSP* 152–3)

And thus what are we left with in *Texts for Nothing*? What remains? As the narrator says, there is nothing but a voice and its trace, the voice of a positionless subject, distributed between states of being, inhabiting the space of what Deleuze and Guattari call the 'non-localizable relation' of becoming. And this is the state of the posthuman in *Texts for Nothing*: inhabiting simultaneous states of being, none of which will allow the subject to come to an end. And here, of course, is the true agony of the Beckettian subject, posthuman or otherwise: the inability to end. Despite the fact that the world of the here is bereft of that which would support life or signs of life, as such – *air, dust, there is no air here, not anything to make dust* – it is a world that cannot cease; there is only the fantasy of finding a space where the subject could materialise and perhaps enter into temporality and causality: 'go where time passes and atoms assemble an instant' (*CSP* 153). The subject, now ecologically distributed between worlds, is endlessly sustained within that dialectic and within even the poorest of world states:

> and were there one day to be here, where there are no days, which is no place, born of the impossible voice the unmakable being, and a gleam of light, still all would be silent and empty and dark, as now, as soon now, when all will be ended, all said, it says, it murmurs. (*CSP* 154)

To be in the world, to be in *this* world, is to find oneself suspended, positionless (there are no days, there is no place) before the very limit, the boundary, between being and non-being. To be in the world thus, and finally, means only ever to register the deprivation of the world and the poverty of its endless, and unavoidable, embrace.

Notes

1. Although written in a different register, Steven Connor's remarks about Beckett's exploration of finitude harmonise nicely with Chambers' notion of the limit: 'It [Beckett's finitude] is a finitude that is never used up, or said and done, a finitude to be fully accounted for, abbreviated or economised on, because there will always be, what there only ever is, more of the here and now. A finitude that, seemingly without let or cease, itself remains finite' ('Beckett's Radical Finitude' 49–50).
2. In *Beckett: A Guide for the Perplexed*, I argue that the subject in *The Unnamable* may be best understood via Blanchot's reading of the affect of trauma in *The Writing of the Disaster*. The speaker of *The Unnamable*, unable to locate the source of his alteration into his present state of (posthuman) being, becomes what Blanchot calls a '*subjectivity without any subject*' (*The Writing of the Disaster* 30), an entity displaying the affect of being without a full claim to being, as such. For a critical expansion on these ideas, see Liz Effinger's 'Beckett's Posthuman: The Ontopology of *The Unnamable*'.
3. The phrase 'grisly afterbirth' is quoted in Enoch Brater's *The Drama in the Text: Beckett's Late Fiction* (9).
4. Morton uses the term 'strange stranger' throughout his work, but most centrally in *The Ecological Thought*.
5. David Farrell Krell puts the matter thusly in *Ecstasy, Catastrophe*: 'Understanding, for Heidegger, is not the faculty that synthesizes categories and intuitions, enabling us to *know* the world. To repeat, knowing the world is a *founded, derivative* mode of being in the world' (44).
6. In *Heidegger and Homecoming*, Robert Mugerauer describes deseverance thusly: 'we bring the world to ourselves to live in it, use things in it, and understand it' (29).
7. For a reading of Beckett's treatment of space up to *The Unnamable*, see John Wall's '"L'au-delà du dehors-dedans": Paradox, Space, and Movement in Beckett'.
8. In some sense I am begging the question of the 'reality' of the fictional character, as such. Of course the speaker of *Texts for Nothing* is not real; he is a character in a series of stories. But I am not convinced that *Texts for Nothing* is merely an extended meditation on the various philosophical complexities of what we may call 'fictional ontology'. I have argued elsewhere (*Beckett: A Guide for the Perplexed*) that *The Unnamable* is a text where Beckett does call into question the various ontological realities of his characters; as the novel unfolds an examination of what it means to be a character within a novel (or an author of a series of

novels), it becomes clear that *The Unnamable* is a meditation on questions of agency within complex discursive realms (it strikes me that Porter Abbott's characterisation of *Texts for Nothing* as a form of the 'meditative personal essay' [*Beckett Writing Beckett* 90] is thus more accurately applied to *The Unnamable*).

9. Agamben's gloss on Heidegger's reading of the animal's poverty in world is important: 'the animal is not simply without world, for insofar as it is open to captivation, it must – unlike the stone, which is worldless – do without world, lack it' (*The Open: Man and Animal* 55). The question for Beckett's subject is critical: how does one do *without* world and yet know that what counts is to *be* in the world? For a reading of this question that continues to interrogate Heidegger, see Haraway's *When Species Meet* (367–8).

10. Derrida's reading of Heidegger's *The Fundamental Concepts of Metaphysics* is informed by a keen sense of the inherent aporias in Heidegger's conception of the animal. In *The Animal That Therefore I Am*, Derrida points out that Heidegger at times contradicts himself in his characterisation of the animal. Derrida notes that Heidegger argues, in contradiction to himself, that the animal is that which *cannot* die (cannot register the fact that death is a possibility) but also that which *can* die (154); Derrida notes further that Heidegger suggests that what defines the being of the animal is its deprivation, its 'not having', but that, at the same time, the animal's state of being 'poor in world' means, by definition, that it 'has world' enough to lose (156). Beyond attempting to demonstrate the inherent aporias at work in Heidegger's reading of the animal, as such, Derrida wishes to suggest that the very ground of Heidegger's analysis of animality and humanity is shaky, at best. Why? Because Heidegger is unable to offer a definition of *world*, the very idea upon which the subsequent analysis of animality and humanity is based. Derrida writes: 'At the point where he [Heidegger] advances like an army, armed with theses, solid, positive theses, it buckles, and he says in the end: decidedly, this concept of world is obscure. At bottom he doesn't know what "world" means' (151). Derrida, nevertheless, still must engage with Heidegger, still must deconstruct his reading of the animal even as he admits that the argument he is dismantling is groundless. And I say 'still must' here with purpose. Because Derrida has made a similar argument before: in 'Finis' he draws attention to Heidegger's insistence that the animal cannot die, an idea that compels Derrida to carefully unfold the relation between 'dying' and 'perishing', a binary that ultimately exposes the contradictions at the heart of Heidegger's reading of the animal (Derrida will make a similar argument in *The Beast & The Sovereign, Volume II*). In '*Geschlecht* II: Heidegger's Hand',

Derrida will unravel the aporias at work in Heidegger's refusal to see the ape as a being in the world, as being unable to wield the 'hand' as a means of giving to the world, rather than merely taking (175); similarly, and to cite one final example, Derrida takes Heidegger to task in 'Heidegger's Ear' for his insistence that the animal is ontologically incapable of parsing the world, incapable of reading the world in terms of comparison and discrimination; the animal, as Derrida characterises Heidegger's reading, is incapable of reading the world in terms of the 'as such'; this deprivation means that the animal cannot register the world in terms other than its own.

11. In *The Open*, Agamben writes (and anticipates perhaps our reading of Beckett's posthuman subject in *Texts for Nothing*): 'if the caesura between the human and the animal passes first of all within man, then it is the very question of man – and of "humanism" – that must be posed in a new way' (16); the question of the animal, as such, for Agamben compels him to interrogate the category of the human.

12. On the question of Heidegger's possible use for ecology theory, see Hanspeter Padrutt's 'Heidegger and Ecology': Padrutt here defines his understanding of what Heidegger's signifies by 'world': 'The world is no longer the universe, "all of the world", the sum of everything, but rather the play of the world in which we are inseparably connected co-players' (26).

13. For another reading of Beckett's posthumanism, and specifically his complication of the 'human/animal distinction', see Karalyn Kendall-Morwick's 'Dogging the Subject' (101). See also Naoya Mori's '"An Animal Inside": Beckett/Leibniz's Stone, Animal, Human and the Unborn' for a brief reference to *Texts for Nothing* and animality; Yoshiki Tajiri's 'Beckett, Coetzee and Animals', for an excellent analysis of Beckett's use of the animal; Steven Connor's now-prescient 'Making Flies Mean Something', although written in a different philosophical register than the present chapter, does offer a way of thinking about Beckett's blurring of demarcated lines between animals and humans.

14. For important work on the subject of Beckett and ecology, see Paul Saunders' 'Samuel Beckett's Trilogy and the Ecology of Negation'; Paul Davies' 'Strange Weather: Beckett from the Perspectives of Ecocriticism'; and Steven Connor's 'Beckett's Atmospheres'.

15. For another reading of the relation between the two spaces of *Texts for Nothing*, see Joanne Shaw's 'The Figure in the Landscape in Jack Yeats and in Samuel Beckett'.

16. On this point, of the posthuman subject as essentially still haunted by the remainders of the human it attempts to leave behind, see Ruben Borg's 'Putting the Impossible to Work'. Borg draws on Neil

Badmington's *Alien Chic* to suggest that one of the 'hypotheses' that emerge from theories of the posthuman is that 'posthumanity is always co-implied with humanity' (164).

17. It is this idea, that the world itself has been diminished in a real, material, and ontological sense, that problematises any attempt, as for example by Robert Pogue Harrison, to read Beckett's world, its material reality, in allegorical terms. The world, its ecological poverty, is *real* in Beckett; it is not, as Harrison argues in his brief reading of *Molloy*, a metaphor for any philosophical position or world view (see his *Forests: The Shadow of Civilization* 151–2).

3

Spaces of Ruin: *All Strange Away, Imagination Dead Imagine, The Lost Ones, Ping, Lessness*

A place, that again.

(*All Strange Away*)

In this chapter I map out a trajectory that I see emerging in the fiction from *All Strange Away* (1963–4) to *Lessness* (1969). My task here will be to analyse the relation between *being* and *space* in what Beckett himself referred to as the 'closed space' fictions: *All Strange Away, Imagination Dead Imagine* (1965), *Ping* (1966), *The Lost Ones* (1966, 1970). I begin with *All Strange Away* as the text which sets out the parameters of the closed space fiction: here we are given precise dimensions of the space a subject either inhabits or into which he projects his memories; as the text unfolds, the subject's space is reduced (from five foot square and six feet high) to a cube measuring 'three foot every way' (*CSP* 173); the space finally becomes a rotunda supporting a dome 'as in the Pantheon at Rome or certain beehive tombs' (*CSP* 176). My interest here is to think through the relation between these interior spaces and the interiority of the subject: is this text offering a way of thinking about material interior spaces and the (metaphorical) spatiality of the subject? (We speak of 'interiority' as a way of referring to the self but perhaps ignore the spatial implications of the word.) As we move to *Imagination Dead Imagine*, the 'residual precipitate' of *All Strange Away*, we notice that Beckett has refined the image of the subject as interiority: here now the subject is beyond what appears to be all markers of (conventional) life: 'No trace anywhere of life' (*CSP* 182), but the *material reality of the space*, now mathematically precise, remains. As I move into a discussion of this text, and map its relation to the unfolding of the closed spaces of *Ping* and *The Lost Ones*, I will return to questions raised in *Texts for Nothing*, but here perhaps answer them in a different register: how are we to understand the relation between the perceiving, remembering subject, the subject who appears only as the catastrophic remainder of a past self, and his location within massively reduced and confined spaces, spaces that appear as testimony, perhaps *witness*, to a seismic shift in the reality of the world, as such? My real interest here, in these closed space fictions, is to analyse what I am calling 'post-catastrophic space' in an effort to map some ecological, that is, deeply *relational*, connection between catastrophic space and catastrophic interiorities/subjectivities. How, for instance, are we to understand the relation between the posthuman and the mathematically precise, almost machined space he inhabits? The space of *All Strange Away*, *Imagination Dead Imagine*, and *The Lost Ones*, especially, are rigorously demarcated to the point where, perhaps, we can begin to think of that space as a *technology* of confinement. The posthuman, as Haraway and Hayles have argued, emerges as a technological event: the human, interacting with technology, becomes other than it was. Do Beckett's short texts present an image of the technologically defined, because confined, posthuman subject? Bruno Latour's question regarding the *anthropos* should detain us here: 'Where are we to situate the human?' (*We Have Never Been Modern* 136). Perhaps we will discover that the question of the *situatedness* of the subject is, for Beckett, the only real question. This chapter will end with a reading of *Lessness*, a text that, I believe, stands as the logical end of the closed space fiction. Here Beckett moves the catastrophic subject away from any technology of confinement and into the external environment, itself marked as post-catastrophic: 'Scattered ruins same grey as the sand ash grey true refuge' (*CSP* 197). Here of course my analysis will be guided by Beckett's own word: *refuge*. How, I ask, does this ruined world act as 'refuge'? How is this ruined world a refuge in ways that the closed spaces of the previous fictions are not? Is the ruined world itself an implicit critique of the logic of the technological regime? What, to look forward to Beckett's 'neither' – a text with which I will conclude this book – is the relation between Beckett's use of the word 'refuge' here and the concept – perhaps an impossible one for the posthuman – of the 'unspeakable home' ('neither')?

All Strange Away/Imagination Dead Imagine

In 1963 and 1964 Beckett composed *All Strange Away*, a text that, as Stanley Gontarski notes in *The Complete Short Prose*, marks Beckett's return to short fiction after *Texts for Nothing*, a decade earlier. *All Strange Away*, and its curious appendix, *Imagination Dead Imagine*, find their origins in an abandoned work called *Fancy Dead*, the remains of which were published as *Faux Departs* in 1965.[1] It is in *Faux Departs* 4 that we encounter a crucial phrase, one that, appropriately enough, haunts *All Strange Away* and *Imagination Dead Imagination*, if only in its absence. The opening of *Faux Departs* 4 reads as follows:

> Imagination dead imagine.
>   Imagine a place, that again.
>   Never ask another question.
>   Imagine a place, then someone in it, that again.
>   Crawl out of the frowsy deathbed and drag it to a place to die in.
>   Out of the door and down the road in the old hat and coat like after the war, no, not that again.
>   A closed space five foot square by six high, try for him there. (*CSP* 272)

The seventh sentence of *All Strange Away* reads: 'Five foot square, six high, no way in, none out, try for him there' (*CSP* 169). Beckett has excised the phrase 'a closed space', but, as I say, the phrase haunts the fiction of the 1960s even as it provides an interpretive entry point into the worlds Beckett offers.

And indeed it is my purpose here, in my reading of *All Strange Away* and *Imagination Dead Imagine*, to attempt to make some sort of interpretive sense of the spaces Beckett represents here. Specifically, I am interested in exploring the viability of a series of ideas or questions in relation to these curious, uncanny, and fundamentally resistant works. What kind of space is being represented here? What kind of mind is imagining these spaces into being? What is the precise ontological status of the imagining, or perceiving, or projecting mind? If the spaces of *All Strange Away* and *Imagination Dead Imagine* function, as I will attempt to suggest, as spaces of memory, is it not possible – and here I offer my central reading – to read these spaces as archival and thus, ultimately, as spaces of mourning?

Spaces of Ruin 99

Here then are the opening lines of *All Strange Away*, lines that immediately signal a relation between space, being, and imagination:

> Imagination dead imagine. A place, that again. Never another question. A place, then someone in it, that again. Crawl out of the frowsy deathbed and drag it to a place to die in. Out of the door and down the road in the old hat and coat like after the war, no, not that again. Five foot square, six high, no way in, none out, try for him there. (*CSP* 169)

The narrator signals that this turn to space – the word he uses here is 'place' and I will return to it specifically – is a turn to an interior space. After the world that we find in, for instance, *Texts for Nothing*, which witnesses the subject in the exterior, natural world, here, in *All Strange Away*, we are in the interior, an interior that is specifically and mathematically ordered: five foot square, six high. This is a space of confinement – 'no way in, none out' – but it is also one of definition and conjuring: 'try for him there.' It seems at the outset, thus, that *All Strange Away* is a deliberately foregrounded allegory of creation, of the creative process: this is an attempt to conjure, via a dying imagination, a subject and a world (albeit a compromised and limited world) for that subject to be in.[2] And Beckett is clear that this conjuring, this attempt to call a being into being, functions at the limit of imaginative possibility: the narrative imagination – and this text does seem to be an allegory of writing, at least at one level – is dead: *imagination dead*; and yet it continues: *imagine*. The imagination, in other words, is perfectly spectral, almost to the point of a kind of parody. This is the continuation of a dead imagination: 'Crawl out of the frowsy deathbed and drag it to a place to die in.' And Beckett continues to signal the spectrality, and thus the posthuman quality, of the imagination, via the economy of the spaces it conjures: 'a place, that again', a phrase he uses twice. Place here is a space of return and repetition; by its very nature of signalling a return, a revenant always already evokes a haunting. The conjuring imagination thus is established immediately as spectral; the spaces it wishes to conjure, by return and repetition, too are spectral and thus perfect, perhaps even unavoidable, haunts or homes for the posthuman subject.

But I wonder if we should pause here and consider what has happened to the idea of space as *Faux Departs* is translated into

All Strange Away. Recall *Faux Departs*: 'A closed *space* five foot square by six high' (*CSP* 272); in *All Strange Away* we read: 'A *place*, that again.' The spectral, because now absent, 'space' has been replaced by the equally spectral, because repeating, 'place'. But should we not consider the semantic shift here, the shift from space to place? I would suggest, following geographer Yi-Fu Tuan, that we consider that place is space transformed into something approaching a kind of familiarity. Space, Tuan contends, is an abstraction; place is a result of the domestication of space: '"Space" is more abstract than "place". What begins as undifferentiated space becomes place as we get to know it better and endow it with value' (*Space and Place* 6). Place thus is something of an hermeneutical event, a translation of abstraction into knowability. Jeff Malpas' crucial readings of Heidegger and place allow us to understand that, for Heidegger, like Tuan, place is space transformed: Heidegger understands place as that which permits being, as such, to emerge. Being, as we have seen, is spatial, as Heidegger argues in *Being and Time*: being is bounded, delimited, by its location in space. But being, as Malpas argues, only comes to know itself as it founds itself in place, as a topology: 'being', he writes, 'has to be understood as, one might say, an "effect" of place . . . being emerges only in and though space' (*Heidegger's Topology* 6). Tuan, though he does not cite Heidegger, adds an idea to his analysis of place that is fascinating and useful for our reading of Beckett: 'if we think of space as that which allows movement, then place is pause; each pause in movement makes it possible for location to be transformed into place' (*Space and Place* 6). We will observe specifically the idea of space as movement in our reading of *Fizzles* – a text that in some sense thematises Heidegger's notion of directionality and de-severance – but here, in these closed space fictions, we are offered what Tuan calls a pause, rest. And it is what occurs within this place of pause, the space of rest, that is crucial; it is what occurs within this domestication of space, this overt attempt – on the part of the narrator, on the part, perhaps, of the narrated subject – to make space readable, useful, and valuable, that should detain us.

I wish in what follows to offer a reading of *All Strange Away* and *Imagination Dead Imagine* that finds its point of inspiration in Derrida's conception of the archive. Specifically I am interested in suggesting that these texts are about the *economy of memory*; memory that comes into being as a projection of desire in what night be called, after Tuan, *paused space*; memory that comes into being as it finds itself *located and housed*; memory that works as an archived residue of the process of impossible mourning. *All Strange Away* and *Imagination Dead Imagine* are, to speak bluntly, about the spatialisation of mourning: mourning becomes space precisely as memory is projected and domesticated 'as' and 'in' place. But there are initial, and critical, interpretive difficulties in any reading of these texts: who, to speak only of the most obvious difficulty, is speaking here? Who is doing the imagining? *Imagination dead imagine*. At one immediate level, given that the narrative voice of *All Strange Away* seems to speak another being into existence – 'Light off and let him be, on the stool, talking to himself in the last person' (*CSP* 169) – it seems that there is a separation between narrative voice and the initially conjured figure. But there is equally no reason not to suggest that this speaker is conjuring his own space, his own space of memory, and is maintaining a critical, perhaps protective distance between himself and the projected space of desire. Perhaps it is even possible to imagine that the work of imagination here is always already lacking any grounding subjectivity or person; that what we are presented with here in *All Strange Away* is a radically displaced voice, a radically ungrounded voice, a subjectivity without any subject, to return to Blanchot. I am uncertain whether it possible to decide, hermeneutically, which of these readings is the most appropriate or correct here, or even if these terms apply. What I do think is crucial to indicate is the difficulty itself: at the very least, there is a distance, perhaps ironic, perhaps protective, perhaps even spectral, between voice and its object, or objects. What is clear, however, is that this conjured 'he', the projection of a dying imagination (or being projecting his own dying desire), exists in a space whose sole purpose seems to be the concomitant conjuring of a lost figure of desire: 'fancy', as the narrator will put it, 'is his only hope' (*CSP* 170). The fancy, like the work of imagination (Beckett's narrator seems to conflate the two terms), may be 'dead' (*CSP* 171), but the work of mourning seems to proceed: the figure projects onto the places of his space memories of the lost Emma (or Emmo): 'See how light stops at five soft and mild for bodies, eight or more, one per wall, four in all, say all of Emma' (*CSP* 171). This work of projected memory reaches its maximum intensity with the following: 'Imagine lifetime, gems, evenings with Emma and the flights by night, no, not that again' (*CSP* 171); the final 'no, not that again' signals perhaps an anxiety of memory, an anxiety of a retention of memory that can only ever be memory and thus a space of pain. Because what follows from this projection of memory and desire would seem to be the full and material conjuring of Emma herself: as if the initial conjured or imagined being – he – has in turn conjured his own remembered lost one, Emma. And it is this work of projection and conjured imagination that should detain us, this seeming material projection or externalisation of memory.

Derrida's notion of hauntology, we recall, allows us to begin thinking about the precarious being of the Beckettian subject, what I am calling here the Beckettian posthuman: the spectral subject, neither here nor not here, neither absent nor present, material nor non-material, is defined, if this is indeed a term that is useful here, by its absolute resistance to knowledge. In *Specters of Marx* Derrida writes this about the spectre:

> *It is* something that one does not know, precisely, and one does not know if precisely it *is*, if it exists, if it responds to a name and corresponds to an essence. One does not know: not out of ignorance, but because this non-object, this non-present present, this being-there of an absent or departed one no longer belongs to knowledge. (6)

The initial conjured subject in *All Strange Away*, like Derrida's spectre, is defined by his ontological imprecision: 'Now he is here' (*CSP* 169), 'he's not here' (*CSP* 170, 171); like the spectre, who again, as Derrida reminds us, is marked, if not defined, by the event of the return – 'the specter is always a *revenant*' (*Specters of Marx* 11) – Beckett's initial figure is a repeating one, defined by his being in a repeating place: 'A place, that again . . . A place, then someone in it, that again' (*CSP* 169). And if the initial figure is spectral, as I would argue, the second figure, Emma, can only be a repetition of a repeating spectre: she is conjured by a conjured figure defined by his status as an effect of a dying imagination that, as I suggested above, is itself spectral because it functions either on the brink of, or just beyond, the event of death: *imagination dead imagine*.[3]

But it is not exactly the status of the two figures here in *All Strange Away* that should detain us, perfect representations of the posthuman though they are. I am more interested here in the spaces within which these figures come into compromised being: the space or place of memory. I am, that is, attempting here to find the appropriate vocabulary with which to speak of the space of return and hauntology. And here we benefit, again, from Derrida's crucial work, in this case *Archive Fever*. It is not my intention to rehearse the rigorous complexities of this text here, having done so before many times, but we should remind ourselves of its central arguments.[4] First, and perhaps for our purposes here, foremost, the archive is always already a spectral space. Oriented not only, or even primarily, to the past, the archive, argues Derrida, instantiates itself as a call to the future, a promise to a time to come:

> The question of the archive is not, we repeat, a question of the past. It is not the question of a concept dealing with the past that might *already* be at our disposal or not at our disposal, *an archivable concept of the archive*. It is a question of the future, the question of the future itself, the question of a response, of a promise and of a responsibility for tomorrow ... A spectral messianicity is at work in the concept of the archive ... (*Archive Fever* 36)

It is not, I think, going too far to suggest that the archive, in its relation to the future, is something of an imaginative, if not imaginary, event: it speaks to what is to come, what cannot be seen, or anticipated, but perhaps hoped for. The archive, in other words, is spectral, like all events of desire. But this complex, this event (perhaps the event of the archive is a gestalt), of imaginative, projected desire only describes the affect of the archive. Derrida is quite clear that the archive is always a materialisation of that affect: the archive is always spatial, material, real. As he traces the etymology of the word *archive*, Derrida is emphatic: the archive

> names at once the *commencement* and the *commandment*. This name apparently coordinates two principles in one: the principle according to nature or history, *there* where things *commence* – physical, historical, or ontological principle – but also the principle according to the law, *there* where men and gods *command*, *there* where authority, social order are exercised, *in this place* from which order is given. (1; italics in original)

The archive is a spatialised, located act of projected, spectral desire; speaking of history and to the future, the archive is always already a place, and space, of desire. And this place is always, must always be, external to the subject. The archive is always, as

Derrida writes, *there*: there to be seen, or indeed secreted away, but always to be seen. The archive defines itself, or is defined, as an externalisation of spectralised desire; the archive, to use Derrida's specific terminology, is consigned to an externality: 'There is no archive without a place of consignation, without a technique of repetition, and without a certain exteriority. No archive without outside' (11). It is this idea – the archive as externalised consignation – that coordinates perfectly with an idea Derrida later elaborates in his reading of the function of the mystic writing pad in Freud (the idea being that the unconscious is indelibly marked by the traces of experience): Derrida proffers the notion that the archive, like the mystic writing pad, is an externalisation of the subject's – or indeed the culture's – unconscious, a process of externalisation that, in a critical way, marks the unconscious as, if only in the act of archiving, separate from the imagining, desiring subject. Acts of memory and acts of projected desire, are seen, enacted, and witnessed by the subject: memory becomes an event of externalisation. This externalisation enacts or instantiates, in Derrida's telling phrase, a *'prosthesis of the inside'* (19).

And it is this idea – archive as prosthesis of the inside; archive as projected space of memory and future desire – that resonates with a reading of Beckett's *All Strange Away* and *Imagination Dead Imagine*. I am drawn to the Derridean notion of the prosthesis because it names a sort of distancing at work between the subject and its memory, between the subject and the place of consignation: the prosthesis functions as extension but also as adjunct to the subject; the image of the archive as prosthesis suggests that memory functions, or can function – and maybe it is functioning here as a distancing protection of the subject – separate from the remembering subject. What is clear, as I suggested at the outset of my discussion, is that the remembering subject here in *All Strange Away*, and, indeed, in *Imagination Dead Imagine*, is at least difficult to pin down: who is doing the projecting here? Is the narrative representing the efforts of a subject to remember; with, for instance, 'try for him there' is the narrator speaking of himself, to himself, yet refusing to enter the first person? Is he, that is, 'talking to himself in the last person'? Or is *All Strange Away*, as a whole, a radically displaced, ungrounded and ungroundable, affect of a sourceless memory? A memory without subject? As I argued above, I think these questions are unanswerable, but the effect of the question, the effect of the inability to ground the narrative voice within a single, or even singular, voice, is to suggest that the memory work being done here, this projected, prosthetised archive work, instantiates what we should call, after Blanchot, and with an eye to our larger discussion of the posthuman, a subjectivity without any single subject. The archive work here, in other words, takes place, as a prosthetic of the inside, within the space of the posthuman just as the posthuman comes into being within the space conjured by the dying, the dead, the posthuman subject.[5]

But this archived posthuman space functions not merely as a sign of displaced subjectivity. This space, first a cube, then a rotunda 'three foot diameter eighteen inches high supporting a dome semi-circular in section as in the Pantheon at Rome or certain beehive tombs' (*CSP* 176), becomes a space with purpose and as such, to return to Tuan, is translated into place, a place, we might be tempted to say, of mourning. But we need to be careful here; we might, as I say, be tempted to read this place – beehive tombs – and the quality of the work enacted or instantiated here – spectres conjuring spectres – as the place and work of mourning, but, as I have argued elsewhere, and as is clear from not merely the logic of this text, but of its critical adjunct, *Imagination Dead Imagine*, the work of mourning, as such, is not being done here, perhaps *cannot* be done here. Mourning, as Freud argues, involves the subject being able to withdraw his or her libidinal identification with the lost object and to find expression for that energy elsewhere: mourning is an effect of translation, in other words.[6] And while the subject who mourns never forgets the lost object – and Freud is clear that mourning is not a forgetting – the lost object ceases to cast its shadow on the still living subject. It strikes me that what Beckett offers here in his representation of the remembering, spectral subject in *All Strange Away* is more closely aligned with what Freud would call melancholy: the inability or unwillingness to mourn the lost object. The melancholic subject is unable, or unwilling, to translate his libidinal energy to anther object and is, consequently, continually haunted by loss, still lives within the space of loss. The archive, as I have argued elsewhere, is the perfect space, if not place, for melancholy to unfold its dark economy, given that the archive is defined as a space of haunting: history is conjured in the archive in order for it to remain, *as remainders*, forever. (Even Derrida's model of the archive, which suggests that the archive is oriented to the future rather than the past, sets the archive up as a space of futural haunting: the archive is spectral and thus melancholic, a priori, in that it invites the spectre of the future into the present.)

The memory work being done here in *All Strange Away* is a refusal of mourning: the remembering subject conjures a place, again. This is a repeated, perhaps endlessly repeating, act of projected memory, an endless act of return, of nostalgia for what was lost: the self, perhaps having died, conjures itself in order to conjure the lost object, Emma. Emma's appearance, the spectre for a spectre, occurs, crucially, in the second part of *All Strange Away* following the title 'Diagram'. A diagram, if we trace the term etymologically, means to mark out a figure; a diagram maps or, more accurately, projects a possible localisation of a figure in space. I am fascinated by Beckett's deliberate use of this term here in the second section of this text because the idea of the diagram so perfectly aligns with the notion of imaginary spaces, spaces of desire: a diagram is always already only a possibility. Emma does not appear as a reification of a memory. Coming into being as the projection of a spectralised imagination, Emma exists, if this is the term, twice removed from being. In some senses, if, that is, we read Emma and the space she inhabits from a Derridean perspective, Emma not only comes into being within the melancholy space of the archive, this prosthesis of the inside, but she in some senses is the perfect allegory of the spectralised nature of the archive itself. Derrida writes: 'the structure of the archive is spectral. It is spectral a priori: neither present nor absent "in the flesh", neither visible nor invisible, a trace always referring to another whose yes can never be met' (*Archive Fever* 84). Derrida's humanising – or is it posthumanising? – of the archive brings us back to the human affect of loss at work here. In *All Strange Away*, the figure of the woman is perfectly spectral – a spectre of a spectre, as I suggest; she can never achieve a status beyond the trace, can only serve as a reminder of what was. She *is* the archival trace 'always referring to another'. She is, finally, the diagrammed archive of loss, endlessly signalling the impossibility of what Beckett will later call 'company':

> So in rotunda up to now with disappointment and relief with dread and longing sorrow all so weak and faint no more than faint tremors of a leaf indoors on earth in winter to survive till spring . . . All gone now and never been never stilled never voiced all back when never sundered unstillable turmoil, no sound, She's not here . . . (*CSP* 180)

Beckett follows this assertion of the trace's vanishing – 'she's not here' – by offering, if only for a moment, the possibility that absence may be mitigated, perhaps we can say prosthetically, by the imagination: 'Fancy is her only' (*CSP* 180). This phrase, one to be placed, almost predictably, under erasure only too soon – 'Fancy dead' (*CSP* 181) – is difficult to parse. Does the phrase suggest that fancy, the imagination, is Emma's only marker of presence on the world? That fancy is her only hope for existence? That she *is* only insofar as she is imagined to be? The fragment is a perfect grammatical index of Emma's hold on this world: partial, only a trace of a whole, a trace soon to be obliterated as the imagination itself subsides into nothingness: 'fancy murmured dead' (*CSP* 181).

Imagination Dead Imagine further complicates the idea of melancholy. Here Beckett telescopes the narrative movement of *All Strange Away* – a body is conjured, it conjures another in its turn – into a single image of two bodies in one space, the rotunda. 'Lying on the ground two white bodies, each in its semi-circle' (*CSP* 182). This image is again, perhaps, the product of a dying imagination. It is again difficult to assert who is doing the imaginative projecting work here: 'No trace anywhere of life, you say, pah, no difficulty there, imagination dead not yet, yes, dead, good, imagination dead imagine' (*CSP* 182). Is this 'you' the imagining subject speaking to himself in the second person? As I say, the question is difficult to answer, but what is clear, perhaps even clearer than in *All Strange Away*, is that there *is*, in fact, life here. This rotunda, with its complicated variations of rising and falling lights and temperatures, variations that speak, again, uncannily to the materiality of the space, is a space where life persists. I am interested in the way Beckett's linking of this text to *All Strange Away* asks us, at least initially, to imagine this space as having a similar economy: that is, one is tempted to read *Imagination Dead Imagine* as a compression of the previous text, a compression in which the economy of melancholy – the obsessive return to the past by conjuring the lost object – persists. *All Strange Away* may be a more explicit allegory of conjuring and memory – the text opens with an imaginative act of calling into being a being who in turn will offer a diagram of his own projected desires – but *Imagination Dead Imagine*, in its insistence on what appears to be the material presence of these bodies, suggests that something more than merely the memories of the subject, the memories of a possible lost happiness, is at stake here.

Beckett refers to *Imagination Dead Imagine* as the 'residual precipitate' of *All Strange Away* and we should pause and consider the metaphor at work here. Beckett's metaphor implies a sublimation of the contents of the previous text, as if, through a process of refinement and elimination, something ineffaceable remains. My suggestion here is that *Imagination Dead Imagine* is about the persistence of life in the face of its loss. What is being archived in this text is not the face of another, nor the memory of one's past life, but life, as such: the residual precipitate here is being itself. Notice how the text does not concern itself with the ephemera of memory, of affect, or of emotion. Here the relentless focus is on the materiality of things: light, darkness, temperatures (hot to cold), space. And while the space of this rotunda, like that of *All Strange Away*, seems at once to be allegorical and real – it may be that this space is a visual representation of the dying imagination's own interiority: 'Go back out, a plain rotunda, all white in the whiteness, go back in, rap, solid throughout, a ring as in the imagination the ring of bone' (*CSP* 182) – Beckett refuses to allow us to dismiss the actuality of the space and the bodies it contains. He is insistent on the mathematics of the space – 'Diameter three feet, three feet from ground to summit of the vault. Two diameters at right angles AB CD divide the white ground into two semicircles ACB BDA' (*CSP* 182) – just as he is insistent on the beingness of the bodies. The bodies here sweat and breathe; despite the fact that they lie uncannily still and thus 'might well pass for inanimate' (*CSP* 184), their eyes open and shut: they are not dead and 'they are not sleeping' (*CSP* 185). The space of *Imagination Dead Imagine*, in other words, is a space of a kind of perpetual material existence. The final lines of the text will complicate our ability to state explicitly that this is a text about persistence – and, thus, what about hope? – but *Imagination Dead Imagine*, as a whole, and even as it works in intimate relation to *All Strange Away*, suggests that this conjured space has an undeniable, ineffaceable claim on the imagining subject. This space, we are allowed to think, even as the text winds its way to a denial of the life it has conjured, will persist despite itself, despite, perhaps, the desires of the imagining subject. And in its persistence the possibility of life returns, in however compromised a form:

> Only murmur ah, no more, in this silence, and at the same instant for the eye of prey the infinitesimal shudder instantaneously suppressed. Leave them there, sweating and icy, there is better elsewhere. No, life

ends and no, there is nothing elsewhere, and no question now of ever finding again that white speck lost in whiteness, to see if they still lie still in the stress of that storm, or of a worse storm, or in the black dark for good, or the great whiteness unchanging, and if not what they are doing. (*CSP* 185)

It is the tension between 'Leave them there . . . there is better elsewhere', with the suggestion of continuity and persistence, and 'no, life ends and no, there is nothing elsewhere' that animates this text and its critical final moments. Does this 'no' evacuate entirely the possibility of the two bodies persisting? Does in fact the tension produced between the idea of the persistence of the bodies and the denial of their lives not allow for an image of uncanny spectrality to emerge? Is Beckett, in some way, not offering an image in these final lines of the subject, effaced, under erasure, but still persisting *even in its erasure*? Perhaps this idea – the persistence of the posthuman beyond place – there is nothing elsewhere – is strengthened by Beckett's sense that *Imagination Dead Imagine*, being the residual precipitate of *All Strange Away*, is connected to that text's economy of repetition and thus persistent return. In other words, what *All Strange Away* and *Imagination Dead Imagine* give us is an uncanny, paradoxical, impossible image of the posthuman subject as spectralised and endlessly returning, but only ever in the abandoned space of a dying imagination. The posthuman, in other words, can only ever be an event of the imagination; but it is an event, as it were, without end.

The Lost Ones

To this point in my analysis of Beckett's short prose there has been an implicit understanding about the nature of what I am calling posthuman space: posthuman space is space inhabited by the posthuman. That is to say, space itself maintains a kind of neutrality, insofar as it functions, at one level, merely to contain the posthuman, to house it, to define its limits and boundaries. My intention here, in my reading of *The Lost Ones* and *Lessness* (and further into *Fizzles*), is to begin teasing out the possibility that, in Beckett, space itself is more than a neutral holding ground for the posthuman, spectral subject. Space, I will argue, insofar as it becomes catastrophic, begins to reflect the posthumanity of the subject housed within its limits and boundaries; moreover, space, insofar as it becomes catastrophic, inscribes catastrophe onto the posthuman subject, translating the subject from mere inhabitant of space into something approaching *an expression of catastrophe itself*. The Beckettian posthuman becomes spatialised insofar as it becomes an adjunct to and of the catastrophe that defines its world.

The term 'catastrophic space' has two inflections here. First, the term refers to space or place that itself carries the mark, trace, or evidence of catastrophe. Beckett's spaces of ruin – found, say, in *Fizzles* or, as we shall presently see, in *Lessness* – offer themselves as locations of (an obviously aporetic) refuge. Second, the term can refer, as in *The Lost Ones* (and indeed *All Strange Away* and *Imagination Dead Imagine*), to space that *itself* houses catastrophe, or radical loss. Here space or place is not itself marked by signs of catastrophe: these are not the 'ruinstrewn' lands of *Fizzles* or *Lessness*. Rather, here, in *The Lost Ones*, space houses the subject of loss, the subject of catastrophe; space here – limited, mathematically formulated, carceral – marks the limits of the subject, defines its trajectory and its possibility.

And it is perhaps with the question of loss, as such, that we should begin our reading of this difficult text. *All Strange Away* and *Imagination Dead Imagine*, I argued, are archival texts, texts that work assiduously to preserve the memory of the lost one. Resurrecting the spectral lost other, or others, these texts mobilise space as a prosthetic extension of the imagining, desiring self. Space, in other words, becomes the objective correlative of the subject's desire, a desire to maintain a connection to what has been lost. *The Lost Ones*, too, obviously stages loss even as it figures the subject as only ever the subject *of* loss. We will return to the question of the ontology of the subjects in *The Lost Ones*, but I wish, at the outset, to spend some time thinking through the relation between the subject and the space that houses it. *Houses*. We notice the first word of the text is, in fact, 'abode' (in French it is *séjour*). This is a complicated and, I would argue, deliberately chosen word: it does of course mean 'home', 'house', or 'residence' in its noun form. But the word is more precise: from the Middle English, and in its verbal noun form of 'abide', the word means 'wait' or 'remain behind'; even more exactly, the word combines the notion of onward motion and waiting. What interests me here, of course, is how perfectly the term defines the subject and the space of the subject here in *The Lost Ones*: in motion, propelled by its loss into an inevitable and unavoidable condition of what Heidegger would call 'directionality' or 'de-severance', the subject is simultaneously condemned, it seems, to inhabit a mathematically limited and limiting space, what the narrator tells us is a 'flattened cylinder fifty metres round and sixteen high for the sake of harmony' (*CSP* 202).[7]

Despite the fact that Beckett explicitly frames this space of loss as an abode, we must not, I think, read the space as archival. While it is true that Derrida draws attention to the fact that the term archive, from the Greek *arkheoin*, refers to a domestic space, 'initially a house, a domicile, an address' (*Archive Fever* 2), the abode here in *The Lost Ones* is not, specifically, a space of memory, of history, or even of a spectral futurity. For one, I am not convinced that time, as such, functions here in any comprehensible way. The narrator will refer to the 'unthinkable first day' (*CSP* 212) of the subject's confinement here; as the text concludes, he suggests the subjects will remain here 'infinitely until towards the unthinkable end' (*CSP* 222). We are in a space and a time that perhaps reminds us of the 'infinite here' (*CSP* 123) of *Texts for Nothing* and as such memory and futurity are empty categories. But this is a space of loss. If it is a space not exactly of the memory of loss, it is, perhaps even more *painfully* – and I am using this word with purpose – a space where the affect, the passion, of loss is the predominant, if not only, feeling. If the archive, as Derrida reminds us, is doubly inflected in terms of its temporal orientation (to the past and to the future), the temporality of the space in *The Lost Ones* is only an infinite here and now of loss. This, then, is a purely and perfectly catastrophic space: this is the space of loss because loss is the only reality here.

There is thus a radical refinement of affect in *The Lost Ones*: loss becomes the only feeling. The subject is only, it seems, subject to the affect of loss. But we should perhaps wonder after this predominant affect. We should wonder what it means that loss is still present in this depleted world. Specifically, what business has the affect of loss here in this catastrophic world? What business has loss here among beings, it seems, so far removed from being human? And this is, of course, our question: what kind of being inhabits this world, this space, this place of loss? Beckett offers several ways of answering this question. The primary way is simply this: these are bodies, not subjects; if even there is intimate contact between these beings, they remain only bodies: 'the bodies brush together with a rustle of dry leaves' (*CSP* 202); there may be 'relatives and friends' (*CSP* 213) present here, as there are husbands and wives (*CSP* 213), but they remain 'strangers two paces apart' (*CSP* 213) and, ultimately, are only ever bodies in search of other lost bodies. This is, in other words, a carceral space where the carceral subject is reduced only to the status of the material body and a single, defining affect, the affect of loss. But still this affect is there, like a spectre of a defunct emotion, a ghost of an emotion that once would have been meaningful. Beckett's logic is ruthless: if loss is the only emotion or affect at work here in this carceral space, the emotion loses its meaning. There is nothing to measure that loss against if loss, the desire to search for the lost, is the only operational affect. Moreover, loss can only be measured and understood as it works in relation to the temporal: I know what I have lost because that loss occurred at some point, *then*. But if these subjects exist in a time so agonisingly slow, or if they live in an eternal present, what sense does loss, as such, make? Hence the mathematically ordered, habitual searching that occurs here: loss has become only instinct, the only instinct of the subject who no longer understands its economy.

To imagine the space of *The Lost Ones* as a space of habitual yet meaningless loss is to approach the truth of its space. And thus we can understand how Beckett's narrator can, accurately, refer to the searchers, or one group of searchers (the third group who will, periodically, be seized with the desire to find a ladder [*CSP* 204]), as a 'quidam' (*CSP* 205), a nobody. We can, thus, understand what the narrator means when he describes others' affectless reactions to the image of a couple engaged in sexual congress; or, crucially, that moment when the narrator details how the bodies periodically stop and look at each other, or at the void. The affect is flat, radically neutral:

> Stranger still at such times all the questioning eyes that suddenly go still and fix their stare on the void or on some old abomination as for instance other eyes and then the long looks exchanged by those fain to look away. Irregular intervals of such length separate these lulls that for forgetters the likes of these each is the first. Whence invariably the same vivacity of reaction as to the end of a world and the same brief amaze when the twofold storm resumes and they start to search again neither glad nor even sorry. (*CSP* 220)

I am intrigued by this last sentence: 'whence invariably the same vivacity of reaction as to the end of a world'. For some of these subjects, called the 'forgetters', the lulls between habitual searching and this staring into the void become, if only very briefly, a new experience. In this lull they seem to see things – the void, others' faces – as if for the first time. And Beckett's language is careful; this flash of seeing truly is invigorating, exciting, even life-giving ('the same vivacity'), if only for a brief moment. But it is this phrase – as if to the end of a world – that should detain us. It is not quite that the narrator is suggesting that seeing the truth of things, seeing, for instance, the face of the other, is seeing the end of a world, but it is 'as if' seeing the end of a world. This phrase is of course deeply ambiguous, tantalisingly so. It is one of very few phrases in *The Lost Ones* that alludes to a time prior to the non-temporality of this enclosed space. Because surely this idea, of the end of a world, does not obtain in this space of endlessness, of, at best, so slow a time passing that none can even notice it. Is it possible that the phrase indicates an event, a brief moment, when the subject is freed from the endless present of this time in the cylinder and vouchsafed a brief flash of memory of the catastrophe that preceded its entry into this space? Does this phrase, in fact, show us, in a complicated way, the nature of the loss in *The Lost Ones*?

Because we should notice how carefully Beckett indicates that these lost ones are not necessarily in search of some lost other, or indeed some lost aspect of the self. As the narrator says: 'None looks within himself where none can be' (*CSP* 211). We may take this phrase at first as indicating perhaps that the searching subject does not expect to find a lost object within, within, perhaps, the space of its own memory or interiority. Perhaps this line indicates that there is no interior space of memory for these searchers. Moreover, as we see at the end of this same paragraph, the searchers are not, in fact, searching for lost companions, lovers, husbands, or wives:

> Man and wife are strangers two paces apart to mention only this most intimate of all bonds. Let them move on till they are close enough to touch and then without pausing on their way exchange a look. If they recognize each other it does not appear. Whatever it is they are searching for it is not that. (*CSP* 213)

My suggestion, and it can only, of course, be a suggestion, is that the loss here in *The Lost Ones* is the loss of world, as such. We have heard that some of these searchers operate under the idea that there is a hidden 'way out to earth and sky' (*CSP* 207); others believe that there is a secret passage 'leading in the words of the poet to nature's sanctuaries' (*CSP* 206). This motivation to find a way out of this space may be operational, but Beckett raises this issue fairly early in the text and does not return to the idea as a major theme. Indeed this phrase, 'whatever they are searching for', does seem to indicate that the desire to find a way out is not quite the predominant desire. What I mean to say here is that the idea of a world 'out there', of 'earth and sky', of 'nature's sanctuaries', this possibly pre-lapsarian world before the catastrophic fall into this space, is not, I would argue, the same idea of world that is invoked in the phrase 'as to the end of a world'. These subjects here in *The Lost Ones* are indeed, as the title directly states, lost; they are in the space of loss, in the sense of not knowing where they are, not knowing how to proceed, not knowing any direction. The loss of world, as Heidegger reminds us, is always and only the catastrophic loss of direction, of directionality. World, as such, is defined by the ability to makes one's way in the world, by the ability to map out a space that, once defined, continues to work as space. Perhaps more accurately, and again to invoke the important work of Tuan, what the subject in *The Lost Ones* is unable to do is to transform this space – mathematically ordered as it is, but mathematically ordered not *by* the subject – into place. This space is not place in the sense that space has become knowable and familiar; this is a space, obviously limited, but continually and perhaps forever to be traversed; this is a space where nothing can be known.

And it is exactly here, in this space of nothing, a space inhabited by the quidam – the nothing – that Beckett, in the text's final paragraph, offers to the reader a deeply ambiguous event, perhaps an event that adds up to what we may call the plot of *The Lost Ones*. Here in this final moment of the text, which, as the narrator seems to indicate, may be the final moment of this space in the cylinder, 'a last body' (*CSP* 222), this 'last of all if a man' (*CSP* 223), perhaps seized with what the narrator has several times during the course of the text referred to as a 'passion' for searching, makes his way to another body, a woman. This event – the man parts the woman's hair and looks at her face and into her eyes – is marked off in a complicated temporality. This man is several times referred to as the 'last' man, the last body; we seem to be in what the narrator refers to as the 'unthinkable end' (*CSP* 222) of this space, its 'last state' (*CSP* 223). I am of course interested in how Beckett offers this image of lastness. This man is the last body, the last man; this act, perhaps, is the last act of passion to occur in the 'last state of the cylinder' (*CSP* 223). But Beckett is careful to qualify his description of the man: this last body is described three times in the final paragraph with the phrase '*if a man*' (*CSP* 223), as if, perhaps, it is unimportant if this is indeed a man; as if, perhaps, what matters is not the sex of the man, but the fact that he is a body. What matters, it seems, is not the body's humanity, but its placement there, in the cylinder, in this last state, to carry out this last act of passion. If this space is not, as in *All Strange Away* or *Imagination Dead Imagine*, precisely posthuman, it is, it seems, on the verge of being so.[8] But even so, even in this space of the limit or boundary of the posthuman, with this *finality* of the human, some trace of the human remains. This word, *passion*, defines the drive of the searcher: a searcher acts on the 'spur' of their passion (*CSP* 221); one is 'carried away by his passion' (*CSP* 222); there is an overall 'passion to search' (*CSP* 219) that would, it seems, threaten to define these subjects. It is curious that in this space of finality, a space where the humanity of the human seems on the verge of flickering out, a space where a man may or may not, in fact, be a man, that this purely human emotion, *passion*, is present. Like a ghost of some lost affect, passion haunts this text. 'Passion' of course means 'pain'. Pain is what drives, spurs, carries these searchers away; pain is what offers a spectre of directionality. And thus we must qualify what was said earlier. These searchers are not exactly lost in an unknowable space; they still feel the vestiges, the traces, of some affect that drives them, spurs them, commands some kind of movement, of trajectivity. But what is the end of this passion, this pain? What results from this directionality? Beckett is careful with his description of the event in these last lines of *The Lost Ones*. Here 'the last of all if a man' parts the hair of the woman:

> On his knees he parts the heavy hair and raises the unresisting head. Once devoured the face thus laid bare the eyes at a touch of the thumbs open without demur. In those calm wastes he lets his eyes wander till they are the first to close and the head relinquished falls back into its place. (*CSP* 223)

I am fascinated by this act for several reasons. At one level the act of gazing into the face of the other operates almost at the level of a parody of the Levinasian event of ethics. The self gazes upon the face of the other, acts as a witness to the terrifying and threatening faciality of the other. The otherness of the other is acknowledged: the self is constituted by that act of gazing. But here there is no real act of witnessing: the face of the other is gazed upon, 'devoured', but is there a reciprocal gaze? Or is there only and ever a kind of blankness? It is also critical to note how the face of the other here is not operating as a confirmation of an other that constitutes the self. The face of the other, and we should attend carefully to Beckett's words here, is translated into a space: 'calm wastes' where the eyes of this last man 'wander'. The man, inhabiting a space that is defined by loss, finds his way into another space itself defined as a space of waste, of nothingness, perhaps of catastrophe. There is no confirmation of self or other in this act of gazing: there is nothing to be seen here, nothing to be witnessed. And thus the man, this last man, returns to his place, this last act of passion having confirmed only the continuity of the space of loss. And indeed the final sentence of *The Lost Ones* also confirms a kind of continuity. If this final paragraph of the text begins with an indication of the possibility of finality – 'So on infinitely until towards the unthinkable end' (*CSP* 222) – this final sentence works only to bring the last man back to an endless beginning:

> So much roughly speaking for the last state of the cylinder and of this little people of searchers one first of whom if a man in some unthinkable past for the first time bowed his head if this motion is maintained. (*CSP* 223)

This act, at once first and last, at once occurring in a singularity of finality and a singularity of an absolute beginning, occurs both in the space of an unthinkable end and an unthinkable past. Here loss is, it seems, always already to be reconstituted, always already to define the subject – itself on the verge of becoming human no more – as endlessly seized by a passion that can only ever reveal nothing.

Ping/Lessness

On the back cover of the Signature edition of *Lessness* Beckett writes (or is quoted as saying) the following:

> 'Lessness' has to do with the collapse of some such refuge as that last attempted in 'Ping' and with the ensuing situation of the refugee. Ruin, exposure, wilderness, mindlessness, past and future denied

and affirmed, are the categories formally distinguishable, through
which the writing winds, first in one disorder, then in another.
(*Grove Companion* 318)[9]

My task here in the final section of this chapter is to speak of
the situatedness of the subject in both *Ping* and *Lessness*. I am
interested in attempting to speak of the idea of dwelling: dwelling in the sense of living in a space; dwelling in the more Heideggerian inflection of the term which will come to mean something
like the relation between being, *as such*, and space. To state my
thesis directly at the outset: the posthuman does not dwell; the
posthuman cannot dwell. To dwell, in the Heideggerian sense of
things, means to find oneself within circumscribed space, to find
oneself limited by the boundary of space. To dwell, which for Heidegger is always synonymous with being, means to find oneself at
the boundary of an observable definitional threshold, a boundary that, in Blanchot's terms, 'de-scribes' the self in relation to its
space (*The Writing of the Disaster* 7). To be a refugee, as Beckett
reminds us, means to find oneself, or to be found, in a space that
makes dwelling an impossibility. Beckett may several times refer to
the refuge in *Lessness* as the 'true refuge', but, as we will discover,
'true' here means only, perhaps, that the space that once did offer
the possibility of dwelling has revealed itself, as an *uncovering*, as
the ruin of what it once was. The refuge, in other words, reveals
itself – and this is its *truth* – in its disassembly, in its deconstruction. Seen for what it truly is too late, the refuge cannot offer the
possibility of dwelling. What is fascinating here, and this is the
reason I pair *Ping* and *Lessness* (and not merely because Beckett
himself does), is that despite the movement from an intact space
in *Ping* to the ruin and 'disorder' of *Lessness*, the spaces themselves are, I will argue, identical ontologically. The space of *Ping*
is entire, but, in a critical way, the space reveals nothing of what
we might call its spatiality: the planes of the walls are described as
'meeting invisibly one only shining white infinite but that known
not' (*CSP* 194).[10] The posthuman does not dwell because the space
of his dwelling cannot, will not, reveal its spatiality. Inhabiting a
space of infinite sameness, the posthuman subject cannot dwell: to
dwell means to be able to recognise the boundaries of space that
reveal the limits of being and thought. In a crucial way *Ping* and
Lessness, both texts of catastrophe insofar as they are texts that
remove the possibility of being, ask: what kind of subjectivity is

possible when spatiality no longer obtains? What kind of subject can emerge from within the catastrophic refuge?

Two quotations from Heidegger's essay 'Building Dwelling Thinking' will act as a guide through this discussion of *Ping* and *Lessness*. In the first Heidegger offers his working definition of space as that which is bounded and defined. Within that boundary not only does a concept of space emerge, but the subject – the being who dwells – comes to be, *as* a subject. The boundary, in other words, is the definitional threshold par excellence:

> Only things that are locations in this manner allow for spaces. What the word for space, *Raum*, designates is said by its meaning. *Raum*, *Rum*, means a place cleared or freed for settlement and lodging. A space is something that has been made room for, something that is cleared and free, namely, within a boundary, Greek *peras*. A boundary is not that at which something stops, but, as the Greeks recognized, the boundary is that from which something *begins its essential unfolding*. (BDT 332)

In the second quotation, one we attended to in our reading of *The End*, Heidegger makes clear the relation between space, dwelling, and being: 'Spaces open up by the fact that they are let into the dwelling of man. To say that mortals *are* is to say that *in dwelling* they persist through spaces by virtue of their stay among things and locations' (*BDT* 335). 'Building Dwelling Thinking' was published in 1954, but Heidegger's concern with the relation between space and being is consistent with his thinking in *Being and Time*. In both texts Heidegger emphasises the relation between being (Dasein) and the space that determines the outline of the possibilities of being. To be is to be within the boundedness of space, within space that is defined just as it in turn defines the limits of the human. We recall Section 1.3 of *Being and Time* and Heidegger's assertion that the '"subject" (Dasein), if well understood ontologically, is spatial. And because Dasein is spatial in the way we have described, space shows itself as a priori' (*BT* 146). What is crucial about the human's relation to that a priori, to the facticity of being in space as a mode of being in the world, is that that beingness comes to be *knowable* to the subject. To be a subject, in Heidegger's sense of things, is to come to know one's place within the world, is to be able to locate oneself spatially: 'knowing the world', he writes 'thus functions as the primary mode of being-in-the-world' (*BT* 59).

Space, it seems to me, in Beckett's *Ping* and *Lessness* is indeed an a priori, in even Heidegger's sense of things. Space is a ground upon which the subject rests or against which the subject itself is highlighted, or limned. Space here – the confines of a box or room; the vast wastes of sand – determines what can be seen of the subject. But, and this is crucial, space does not necessarily provide the grounds for the *subject* to know either itself or the space that determines it, *as* subject. This is perhaps all to say that space provides the grounds for the witnessing of the subject; space provides the narrator (and perhaps the reader?) – who functions as a witness to the posthuman subject – the means to see the subject; but the subject, posthumous, posthuman, post-*being*, remains in a space that, for him, cannot be a space, as such: the posthuman, as I am suggesting, cannot dwell.

And within the first two sentences of *Ping* Beckett explicitly thematises the idea of the relation between space, knowledge, and witnessing: 'All known all white bare white body fixed one yard legs joined like sewn. Light heat white floor one square yard never seen' (*CSP* 193). The phrase 'all known' implies an incompletion. Does the truncated grammar allow itself to be read as *all that is known*, as in *all that is known is this bare white body*? Who is doing the knowing here? Who, in the second sentence, is not seeing the white floor one square yard?[11] Is this body – can we call it a subject? – aware of its surroundings? I ask about the possibility of calling this body a subject and, as in *The Lost Ones*, the answer is complicated: this is a body, it seems, without interiority, or, at best, with only the traces of interiority. If subjectivity is determined at least in part, by the subject's sense of itself within history, within space, within time, then this body would seem to lack these prerequisites. Or almost. This incessant marker of exteriority, this *ping*, this echolocating sign of exteriority, inscribes, perhaps, a trace of the past: 'Ping murmur perhaps a nature one second almost never that much memory' (*CSP* 194); 'Ping murmur only just almost never one second perhaps a meaning that much memory almost never' (*CSP* 194). Beckett's diction, effacing, self-cancelling, makes it impossible to locate the viability of this possible memory. But the trace of a possibility of a memory perhaps – perhaps being Beckett's favoured word – exists. And if later the body, sensing – if it can indeed sense – that it is 'not alone' and 'imploring that much memory almost never' (*CSP* 195);

if there occasionally will irrupt into this space a 'flash of time' (*CSP* 195); if, that is, there remain the traces, the spectral traces, of a past interiority, a past subjectivity, then the present state of the body, its present state within space, and indeed within time, would seem to annul those traces completely. Here there is 'only just almost never one second always the same all known. Given rose only just bare white body fixed one yard invisible all known without within' (*CSP* 194). *Without within*: exteriority and interiority efface each other; exteriority and interiority lose, in point of fact, all meaning as the difference between categories vanishes into invisibility. With exteriority and interiority cancelled space itself becomes a spectral category. The white walls, floor, and ceiling of the body's enclosure are 'never seen' (*CSP* 193, 195): the very geometry of the enclosure cannot be seen or, crucially, known.[12]

And thus what is perhaps the critical line in *Ping*: 'Planes meeting invisibly one only shining white infinite but that known not' (*CSP* 194). What does it mean, what *can* it mean, to dwell within this eternal 'one second', to dwell within space that cannot be known as space? I return to Heidegger and his notion of the boundary: 'A boundary is not that at which something stops, but, as the Greeks recognized, the boundary is that from which something *begins its essential unfolding*' (*BDT* 332). What Beckett offers us here in *Ping* is a state of bare life – life only barely being life; life as a trace of itself – within space that effaces the possibility of boundaries and thus of any notion of spatiality, as such. In Heidegger's sense of things the boundary is what delimits space, allows space, which in turn contains the possibility of Dasein to emerge as a viability. Within this demarcated space – *space that is invisible in its demarcation to the subject* – subjectivity, as such, becomes an impossibility. Or to put it in explicitly Heideggerian terms, the subject here in *Ping* does not emerge as a subject of being, within being: 'To say that mortals *are* is to say that in dwelling they persist through spaces by virtue of their stay among things and location' (*BDT* 335). There is, we must admit, a kind of (dogged) persistence at work here: the subject, what I am calling the posthuman subject – the subject cannot be a human subject in Heidegger's sense of things – persists as a trace to itself, a trace of a former life. The subject here persists in its spectrality, but spectrality is not full humanity. Moreover, if, as Heidegger suggests, mortals exist insofar as they 'stay' among things and locations, we have here a subject without things, without locations. We may be tempted to use Agamben's notion of *bare life* to describe this state, but this is not, strictly speaking, accurate. Bare life, in Agamben's terms, still refers to a life recognised as that which can be reduced; the subject has enough being, subjectivity, to have it stripped away into what Beckett would call the 'mere minimum' of humanity. The subject here in *Ping* – and perhaps this will be true of the subject in *Lessness* – cannot, it seems, be reduced any further: it is being, *sublimated*, the residual precipitate of what once was.

I suggested above that the traces of memory that still persist here in *Ping* are annulled, or would seem to be annulled, by the present state of the posthuman subject. Existing in one endless second, in a featureless, positionless space, the subject cannot claim any subjectivity. But still the traces of memory persist and it seems that we are in, once again, familiar spectral territory: the posthuman, perhaps posthumous subject, barely animated by traces of a past: the human 'in' the posthuman endures.[13] But Beckett here in *Ping* complicates things somewhat by the use of one word, a word that occurs only once in the text and thus resonates critically. As it becomes clear that this subject still carries traces of a past, a memory that works in a perhaps perverse sense to give him the sense of not being 'alone'; as the subject recalls, or has recalled for him – is this *ping* not an exteriorised irruption, a *punctum* that compels memory? – a memory of 'eye black and white half closed long lashes imploring that much memory' (*CSP* 195), we read the following: 'Afar flash of time all white all over all of old ping flash white walls shining white no trace eyes holes light blue almost white last colour ping white over' (*CSP* 195). I am intrigued by the phrase 'Afar flash of time' given the way it spatialises time, places time at a far distance. The phrase occurs immediately after the memory of the eyes imploring and suggests a radical distancing: as if the memory occurs not only *back* in time but *away* in the distance. Memory is spatialised in a way that suggests that the only real spatialisation at work here in *Ping* is the space of memory. Material space, as we have noticed, does not function to allow the subject to locate himself. There is, for all intents and purposes, no space to speak of; space, at least in this one phrase – a phase, again, used only once but resonant because of this – is revealed in the *flash of time*. Time, I would argue, is not functioning as a metaphor of memory here. Time itself is being revealed in this flash. The awareness of time having passed, perhaps, but perhaps also a revelation of this one second that truly is the only temporality at work here. This is a complicated sentence, to be sure. Because the phrase 'flash of time' is immediately echoed in 'flash white walls shining': if the flash of time reveals the subject in this one second, this non-time of the 'always the same' (*CSP* 194), the flash of time, echoed into the walls of this non-space is, perhaps, *nullified* as time. The spatiality implied by 'afar' in 'Afar flash of time', now echoed into the flash of the non-space of the white shining walls, is, I would suggest, cancelled, effaced as, once again, the white walls cancel the possibility of location, of positionality. Perhaps this is all to say that this phrase, again occurring only once in *Ping*, is the most agonising phrase in an agonising text: holding the possibility of spatiality – of at least the possibility of seeing the past and negotiating a relation to it – the idea, as soon as it is proffered, vanishes into the undifferentiated time and non-space of eternal white.

If *Ping* ends with the effacement of the possibility of location, of what I am calling 'positionality', *Lessness* begins with a curious assertion of place: 'Ruins true refuge long last towards which so many false time out of mind' (*CSP* 197). A great deal in this first sentence should detain us: how, for instance, is a ruin a *true* refuge? What does a *true refuge* (a phrase repeated eighteen times in *Lessness*) consist in? Beckett, we recall, draws our attention to the genealogical, perhaps even genetic relation between *Ping* and *Lessness* in the description on the back cover of the text and speaks of the idea of refuge – '"Lessness" has to do with the collapse of some such refuge as that last attempted in "Ping" and with the ensuing situation of the refugee' (*Grove Companion* 318) – but he does not deploy the term *true* here. My interest is to explore what this phrase *true refuge* can mean here in *Lessness*: how, if at all, does 'situatedness' obtain within the ruin? What can the idea of the *situation* of the refugee mean when space, as such, perhaps no longer functions?

Refuge, of course, is a central term in *Lessness*, just as it becomes crucial for Beckett in later texts (I think here especially of 'neither': 'To and fro in shadow from inner to outershadow/from impenetrable self to impenetrable unself by way of neither/as between two lit refuges whose doors once neared gently close,/once turned away from gently part again' [*CSP* 259]). Given the term's meaning, however, it may strike us, at least initially, that the use of the term is curious. In a text as still as *Lessness* appears to be – and indeed the question of the mobility of the subject perhaps is *the* question

– the idea of refuge indicates immediately that we are in a place of arrival, *after* some kind of motion. 'Refuge', etymologically, is a place to fall back to, a place of hiding or secrecy: the idea of refuge, in other words, implies some past movement. Thus, if we gauge the word's resonance in *Lessness* we must, at least at the outset, read this space as a space of having come after some kind of movement, given the seeming stillness of the 'little body' that is in place here. But in what way is this refuge *true*? Given the state of the refuge, its absolute ruin, is Beckett deploying the term ironically? Is he forcing us to recall how the refuge, the space of enclosure in, say, *Ping*, in its impossibility – space there is not space at all, in the strictest sense – is false? Is he suggesting that this is a true refuge in that it succeeds in sheltering or hiding the subject? Because it does not: the little body here will feel the 'passing deluge' (*CSP* 197) in this shelterless shelter: 'On him will rain again as in the blessed days of blue the passing cloud' (*CSP* 197). The term *true* here must, be read ironically, but not in the obvious sense. It is not that the ruin is not a shelter. The truth of this refuge is more in line with the Heideggerian notion of the truth, of what he calls *aletheia* or 'unconcealment' (*Unverborgenheit*). *Aletheia* is the revealing, the uncoveredness of something: truth is the means by which the real substance, the real shape of a thing is revealed. What is given to us at the outset of *Lessness* is the absence of refuge: the ruin offers us a shape of what the space of refuge may *have been*: 'Blacked out fallen open four walls over backwards true refuge issueless' (*CSP* 197).[14] The true refuge, and this is perhaps Beckett's most devastating commentary on the possibility of space, of location, is the absent refuge, the imaginary refuge, the spectral refuge: the refuge that once may have existed, but in all likelihood did not.

And this image of the depleted refuge, the refuge now true because depleted, is married to the image of the depleted subject: 'Grey face two pale blue little body heart beating' (*CSP* 197). The depleted refuge is the perfect space, the objective correlative, to the depleted subject, the subject who now becomes the affect of lessness itself. Here, as in previous texts, there is no time, no possibility of futurity. Here, there is only 'changelessness' (*CSP* 197); here, perhaps as opposed to *Ping*, there is not even sound: 'Never was but grey air timeless no sound figment the passing light' (*CSP* 197). There is a certain brutal irony in this state of depletion: despite the intractable lessness of things, the subject is given a superabundance of endlessness, of sameness, of changelessness, of greyness. And, in some crucial way, this is the point: the undifferentiated colour, the undifferentiated planes, the effacement of any difference between sky and earth, absolutely delimits, once again, the possibility of seeing space, of comprehending space. Indeed, even though Beckett himself will offer *Lessness* as moving a step forward from *Ping* in the destruction of the refuge, the figuration of space is uncannily similar. In *Ping* there is no possibility of distinguishing the various planes of the enclosure: the idea of space thus is nullified. Here, in a similar way, the idea of spatiality is effaced. Beckett figures the various zones of this world as, in a sense, claiming the subject, absorbing the subject into its undifferentiated sameness: 'Scattered ruins same grey as the sand ash grey true refuge' (*CSP* 197); 'No sound no stir ash grey sky mirrored earth mirrored sky' (*CSP* 197); 'Little body same grey as the earth sky ruins only upright. Ash grey all sides earth sky as one all sides endlessness' (*CSP* 198).[15]

And what can occur within this negated space? Having established in the second paragraph that movement, as such, is not a possibility – 'no sound no stir' – the narrator offers the following: 'He will stir in the sand there will be stir in the sky the air the sand' (*CSP* 198); the narrator offers the possibility of futurity – *he will* – but follows this sentence immediately with 'never but in dream the happy dream only one time to serve' (*CSP* 198). Time can only function here in *Lessness* as a dream, a 'figment' (*CSP* 197) – 'figment the passing light' (*CSP* 197) – an act of imagination (we recall the use of the word *fancy* in *All Strange Away*). And not only time of course, but movement, de-severance, to use Heidegger's term, cannot obtain within the space of the imagination:

> Slow black with ruin true refuge four walls over backwards no sound. Legs a single block arms fast to sides little body face to endlessness. Never but in vanished dream the passing hour long short. Only upright little body grey smooth no relief a few holes. One step in the ruins in the sand on his back in the endlessness he will make it. Never but dream the days and nights made of dreams of other nights better days. He will live again the space of a step it will be day and night again over him the endlessness. (*CSP* 198)

In this final sentence, one that anticipates the relation between movement and spectral being in 'neither', Beckett carefully articulates the agonised spacing of desire. Indeed, as becomes clear in *Lessness*, the only space that functions here is that which measures the distance between the present state of depletion and the event of the dream, the figment, the desire for movement as the desire for being.

Another word for this space of distance, of course, is despair. I am not deploying the term in any real theological sense of the term. Despite Beckett's clear evocation of a post-lapsarian world – the refuge is a fallen one; the world is depleted; the subject will, perhaps like Milton's Satan, 'curse God again as in the blessed days' (*CSP* 197) – there is no sense in speaking of a theological metaphysics at work here. But perhaps we can retain the spatial logic of the idea of despair which (as Milton so perfectly demonstrates in *Paradise Lost*) always measures the real and spiritual distance between the subject and God, the subject and meaning, the subject and significance: despair measures and maps distance. But Beckett even complicates the idea of despair here in *Lessness* by calling into question the simple logics of distance and nostalgia. The subject here does not only yearn for what has been lost; the subject does more than wish to return to a pre-lapsarian world of plenitude. If movement – the idea of stirring – is Beckett's visual metaphor for plenitude, for being *as such*, we notice that the ideas of movement and stillness exist in a kind of critical simultaneity. The idea of movement, in other words, is not cancelled or effaced by the idea of stillness: the idea of futurity and mobility – 'he will live again the space of a step' – is held in suspension with 'never but in dream the days and nights'. Beckett offers the maximum compression of the idea of suspended possibility, of the simultaneity of movement and stillness, as *Lessness* comes to its conclusion:

> Slow black with ruin true refuge four walls over backwards no sound. Earth sky as one all sides endlessness little body only upright. One step more one alone all alone in the sand no hold he will make it. Ash grey little body only upright heart beating face to endlessness. Light refuge sheer white blank planes all gone from mind. All sides endlessness earth sky as one no sound no stir. (*CSP* 201)

Beckett's despair, the despair of the posthuman subject, is the despair of this endless possibility of opposing actions or events. The subject moves, perhaps only in dream; the subject does not, or cannot, move. Placed within a refuge that can only ever recall the plenitude of a true refuge, the subject, himself reflecting perfectly the depletion of his environment – he is as grey as his surroundings – can only be understood, ontologically, as neither one thing nor another. His status as what Paul Virilio would call a trajective being is radically undecidable. Able, perhaps at a point in the future, to measure the space of a step, but simultaneously unable to issue forth from his ruin – the true refuge is 'issueless' (197) as Beckett repeatedly indicates – the subject is radically, unalterably, and endlessly neutralised. The true agony of the neutral, the true despair of the neutral, is not the agony of loss. The true agony of the neutral – and this now becomes the true agony, and affect, of the posthuman – is the agony in the impossibility of loss, the impossibility of placing loss at a distance in order to see it as such.

Notes

1. Beckett himself referred to *Imagination Dead Imagine* as the 'residual precipitate' of *All Strange Away* (quoted in Ackerley and Gontarski, *The Grove Companion* 273).
2. On this idea of the text as allegory of fiction-making, see Shane Weller's 'Beckett and Late Modernism'.
3. For a reading of Derrida's relation to the figure of the posthuman, see Cary Wolfe's *What Is Posthumanism?*, especially chapter 3. For Wolfe, Derrida's practice of deconstruction is always already a form of posthuman theorising given its tendency, as he writes, to 'refuse to locate meaning in the realm of either the human or, for that matter, the biological' (xxvi). Wolfe's reading of the relation between spectrality and the posthuman, and its voice – a signal of vanished presence – is critical.
4. For a full treatment of the Derridean archive in relation to contemporary literature, see my *Melancholy and the Archive*.
5. On the idea of the prosthesis and its relation to the human, or its 'end' in the posthuman, see Bernard Stiegler's *Technics and Time*. And while David Wills suggests that the prosthesis operates perhaps primarily as a figure of the supplement, and thus is central to all 'human' experience, his reading of the economy of the prosthesis is crucial (*Prosthesis*). See also Gray Kochhar-Lindgren, who argues that the posthuman, as such, is a problematised notion given that the human has always already been 'machinic' (*TechnoLogics*). And, of course, the *locus classicus* for a discussion of the prosthesis is Marshall McLuhan's *Understanding Media: The Extensions of Man*, where he ominously refers to the human–prosthesis relation as a 'suicidal autoamputation' (43).
6. In 'Mourning and Melancholia', Freud characterises the process of mourning in terms of an 'economics of pain' (252); this effort of

Spaces of Ruin   127

translating and transferring one's libidinal energy away from the lost object in effect allows the loved one to die.

7. On the question of the nature of the cylinder, see Antoni Libera, who argues that 'Life in the cylinder is a model of human history' ('"The Lost Ones": A Myth of Human History and Destiny' 151); Wanda Balzano offers the idea that the text is a 'Literary diagram of the epistemological position of mankind in the twentieth century' ('Searching for Beckett's Real Worlds in *The Lost Ones*' 20); Mary Catanzaro suggests, after Garin Dowd's 'Figuring Zero in "The Lost Ones"', that the cylinder is a 'technology of spatial organization' ('No Way Out' 188); David Houston Jones' reading of *The Lost Ones* as a fantasy of cybernetic information-gathering organised around some 'unspoken atrocity' (*Samuel Beckett and Testimony* 167) perhaps is indebted similarly to Dowd, whose reading of the cylinder positions *The Lost Ones* as an examination of the limits of Agamben's bare life. Jones, more to the point in the context of my own reading, suggests that *The Lost Ones* 'provides a glimpse of what posthuman testimony might mean in Beckett's work' (143).

8. On this point, see Gabriele Schwab's important reading of *The Lost Ones* in *Imaginary Ethnographies*. Here Schwab critiques allegorical readings of the text as seeming 'too referential and literalist' (167); Schwab is most concerned to suggest that we read *The Lost Ones* intertextually (via Dante) and begin to understand how Beckett 'constructs the transitional space between the human and the posthuman' (167).

9. Paul Davies' reading of the economy of Beckettian containment is an appropriate gloss on Beckett's own words: 'Beckett's images of containment and confinement derive their poetic impact only in conjunction – implicit and sometimes explicit – with his figurings of the dispersal of that containment' ('Strange Weather' 75).

10. On the question of the space, and its total revelation, see Peter Boxall's 'Still Stirrings: Beckett's Prose from *Texts for Nothing* to *Stirrings Still*'; he argues that *Ping*, like *The Lost Ones* and *Imagination Dead Imagine*, presents spaces in which 'nothing is hidden', suffused as they are by 'omnipresent' (41) white light.

11. Gontarski's reading of the complications of witnessing in *Ping* is crucial; in *Ping*, 'the reader's focus is not only on a figure in a closed space, but on another figure and a narrator imagining them. We have then not just the psychologically complex but narratologically transparent image of an apperceptive self, but an apperceptive self imagining itself apperceiving itself, often suspecting that it, too, is being imagined and perceived' ('Where Never Before' 146–7).

12. I am reminded here of what Derrida says in *Echographies of Television* regarding the ontology of the subject who, perhaps like the

spectre, has slipped past all bounds of comprehension: 'For an infinite being, there is no meaning' (111); meaning depends, in other words, on the presence of boundaries.
13. We might compare my idea of the trace of human persistence to Alys Moody's reading of *Ping* and the posthuman; she argues that the text's rhythmic patterning 'decouples feeling from narrative and meaning, and produces an inhuman, indifferent affect, devoid of subject' ('A Machine for Feeling' 88).
14. As Mark Wrathall argues in *Heidegger and Unconcealment*, 'Unconcealment is a privative notion – it consists in removing concealment' (1); that is to say, the truth of a thing is revealed only in its removal from hiddenness. Beckett's unconcealment often stands as the absolute removal of totalities in order to show the essence of a thing.
15. L. A. J. Bell's reading of the remains and residue in *Lessness* is important: 'In "Sans" [*Lessness*], everything is reduced to fine sand, tiny remnants of disseminated entities . . . The sand, ash-grey, is the Derridean "presque rien" par excellence, the ash of holocaustal fire' ('Between Ethics and Aesthetics' 41).

4

Space and Trauma: *Fizzles*

And dream of a way in space with neither here nor there where all the footsteps ever fell can never fare nearer to anywhere nor from anywhere further away.

(Beckett, *Fizzles* 8)

It is indeed impossible to imagine our own death.

(Freud, 'Thoughts for the Times on War and Death')

Loss is impossible.

(Blanchot, *The Step Not Beyond*)

I

This chapter attempts to understand the constitution of the subject in Samuel Beckett's *Fizzles*. I am concerned to suggest that these eight short texts present a radical decomposition of philosophical notions of the subject, as such. The subject(s) of these texts, for instance, speaks of itself as being 'destitute of history' (*F* 12), of having existed in a time 'so long ago as to amount to never' (*F* 13), of having given up 'before birth' (*F* 25). Thus, in specific relation to temporality, we are presented with a subject without history, without memory, without, that is, those categories that constitute the subject as subject. And yet, even in this state to which 'none of his memories answer' (*F* 7), some affect of the subject persists, despite itself. It is my concern here to understand how we may conceive of this persistence of affect. Perhaps one way is to read *Fizzles* as a kind of allegory of Blanchot's notion of the post-traumatic subject. In *The Writing of the Disaster*, Blanchot, responding to Levinas' conception of subjectivity (as constituted in the world via relations between self and other), offers a reading of what I am characterising as the post-traumatic subject: 'one ought', he writes, 'perhaps to speak of a *subjectivity without any subject*: the wounded space, the hurt of the dying, the already dead body which no one could ever own, or ever say of it, *I*, *my body*' (30). It is Blanchot's phrase 'wounded space' that should detain us here, for surely *Fizzles* is at one level 'about' the subject 'in' space, both exterior (texts 1–3) and deeply, and radically, interior (texts 5–8). 'Trauma', of course, means 'wound', and part of what I wish to explore here is how the remains of post-traumatised subjectivity in *Fizzles* is demarcated, or indeed effaced, within space. Space, spatiality, and movement through space are central, for instance, to a Heideggerian understanding of the subject. Indeed Heidegger, as we have seen in *Being and Time*, will argue that the movement through space, what he calls *de-severance*, constitutes the subject: 'Dasein is essentially de-severance – that is, it is spatial' (*BT* 143); 'the "subject" (Dasein), if well understood ontologically, is spatial' (*BT* 146). There is indeed movement in *Fizzles*; the subject is presented, especially in the early texts, as negotiating a relation through space: he moves through a 'ruinstrewn land' with 'little panic steps' (*F* 27). But how is that movement constitutive of a subject if, as I argue, he lacks those essential markers of subjectivity (history, memory)? What can *de-severance without any subject* mean? Beckett, as I will ultimately argue, is asking us to conceive of a new kind of subjectivity: one without memory, without history, but located within a space of ruin – a 'place of remains' (*F* 55) – that in its turn constitutes an affect of the subject-as-ruin: 'sepulchral skull is this then its last state' (*F* 60).

The texts comprising *Fizzles* were originally published in French beginning in the early 1970s; *Fizzles* was published in English in *For to End Yet Again* in 1976. Beckett himself was unsure about the date of writing of these texts but surmised, according to the editors of *The Grove Companion to Samuel Beckett*, that perhaps they were written beginning in the early 1960s.[1] Deirdre Bair, on the other hand, speculates that the texts date from the late 1960s or early 1970s; she characterises some as 'exercises' (*Samuel Beckett* 639) written for Jerome Lindon's *Minuit* while noting that another, 'Still' (Fizzle 7), appeared in John Calder's *Signature Anthology*. Others, as she suggests, were 'simply passages that he [Beckett] could not expand further' (*Samuel Beckett* 638–9). Clearly, these texts have something of a stuttering publication history; moreover, *Fizzles* seems, at least from Bair's perspective, to have an essential fragmentariness and incompleteness about it. The fact that 'fizzles', the English translation of the French '*foirades*', can mean 'sputter' or 'hiss' or the act of breaking wind quietly (*Grove Companion* 198) should remind us of Beckett's own habit of characterising his work as a species of failure. It is not my purpose to read Beckett's own criticism of his work as an interpretive entry point to suggest, as I have done elsewhere, that the idea of failure should guide our reading.[2] I am more interested to note, merely at the outset, and perhaps as a way of beginning to think about the various affects of trauma that articulate this work, that *Fizzles* is a work that Beckett has allowed to *return*, years after its original composition. If these texts were indeed conceived in failure, written as failure, it is important to note that Beckett, at some point, and for reasons perhaps unknowable to us, allowed them to appear (for him, to reappear). I am not suggesting, at least in the form of a strong argument, that the writing of these texts specifically instantiated some form of trauma for Beckett (we do know that writing was painful for him[3]), but I am merely suggesting that they may stand, as published texts, as a kind of testament to the agony of creation and, as such, represent, perhaps only structurally, a kind of discursive echo of the economy of trauma, an economy, as Freud originally theorised, conditioned by repetition and uncanny return.

And a discussion of trauma should perhaps be our entry into *Fizzles*, if only to set up a theoretical structure that these texts will ultimately radically call into question. As I suggested above, my goal here is to analyse the subject in *Fizzles*, a subject who appears only to be what we may call merely a trace of subject. That is to say, *Fizzles* offers a representation of subjectivity that calls into question the very idea of subjectivity itself. What should be noted here at the outset is that theories of trauma, as is true for any theory of the mourning subject, seem ultimately to beg the question of subjectivity; that is to say, and to modify an idea I have discussed elsewhere, theories of trauma need the subject to be in place. Trauma, as an affect of temporality, works in fact to integrate a notion of subjectivity, indeed must orient a subject in time and space.[4] Even as the traumatised subject finds herself displaced across time, as we will see, the subject, as such, must be in place for the trauma of trauma to express itself. In some ways my goal here will be to explore the various implications of a single question: what can the idea of trauma mean for a subject beyond subjectivity? But let us begin with Freud and 'Beyond the Pleasure Principle', the *locus classicus* of any contemporary discussion of trauma. Here Freud suggests that the economy of trauma is characterised by its disruption of temporality; the traumatised subject – and Freud here is thinking primarily of participants in the recently ended First World War – finds himself, through flashbacks and traumatised dreams, back in the moment of trauma. Traumatised dreams, instead of offering the subject a vision of what is ultimately to be desired, temporally displace the subject and present instead a return to various scenes of horror:

> Now dreams occurring in traumatic neuroses have the characteristic of repeatedly bringing the patient back into the situation of his accident, a situation from which he wakes up in another fright. This astonishes people far too little . . . If we are not to be shaken in our belief in the wish-fulfilling tenor of dreams by the dreams of traumatic neurotics, we still have one resource open to us: we may argue that the function of dreaming, like so much else, is upset in this condition and diverted from its purposes, or we may be driven to reflect on the mysterious masochistic trends of the ego. ('Beyond the Pleasure Principle' 282–3)

Freud breaks off his analysis here as if shaken by the implications of his own thoughts. It is beyond our purposes here to trace Freud's development of the idea of the death drive – that the ultimate goal of all life is to return to, and repeat, the condition of nothingness that precedes and exceeds life – but we should, again, note that for the death drive to express itself, just as is true for the expression of the masochistic economy of traumatic dreams, a subject must be in place.

And indeed my reading of the Freudian economy of trauma begins with the suggestion that it is grounded on an essentially conservative model of subjectivity. Freud's entire psychoanalysis, despite its foundational ideas of the subject at odds with itself (ego ruled by superego; id unconsciously underpinning all actions; drives that precede and exceed the subject's conscious knowledge), is one that works nostalgically in the hope that an original scene of trauma can be revealed and that the subject may recover – a crucial word – some measure of knowledge of its own history. And this is the point: the Freudian model of trauma suggests that a history is there to be recovered; the subject, in other words, is *historically* located. Thus even as Freud suggests that the victim of trauma is 'obliged to repeat the repressed material as a contemporary experience instead of, as the physician would prefer to see, remembering it as something belonging to the past' (288), he still ultimately holds out the model of recovery as a historical possibility: in other words, history is there to be recovered; trauma, as it plays out over an albeit fractured historical temporality, still functions within an horizon in which a historically located *consciousness* may be recovered. Trauma thus is historical; consciousness is historically located; subjectivity, in the Freudian model, still obtains within the economy of trauma.

It thus seems that a Freudian, or even a post-Freudian, model of trauma may not be the most viable theoretical starting point for an understanding of the Beckettian subject that is articulated, or articulates itself, within *Fizzles*.[5] It strikes me as entirely feasible to suggest that the subject – or subjects – in *Fizzles* exists within some kind of post-traumatic space and time (an assertion that is true for any of Beckett's major subjects from *Molloy* onwards). But given the subject's uncanny understanding of itself as post-history – as 'destitute of history' – it becomes increasingly difficult to hold out any hope of recovering the subject's relation to an originary event of trauma. Moreover, and this in some sense is the task of this chapter, we may be compelled to begin rethinking our use of the term 'subject' here, if subjectivity, as a theoretical construct, is always already linked to some sense of historicity. That is to say, subjectivity is historical; the Beckettian subject is post-historical in the sense that history, or historicity (one's definitional relation to history, the past), is no longer a viable model of Being. We cannot, I would suggest, use a model of trauma to read Beckett's subject, but we must attend to how the subject essentially *is* post-traumatic. How then, our question becomes, do we begin reading and understanding the post-historical, post-traumatic subject? Specifically for my purposes here the question is: how do we read the post-historical subject's relation to what we may call traumatised space?

And thus perhaps Blanchot's model of the subjectivity without any subject will be of use. At a critical moment in *The Writing of the Disaster*, a text which, in my reading, attempts simultaneously to give an affective and theoretical sense of what it means to be in the space of the *after* – after trauma, after the disaster – Blanchot turns to Levinas:

> Levinas speaks of the subjectivity of the subject. If one wishes to use this word – why? but why not? – one ought perhaps to speak of a *subjectivity without any subject:* the wounded space, the hurt of the dying, the already dead body which no one could ever own, or ever say of it, *I, my body*. (30)

This phrase, *subjectivity without any subject*, should detain us, should call to mind the being that articulates itself, or is articulated, in Beckett's *Fizzles*. This phrase suggests to me a way of beginning to understand what it means to be after the event of trauma. Note how Blanchot offers what appears to be a series of categories of subjectless subjectivity; it is critical for my purposes here that his first category is spatial: the wounded *space*. If this phrase refers to the subjectless subject, Blanchot suggests that we should conceive of that entity in spatial terms; equally critically we need to remind ourselves that the term wound (in French the phrase is '*la place blessée*') does mean trauma: the subject has, in effect, become a space of trauma. I will, in what follows, wish to suggest that this idea of wounded space applies not only to the subjectless subject but also to the space he inhabits or moves through, this 'ruinstrewn land' (this is perhaps to assume that there is a difference between the subject and his space, a point to which I will return), but we should not ignore the fact that the series of categories that follows Blanchot's definition of post-trauma all speak of the body: 'the hurt of the dying, the already dead body which no one could ever own, or ever say of it, *I, my body*'. Blanchot's words here suggest a way of conceiving of the subjectless subject as a pure, powerless body, a body separated from all markers of identity and ownership. And yet there is subjectivity there; what does this mean? It means that we have, in this post-traumatic entity, the *affect* of subjectivity, the sense of subjectivity, the sense, perhaps, of personhood, but it is no longer attached or anchored to any material body: subjectivity has broken free of the subject, or has been wrested away from the subject and now floats freely, without being grounded in a constituted ego.

In what follows I wish to keep in mind Blanchot's idea of subjectivity without any subject. It is my purpose to attempt to relate this model of being to Heidegger's conception of being within space and ultimately perhaps to attempt to outline a conception of posthuman traumatised space, as such. But perhaps we are already in a space of aporia as we relate the notion of the subjectless subject to Heidegger's notion of the relation between Dasein and spatiality. While Heidegger is clear that Dasein, as such, is spatial, defined by what he calls 'de-severance', we must acknowledge that Heidegger is not necessarily offering a model of post-traumatic ontology or indeed some anticipation of posthuman subjectivity. *Being and Time* is an attempt, essentially, to define Dasein, that is, the beingness of being; this is an attempt, as is clear, to define what the subject-as-Dasein is. In other words, the subject-as-Dasein for Heidegger is not purely a space for some free-floating affect to be articulated, as is clear when he writes 'the "subject" (Dasein), if well understood ontologically, is spatial' (*BT* 146). My interest here thus is not to attempt to square Heidegger's notion of Being with the model of post-trauma found in Beckett's *Fizzles*. Instead I am attempting to understand what it would mean for movement *not* to be tied to Being; what does a desire for non-de-severance look like? Is de-severance without Being the pure affect of trauma?

II

I wish, as I turn now to Heidegger and Beckett, to quote a passage from the final *Fizzle* (8). It is here that the purest expression of the desire to be without being, to be without subjectivity, *to be pure movement without being*, is made. I quote it so that it may guide what follows:

> And dream of a way in space with neither here nor there where all the footsteps ever fell can never fare nearer to anywhere nor from anywhere further away. (*F* 60)

It is of course the word 'space' and the idea of movement through space in the above quotation that captures my interest. What does the term 'space' mean in the context of *Fizzles*? What *could* the idea of movement through space mean in the context of *Fizzles*? Space, for Heidegger, is that location where being itself finds itself as movement. That is to say, space, for Heidegger, is the locus of an essential consciousness of the relation between self and environment. Being comes to realise itself, as Being, as it moves, as it closes the distance between itself and objects, sites, markers in the world. In Part One Section Three of *Being and Time* Heidegger continues to unfold his notion of Dasein, as being-there in the world. Here his concern is to understand the subject's orientation in space as that position from which Dasein, as such, comes into being; that is to say, Heidegger here is interested in exploring the 'there' component of Dasein as being-there. This being-there begins with the subject's understanding of having been placed within the world, and its 'regions' (*BT* 105); the subject's position in space – and as space; this is critical: the subject is both *in* space and in a critical sense *is* space, is the experience of spatiality as such; the subject is not simply located in space, a space in which it may encounter other beings – amounts to a ontological position, one defined by what Heidegger calls de-severance and directionality, terms, as I have read them throughout this study, that stand as a priori drives that define the subject not only 'in' space, but, as mentioned, 'as' space, as such:

> Dasein ... is 'in' the world in the sense that it deals with entities encountered within-the-world, and does so concernfully and with familiarity. So if spatiality belongs to it in any way, that is possible only because of this Being-in. But its spatiality shows the characters of *de-severance* and *directionality*. (*BT* 138)

De-severance for Heidegger is a state of being that allows the subject to find herself, orient herself, within the world. More than simply a mode of spatial orientation, de-severance defines the subject ontologically and hermeneutically: de-severance, in other words, is a way of understanding the world *as a world in which one is placed*. To move within this world, to be what Virilio calls the traject,[6] is not simply to find oneself in the world, but is a means of discovering the worldliness of world; it is, in other words, to discover the being-there, the Dasein, of the subject:

> When we speak of de-severance as a kind of Being which Dasein has with regard to its Being-in-the-world, we do not understand by it any such thing as remoteness (or closeness) or even a distance. We use the expression 'de-severance' in a signification which is both active and transitive. It stands for a constitutive state of Dasein's Being – a state with regard to which removing something in the sense of putting it away is only a determinate factical mode. 'De-severing' amounts to making

the farness vanish – that is, making the remoteness of something disappear, bringing it close. Dasein is essentially de-severant: it lets any entity be encountered close by as the entity which it is. (*BT* 139)

Two points are crucial here: de-severance 'stands for a constitutive state of Dasein's Being'; de-severance is a condition of spatiality and movement that works to reveal the world: 'it lets any entity be encountered close by as the entity which it is' (*BT* 139). The implication of this second quotation is that de-severance, by removing the remoteness of things in the world – perhaps the world itself – reveals the condition of things; or, if it does not on its own reveal the truth of things, it lays the ground for the possibility of the revelation of the essence of the thing, 'which it *is*'. This is to say that de-severance defines both the essence and ontology of the subject – indeed Heidegger makes this idea explicit: '*Dasein is essentially de-severance – that is, it is spatial*' (*BT* 143) – and the conditions for hermeneutically comprehending the world, as space and through space.

The conditions for mapping out space, as such, are governed by what Heidegger calls directionality: as it is placed within the world, and as the subject's relation to the world is defined by its essential concern and care for its being within the world, the subject's mode of being spatially – that is, its mode of being that allows itself to orient itself in the world and discover the meaning of that world – is articulated by directionality. Directionality is what governs the orientation of de-severance; directionality defines the limits and protocols of the processes of de-severance; directionality orients the subject in space just as it defines the subject as that which in its turn understands itself as spatial:

> Out of this directionality arise the fixed directions of right and left. Dasein constantly takes these directions along with it, just as it does its de-severances. Dasein's spatialization in its 'bodily nature' is likewise marked out in accordance with these directions ... De-severance and directionality, as constitutive characteristics of Being-in, are determinative for Dasein's spatiality – for its being concernfully and circumspectively in space, in a space discovered and within-the-world. (*BT* 143–4)

What is crucial here for our reading of Beckett's *Fizzles* is Heidegger's insistence that Dasein – being, subjectivity – is defined spatially; that Dasein comes into being via a realisation of its orientation in space, space that demands to be read and comprehended hermeneutically. Being itself, in other words, is spatial; ontology is spatially realised; to be a subject is to find oneself in a condition of thrownness in space. Heidegger once again: 'the "subject" (Dasein), if well understood ontologically, is spatial' (*BT* 146). And of course the questions now become: what does this Heideggerian notion of spatial ontology tell us about Beckett's *Fizzles*? How can we understand a post-traumatic spatial ontology? If space is constitutive of Dasein/subjectivity, what kind of space has produced the uncanny ontological condition of the subject in *Fizzles*?[7] Are we being asked, now, in *Fizzles*, to begin to think about post-traumatic space as constitutive of a post-traumatic, posthuman subjectivity?

I wish to begin answering these questions with an assertion: *Fizzles* is the representation of a space of fantasy. Specifically, *Fizzles* is what I will be calling a phantomic space: a space wherein an authorial I projects the scene of his phantasmic effacement, disappearance, even death. My reading of the trajectory of *Fizzles* as a whole thus is quite simple: it tracks the steady elimination of subjectivity and of personhood; as the texts unfold to remove the 'I', to remove the need to say 'I' – 'to say I no more' (*F* 27) – subjectivity fades and affect, an affect of trauma, of trajectivity, of movement within a ruined space towards a hope for stillness (a hope that is aporetically articulated in Fizzle 8 as a hope for a kind of movement of non-movement), takes precedence. I thus read *Fizzles* as an allegory of self-splitting, of the creation of the self as what Abraham and Torok would call the 'lost object'. In 'The Lost Object – Me', Abraham and Torok detail how the self begins to fashion itself as a cryptic space, a phantomic space. This fashioning begins, they argue, with the subject in possession of (or is it 'by'?) a memory that is unspeakable:

> it is a memory entombed in a fast and secure place, awaiting resurrection . . . This segment of an ever so painfully lived Reality – untellable and therefore inaccessible to the gradual, assimilative work of mourning – causes a genuinely covert shift in the entire psyche . . . This leads to the establishment of a sealed off place, a crypt in the ego. (141)

In *The Ear of the Other*, Derrida offers an important gloss on Abraham and Torok's notion of the economy of refused mourning:

Now, what is the crypt in this instance? It is that which is constituted as a crypt in the body for the dead object in a case of unsuccessful mourning, mourning that has not been brought to a normal conclusion . . . Not having been taken back inside the self, digested, assimilated as in all 'normal' mourning, the dead object remains like a living dead abscessed in a specific spot in the ego. It has its place, just like a crypt in a cemetery or temple, surrounded by walls and all the rest. (57)

The question for readers of *Fizzles* of course is this: what is being (unsuccessfully) mourned here? If the creation of the crypt – and my sense here is that *Fizzles*' various texts move towards Fizzle 8 in which what we may call the totalised crypt is revealed – is instantiated by the claims of some kind of unspeakable memory, the unspeakability of which, according to Abraham and Torok, results from a loss – the 'loss that resulted from a traumatism' ('The Lost Object – Me' 141); what is this memory, what is this loss, this trauma in *Fizzles*? This question, as I suggested in my discussion of the Freudian model of trauma, may be an unanswerable one (and thus would seem to correspond perfectly with Abraham and Torok's notion of the a priori occulted nature of the originated trauma). Moreover, and this is quite crucial for Beckett, the question may not be the correct one. It may in fact be that the entire question of the original scene of trauma, betraying as it does a kind of nostalgia for origins, further betrays the claims of the reality of the subject before us, here, now, in *Fizzles*. That is to say, our responsibility here is perhaps to accept that the Beckettian subject is a priori post-traumatic, a priori destitute of history; its condition is a kind of Heideggerian thrownness into post-trauma, a thrownness that bypasses, or overshoots, the time of trauma, as such. The real question is this: how can the subject, this 'I' who wishes no longer to say 'I', this I who wishes to bury itself in the crypt of its own space of fantasy, *realise* the crypt? How can the position of being beyond subjectivity – the subjectivity without any subject; the haecceity – be maintained beyond merely being the projection of a kind of fantasy? My question is readily answered: it cannot. And here, thus, is the true trauma of the text, a trauma that does not instantiate the subject but a trauma that forever conditions the impossibility of its desire. The position of being beyond being, traumatically, cannot be: it remains, to return to and anticipate that crucial word in Fizzle 8, a *dream*.

But let us track the creation of the crypt, its conditions, its protocols. The 'he' of Fizzle 1, 3, even perhaps of 8, stands in dialectical relation to an 'I' who wishes to become that site of imagined subjective disappearance. That is, as the I projects himself into the he – the he that will eventually dissolve into movement and place – the I achieves some kind of transcendence or sublimation: the I becomes the he and the he is effaced into pure affect, what Blanchot calls subjectivity without any subject. The first text of *Fizzles*, an almost perfect allegory of Heideggerian thrownness, presents the subject, this 'he' – we are not yet given the authorial 'I' – as movement itself: 'he is forth again, he'll be back again' (*F* 7); 'He halts, for the first time since he knows he's under way, one foot before the other, the higher flat, the lower on its toes, and waits for a decision' (*F* 8). But this is movement – Heidegger would call it directionality – without direction; that is, the subject here is a purely passive object of forces that precede and exceed it; the subject's passivity, in other words, presages the discovery that this 'he' is a projection, an artistic creation, of an authorial I, an I who creates this subject as 'destitute of history', as having 'been so long ago as to amount to never'. This 'he', in other words, is gradually revealed not to be the precise subject of *Fizzles*; he is merely a screen onto which the authorial I projects, almost as a thought experiment, an idea of subjectivity that cannot on its own sustain itself, but might allow the creation of another, I call it cryptic, state of being.

And Fizzles 2 and 3, spaces where the authorial I first asserts itself most strongly, force us to reconsider the diagnosis of the subject's relation to history in Fizzle 1 as we retrospectively view the 'he' of *Texts for Nothing* 1 purely as a character, a textual figuration. To speak of his trauma, his ahistorical nature is not, thus, entirely satisfactory. Fizzle 1, we must see now, is merely a preparatory sketch in which the authorial 'I' begins to shape the affect he will eventually project himself into as the texts unfold. What is fascinating is to observe how the authorial 'I' has created a space into which he will project himself as a space of trauma; it is as if the authorial 'I' is acknowledging that his eventual projection and disappearance into this 'he' necessarily must involve some radical reconfiguration of self, history, and memory. He must create a traumatic space in order successfully to disappear, in order successfully to 'say I no more'. What follows in Fizzle 3 onwards is the authorial I's theoretical positioning of himself as other (this he) that becomes only movement within a ruined space, movement towards eventual stasis in Fizzle 7. The traumatic affect that weaves its way throughout *Fizzles*, in other words – and this is the crucial point – is entirely fashioned by the authorial 'I', fashioned in order to allow himself to slip free of subjectivity and personhood.

And thus we are called on to track the disappearance of the authorial 'I' in Fizzles 3 and 4. The 'I' places his avatar/character in the 'ruinstrewn land' (*F* 25) only to disavow any intimate, even ontological connection to him:

> he has trodden it all night long, I gave up, hugging the hedges . . . to catch his breath, then listen, ruinstrewn land, I gave up before birth, it is not possible otherwise, but birth there had to be, it was he, I was inside. (*F* 25)

From a Heideggerian perspective the authorial 'I' is in the position of casting his avatar into the world in a kind of condition of thrownness: it is the 'he' who moves, he who becomes trajectivity – 'it was he had a life, I didn't have a life' (*F* 26). The avatar, safely projected into this wasteland, is merely a hypothetical site for some kind of being beyond Being; his condition allows the authorial 'I' to both be Other and disavow that condition of Otherness as being related in any way to him. And yet through his avatar, the 'I', at least as the first part of Fizzle 3 unfolds, can experience the limits and boundaries of a kind of being:

> ruinstrewn land, night recedes, he is fled, I'm inside, he'll do himself to death, because of me, I'll live it with him, I'll live his death, the end of his life and then his death, step by step, in the present. (*F* 26)

Critical here is the way Beckett links movement – call it directionality – with Being; it is the avatar's movement – eventually to be stilled, of course: the entirety of *Fizzles* is working towards that 'magic' moment of trajectivity without movement – 'a way in space with neither here nor there' (*F* 60) – that allows the authorial 'I' to imagine being and then to imagine being no more:

> he is fled through the hedge, no more stopping now, he will never say I, because of me, he won't speak to anyone, no one will speak to him, he won't speak to himself, there is nothing left in his head, I'll feed it all it needs, to say I no more. (*F* 27)

I take this moment as the authorial I's expression of a desire to move beyond the baseline condition of subjectivity: the ability to say 'I'. This process begins by projecting a version of the self into space and then silencing it; dialectically, as I suggest the I's hope is, this silence will rebound back and end all need for subjectivity, all need to say 'I'. And thus, as we see in Fizzle 4, the fantasy of the avatar's death begins to sound like an expression of a desire for pure silence, pure solitude:

> if he rattles it's he who will rattle, I won't rattle, he who will die, perhaps they will bury him, if they find him, I'll be inside, he'll rot, I won't rot, there will be nothing of him left but bones, I'll be inside, nothing left but dust, I'll be inside, it is not possible otherwise. (F 32)

Crucial here is that this fantasy of the avatar's death is not the fantasy of the I's death: *he* will not rot, but he will be present in a posthuman condition of being beyond death. Fizzle 5 thus sees the subject in a 'closed place', a space beyond the need for speaking: 'What goes on in the arena is not said' (F 37). It is here that we may assume the subject has found himself, not yet purely still: 'Arena black vast. Room for millions. Wandering and still. Never seeing never hearing one another. Never touching' (F 37). It is unclear whether this place is in fact inhabited by millions or merely has the potential to be inhabited by millions. What is critical is that this a *space* for some kind of subjectivity to be in complete isolation yet potentially surrounded by the company of millions: 'So many bodies visible on the bed' (F 38). *Here then is the achievement of fantasy: to be in space, but not to be.* What does this mean? This is a space where subjectivity itself does not obtain: but then who speaks here in the description of this posthuman space?[8] Is it the authorial 'I', having rid itself of its avatar, having achieved something like a condition of being beyond being? We may presume, but we cannot know. Fizzle 5 is purely a description of a place with no indication from whose perspective that description arises. And while an 'I' returns, almost spectrally, in Fizzle 6, 'Old earth, no more lies, I've seen you' (F 43), the 'I' vanishes completely in Fizzles 7 and 8 to be replaced by the pure affect of space that is presaged in Fizzle 5.[9]

To be in space but not to be. This statement, this achievement of the subject in *Fizzles*, is at phenomenological odds with

Heidegger's essential conception of being, as such. To be, according to Heidegger, is to find oneself in space:

> *'ich bin'* ['I am'] means in its turn 'I reside' or 'dwell alongside' the world, as that which is familiar to me in such and such a way. 'Being' [Sein], as the infinitive of *'ich bin'* (that is to say, when it is understood as an *existentiale*), signifies 'to reside alongside. . .' 'to be familiar with. . .' *'Being-in' is thus the formal existential expression for the Being of Dasein, which has Being-in-the-world as its essential state.* (BT 80)

As we have seen above in Fizzle 1, this being-in is the initial step, the preparatory step, to a discovery of the dimension of the world that grounds the subject. This discovery – which I remind us, is a hermeneutic discovery – is granted to the subject through directionality and de-severance. The subject is thrown into the world and discovers that world through the movement of directionality and de-severance. However, our subject, at least as it unfolds over Fizzles 5–8, works assiduously not to move, not to de-sever, not to allow directionality to drive it on. The subject strives, as in Fizzle 7, for stillness and stasis. Moreover, the subject here has worked to remove itself from any sense of history, memory, any subjectivity, as such. What then is Beckett presenting to us here in *Fizzles*? How are we to understand this subjectivity without any subject, this trajectivity without movement? I wish to return to my suggestion that we read *Fizzles* as the projection of an authorial fantasy, the creation of a phantomic space.

Let us return to that moment in Fizzle 4 where the I imagines his avatar dying:

> if he rattles it's he who will rattle, I won't rattle, he who will die, perhaps they will bury him, if they find him, I'll be inside, he'll rot, I won't rot, there will be nothing of him left but bones, I'll be inside, nothing left but dust, I'll be inside, it is not possible otherwise. (F 32)

This image, one that presages the elaborate funereal fantasy of Fizzle 8, is an almost perfect expression of what we may call a cryptological fantasy: the fantasy of being buried, the fantasy of finding oneself instantiated within a space of ruin. The authorial I, to return to Abraham and Torok, has perfectly fashioned himself as the lost object: lost to all, including himself. Because it is after Fizzle 4, with the exception of the spectral Fizzle 6, that the speaking I disappears from *Fizzles*. The I has vanished just as the need any longer to say I has disappeared in the fantasy of effacement and encryption. We may be reminded of Blanchot, again: 'one ought perhaps to speak of a *subjectivity without any subject*: the wounded space, the hurt of the dying, the already dead body which no one could ever own, or ever say of it, I, *my body*' (*The Writing of the Disaster* 30). The disappearance of the I into the space of the text, the ruinstrewn landscape of the text, is presaged here in Fizzle 4: the he is dead, the I now is hidden, encrypted, within this disappearance, this death. What emerges thus is the subjectless subject, an affect of disappearance – or affect as the *sign* of the subject's disappearance – which still seems grounded in some kind of space. In my examination of Fizzles 7 and 8, the critical culminating texts in *Fizzles*, I wish to attempt to develop a way of thinking about the subjectless subject in its space. What kind of being emerges here in this subjectless space? What, exactly, *could* a subjectless space mean? From a purely Heideggerian perspective, of course, space means insofar as a subject instantiates itself within it. Space, on its own, without a subject, is of little hermeneutic significance. Thus Heidegger: 'the "subject" (Dasein), if well understood ontologically, is spatial' (*BT* 146). What then about space without a subject? If Dasein is spatial does this not imply that space, as such, to be comprehended as such, requires a subject?

Fizzle 7 begins:

> Bright at last close of a dark day the sun shines out at last and goes down. Sitting quite still at valley window normally turn head now and see it the sun low in the southwest sinking. Even get up certain moods and go stand by western window quite still watching it sink and then the afterglow. (*F* 47)

Who is sitting here? Whose eyes watch the setting sun? In my reading we have here the fantasy projection of a subjectless space, a space of affect and minimal motion. The 'plot' of this narrative would seem to be the tracking of a subject who laboriously, painstakingly, puts his head to his hands; and that is all. The achievement of the authorial I is to have removed itself from the discourse of the space of the discourse; the achievement is of a radically objective view of itself as minimally inhabiting a space via a minimal movement:

> Legs side by side broken right angles at the knees as in that old statue some old god twanged at sunrise and again at sunset. Trunk likewise dead plumb right up to top of skull seen from behind including nape clear of chairback. (F 48)

But this fantasy of stillness, this desire for stillness, is betrayed, minimally betrayed, by movement; despite all desire, in other words, movement still betrays the subject; the authorial I may have buried itself deep in the now-defunct exteriorised subject (this 'he'), may have achieved that fantasy of no longer saying I (but who speaks here? From where does this discourse that comprises *Fizzles* arise?), but there is still movement and movement betrays, that is, reveals, subjectivity. In other words, in Fizzle 7, the authorial I is not encrypted quite enough yet:

> Quite still then all this time eyes open when discovered then closed then opened and closed again no other movement any kind though of course not still at all when suddenly or so it looks this movement impossible to follow let alone describe. (F 49)

Upon discovery – but by whom? By the authorial I? That is, the subject of *Fizzles in toto*? – being is revealed through movement. It takes only the minima (a word used in Fizzle 1) of movement for being to be revealed. This is, perhaps, Being without subject, but it is still Being. Even if the movement of the eye – and how can we not hear the Beckettian pun on eye/I at this point? – is impossible to follow, let alone describe, it is still movement. What does this add up to, this impossible movement? This movement, impossible, is the spatial, we might even say objective, correlative to the impossible subject that emerges in this authorial fantasy: Being without Being; movement impossible to follow; directionality without directionality. And yet, for all that, for even its impossibility, the desire for perfect stillness is betrayed.

And thus the melancholic and elaborate cryptological fantasy of Fizzle 8.

Why melancholic? Because Fizzle 8, as its title indicates, is instantiated out of an absolute repetition of the end: the end that cannot be the end; the end that only ever recapitulates what once was. Melancholy, as Freud tells us, is the inability to do away with the past; melancholy is the inability – or unwillingness – to allow the past *to be* the past. The inability to end, which may in Fizzle 8 translate into an unwillingness to end, speaks simply of a melancholic logic of endless return to the beginning of the end, as the first line makes clear: 'For to end yet again skull alone in a dark place pent bowed on a board to begin' (*F* 55). This image recalls, of course, the primary image of Fizzle 7, the achievement of a kind of classic melancholic pose: the melancholic – one thinks of Dürer's *Melencolia I* here – head in hand. In Fizzle 7, I would suggest, the authorial I, deprived (itself) of subjectivity, finds itself, however, haunted by its inability to achieve the perfect stillness that would, in Beckett's universe, emblematise the perfect end of subjectivity and the affect of subjectivity: the end of movement, the denial of the spatiality of space, would signal the end of Being. But Fizzle 7 tells us only that a minimal movement is minimal being and thus, from the space of melancholy of Fizzle 7 we move into the complex phantasmic space of Text 8, the space of pure cryptological fantasy, the space, crucially, where the plea for being without being is made even as it is acknowledged to be an impossibility. I remind us of the lines we are inexorably moving towards: 'And dream of a way in space with neither here nor there where all footsteps ever fell can never fare nearer to anywhere nor from anywhere further away' (*F* 60). This fantasy, I will argue, can only be articulated in the space of a kind of writerly projection of possibility; that is to say, and to recapitulate, *Fizzles* is an allegory of writing the self into oblivion, a fantasy of achieving that space of writing that Blanchot calls the neutral and what Beckett's narrator hopes is the space of the absent, no longer speaking, I. The fantasy here has been a discursive one: to remove the self within the space of a phantomic writing, to neutralise the claims of the I, just as any exteriorised subject – the 'he' – is effaced in order to create the blank screen of absolute negation. In 'Literature and the Right to Death', Blanchot characterises the discursive neutral space of writing that all authors hope to achieve; the attempt here, he suggests, is to speak of

Space and Trauma   147

> The horror of existence deprived of the world, the process through which whatever ceases to be continues to be, whatever is forgotten is always answerable to memory, whatever dies encounters only the impossibility of dying, whatever seeks to attain the beyond is always still here. (F 52)

Writing, in other words, can only ever be a melancholic space of impossible transcendence; writing can only ever be a space of fantasy where the neutralisation of the subject is only ever a purely discursive act; writing initiates, in other words, what Blanchot calls the step *not* beyond: being is never, can never be, left behind.

And in some ways Fizzle 8 maximally compresses the entire trajectory of the *Fizzles* as a whole: the second and third lines – 'Long thus to begin till the place fades followed by the board long after. For to end yet again skull alone in the dark the void no neck no face just the box last place of all in the dark the void' (F 55) – offer an image of the subject, a fantasy image of the subject, reduced to what Beckett in *Worstward Ho* will call the 'mere minimum': 'no neck no face'. With faciality gone all that is left is the affect of the void; in terms I have been employing throughout this chapter what we are given here is a perfect image of the crypt: 'Place of remains where once used to gleam in the dark on and off used to glimmer a remain' (F 55). Subjectivity and the expression of subjectivity – movement – are reduced here to a mere glimmer, 'in lieu of going out' (F 55). A glimmer – and what does this word signify? Thought? Affect of thought? – in lieu of directionality and movement, movement that would trace the lineaments of the subject's world. We are here, in Fizzle 8, in other words, within the maximally compressed space of interiority: a cryptological space where the authorial I – the writerly I – has reduced itself to the mere glimmer of subjectivity. And yet, for all that, for all the achievements of this radical neutrality, there remain – in all senses of this term – markers of the subject. We may be able to read the 'skull' as a mere metaphor of interiority – a trope anticipated here and worked out more fully in, again, *Worstward Ho* – but, like a spectre, like all things that once were repressed, an eye appears, and more than merely within the discursive logic of cliché or common expression: 'grey sand as far as eye can see' (F 56). This may be an *eye/I* without immediate subjective grounding – as yet no pronominal designation appears in the text – but almost immediately after the appearance of the 'eye' an Other appears, the expelled: 'There in the end same grey invisible to any other eye stark erect amidst his ruins the expelled' (*F* 56). Invisible to any other eye: what does this mean? Is this an admission that what is being seen – the expelled – can only be seen by this perceiving eye because what the eye sees is, narcissistically, the subject himself? Is this instance of vision a traumatic moment – albeit in a register so dimmed as to be almost subliminal – of the return of the repressed? Can, in other words, the perceiving eye maintain the essential separation between itself and the expelled, maintain it enough to sustain the fantasy of absolute solitude? Or is this encounter with the expelled, the expelled amidst his ruins – and I read 'his' here to refer back to the perceiving eye, the authorial I/eye – merely the last gasp of fantasy of effacement and burial? Because what is occurring here in Fizzle 8? At a very basic level Fizzle 8 maps out a movement between a perceiving eye and a perceived object – the expelled – who seems to be carried into a space (by 'two white dwarfs') and left, almost buried. This expelled surely is the last vestige of the authorial I, the last remains of what needs to be cast out in order for the absolute solitude of neutrality to be achieved. Fizzle 8, in other words, and as its title indicates – *to end yet again* – is a recapitulation and return of the major phantasmic trajectory of the entire text, the fantasy of effaced exteriorised subjectivity: a version of the self is created to be buried in order for the perceiving I to be radically alone and beyond the need for Being. And here, to return to our major focus, that elimination of the need for being is expressed as the desire for the elimination of all motion, movement, directionality. The exteriorised other – the expelled – himself finally finds a kind of rest:

> Last change of all in the end the expelled falls headlong down and lies back to sky full little stretch amidst his ruins. Feet centre body radius falls unbending as a statue falls faster and faster the space of a quadrant. Eagle the eye that shall discern him now mingled with the ruins mingling with the dust. (*F* 59)

And while around him there still is a semblance of motion – the two dwarfs carry out the task of motion, seemingly without purpose – the expelled now seems to have achieved the authorial eye's desire: stillness, if not burial.

And yet, we are presented, finally, with the expression of a desire for an end to all motion, motion that would appear to have ceased with the final fall of the expelled. And so, how are we to read these final words?

> Sepulchral skull is this then its last state all set for always litter and dwarfs ruins and little body grey cloudless sky glutted dust verge upon verge hell air not a breath. And dream of a way in a space with neither here nor there where all the footsteps ever fell can never fare nearer to anywhere nor from anywhere further away. No for in the end for to end yet again by degrees or as though switched on dark falls there again that certain dark that alone certain ashes can. Through it who knows yet another end beneath a cloudless sky same dark it earth and sky of a last end if ever there had to be another absolutely had to be. (F 60–1)

It is here that *Fizzles* resonates most purely with almost perfect melancholy: this skull, what in *Worstward Ho* Beckett will call the 'seat and germ of all' (*NO* 100), is explicitly acknowledged as a melancholic space of ruin; this is a *sepulchral* skull, the skull now explicitly a tomb or crypt for what now will always be a repetition of being and non-being: 'all set for always litter and dwarfs ruins and little body' (F 60). This sepulchral space will inevitably stage again this essential dialectic between effacement and an acknowledgement of the impossibility of the end of being. The line – *and dream of a way in a space with neither here nor there* – is the perfect distillation of the fantasy: it is a *dream* of a kind of Being in non-Being. In Heideggerian terms, 'a way in a space with neither here nor there' could only ever be an expression of a desire for directionality without directionality, what Blanchot terms subjectivity without any subject. This is an expression of a desire for perfect stillness in motion, a state achievable only in this last state in the sepulchral skull. But we notice that immediately following this expression of the dream, there is the denial: 'no for in the end for to end yet again by degrees or as though switched on dark fall there again' (F 60–1). The force of repetition – always the bane of Beckettian subjectivity[10] – compels this subject to acknowledge that there can be no perfect stillness within the inexorability of the temporal: 'dark falls again'. There can be no hope to be 'absent for good from self and other' (as Beckett puts it in 'neither': *CSP* 258). If the subject is to be compelled back into time's flow he will inevitably, perhaps traumatically, find himself back within the cryptic ruinstrewn landscape: 'yet another end beneath a cloudless sky same dark it earth and sky of a last end' (*F* 61). And within this ruinstrewn landscape there will inevitably be motion, and with motion there is being.

If there is trauma here then it can only be understood as the trauma of the impossibility of non-Being, stasis, and non-directionality; more exactly this is the trauma of discovering, repeatedly over the course of eight minute yet intensely resonate texts, that being can only ever be nullified if motion and trajectivity are severed from Being, as such. But is this not a curious kind of trauma? Trauma is the affect arising from the weight of history; trauma is a state of knowledge of the inevitability of the past's full presence in the now. In classical, one might say orthodox, terms, trauma is an affect that is precipitated by the sudden irruption of the real into the symbolic; but that irruption – a sudden accident; a sudden loss – is precisely that: a sudden, *singular* shock. The subject's trauma here in *Fizzles* is a trauma of a kind of weak repetition, a discovery, yet again, that the end, yet again, can never be achieved. It is true that trauma, in its classic articulation, sets up a kind of feedback loop wherein the victim experiences his/her sudden shock again and again, in the logic of a kind of lethal repetition, a repetition that threatens the integrity of the subject; the subject's sense of herself within a stably unfolding temporality is ungrounded by the economy of lethal return, as Freud tells us (and as I quoted above).

Trauma, in other words, is initiated by loss and *continually initiates* loss. The Beckettian subject's trauma, however, is not initiated by loss, but by the discovery of the *impossibility* of loss. Does this not suggest a curious negation of the very idea of trauma as a sudden, unexpected, singular irruption of the real into the symbolic? Does this understanding of the impossibility of loss not imply, as I suggested at the outset, that the idea of trauma, as such, may be of little use in our thinking about the Beckettian subject? Earlier I suggested that the idea of trauma may not be useful given that trauma demands a subject to be present to feel the full weight of history; *Fizzles*, indeed like almost any Beckett text written after *The Unnamable*, does its best to eliminate the subject, to fashion the subject as 'destitute of history', as what I call the posthuman *spectre without spirit*; more, the writing subject in *Fizzles* has done its best to neutralise signs of itself in its own discursive production. In a neutral text, as Blanchot himself may ask, how can history obtain? In a text in which the narrative voice places itself outside of subjectivity, beyond subjectivity, exterior to subjectivity, how can we suggest that a moment of trauma, as historical praxis, could possibly emerge? Let me return to Blanchot and his thinking on the neutral voice:

> Let us (on a whim) call it spectral, ghostlike. Not that it comes from beyond the grave, or even because it would once and for all represent some essential absence, but because it always tends to absent itself in its bearer and also efface him as the center: it is thus neutral in the decisive sense that it cannot be central, does not create a center, does not speak from out of a center, but on the contrary, at the limit, would prevent the work from having one. (*The Infinite Conversation* 386)

Surely this description of the neutral voice resonates perfectly in *Fizzles*, a text whose narrative voice is so attenuated as to be phantom-like. Indeed, the neutral voice is spectral in the sense that it has attempted to efface all traces of itself in an encrypted, if not dead, or dying, exteriorised subject. All this is perhaps to say that the idea of trauma cannot obtain given the radical neutralisation of voice and thus subjectivity: trauma without subjectivity, like mourning without a subject, is simply a concept beyond understanding.

But as I read this final Fizzle, with its articulation of the idea that return and repetition prevent the absolute effacement of the subject, I am reminded of a very troubling line in Blanchot's *The Step Not Beyond*: 'loss is impossible' (68). Surely the attempt to efface the subject, the attempt to eradicate the subject within discourse, and even the discourse of history, is revealed here as an impossibility. *Loss is impossible*. Surely what this final text suggests, in its resonant mobilisation of the idea of the impossible end – *for to end yet again* – is that the subject is present even as it attempts to efface itself. For truly what we have traced throughout *Fizzles* is an attempt made by the subject to remove itself, to encrypt itself in phantomic space, to bring about the end of deseverance and directionality: but even in that attempt, even in that discursive, that is to say, writerly, attempt to bring about the absolute neutralisation of the subject, a subject has been present to bring about the (impossible) end of the subject. *Loss is impossible*. An absolute effacement of the subject, within discourse, within discourse mobilised by a writing consciousness, is impossible. Let me quote once again the final lines of Fizzle 8:

> No for in the end for to end yet again by degrees or as though switched on dark falls there again that certain dark that alone certain ashes can. Through it who knows yet another end beneath a cloudless sky same dark it earth and sky of a last end if ever there had to be another absolutely had to be. (F 61)

I do not wish grossly to wrest this final 'to be' from its context, a context that melancholically suggests the inevitable return of another day, that is to say, the course of temporality and thus history, but it strikes me as crucial that the infinitive *to be* is the final phrase of this text, repeated twice, in fact, in the final line. It is as if the text in its attempt to remove all signs of being – being as history, being as movement, being as thought – inevitably inscribes, in the end, the very thing it wishes to efface. And so, where does this leave us? The text has attempted to present a posthuman subject destitute of history and thus beyond the claims of trauma; the text has attempted to remove all signs of subjectivity via an elaborate process of effacement and encryption, a process that, in its turn, would remove the subject from any attachment to trauma. And yet, the subject returns, the subject remains, the subject can never be lost. I suggested above that this is a kind of attenuated trauma, the trauma of the impossibility of disappearance, of loss. But truly if *Fizzles* is, as I suggest, an extended examination of the idea that the loss of subjectivity is impossible, which does also mean the impossibility of the loss of history, we are presented with an image that is more than simply one of attenuated trauma: the true horror of *Fizzles* resides in the perfect nightmare of eternal return, a nightmare image of continuous and inexorable connection to an impossible-to-realise desire to end. *Loss is impossible.*

Notes

1. Ackerley and Gontarski, *The Grove Companion to Samuel Beckett* (199–200).
2. See my 'Does Mourning Require a Subject?' for an example of an interpretation guided by Beckett's own assessment of the success of the work, in this case *Texts for Nothing*.

3. I discuss aspects of Beckett's attitude to the agony of writing in *Beckett: A Guide for Perplexed* (see chapter 2 and the conclusion).
4. On the experience of trauma as (paradoxically) integrative – in the sense that it orients the subject towards some sense of history, as such – see Lauren Berlant's *Cruel Optimism* (80–1).
5. Readings of the relation between subjectivity and trauma, of course, abound. The work of Cathy Caruth (*Unclaimed Experience*), Dominick LaCapra (*Writing History, Writing Trauma*), Dori Laub and Shoshana Felman (*Testimony*), Eng and Kazanjian (*Loss*), and Ruth Leys (*Trauma: A Genealogy*) is crucial and has proven critically influential. With the exception of LaCapra, who mentions Beckett's work, if only tangentially, none of these writers engages with Beckett's work on the subject (and trauma) in any detail, or at all. This fact may strike us as odd given that Beckett's texts seem, at least initially, to be perfectly about trauma. What I am attempting to demonstrate here (and this also is an explanation as to why I am not engaging with trauma theory as such in this chapter) is that Beckett's model of the subject, coming close to a posthuman subjectivity, resists the recuperative logic of trauma theory. Trauma, as I have argued elsewhere, assumes a subject; the writings of all major thinkers of trauma theory assume a subject to feel the effect of trauma and record and testify to that effect. Beckett never assumes a subject; he never assumes a subject to feel or have felt the claims of trauma in ways that would recuperate the event of loss as a locatable historical event. Trauma theory, I would suggest, even in its most radical instantiations, is ultimately a conservatively *humanist* endeavour: it is a theory of the subject therefore that seems oddly out of place in a discussion of Beckett, and perhaps especially *Fizzles*.
6. Allow me to quote Virilio once again: 'I do not work on the subject and object – that is the work of the philosopher – but rather on the "traject". I have proposed to inscribe the trajectory between the subject and the object to create the neologism "trajective", in addition to "subjective" and "objective"' (*Politics of the Very Worst* 39–40).
7. I am reminded of Marjorie Perloff's reading of *Fizzles* in *The Poetics of Indeterminacy*. Perloff's notion that in Beckett's *Fizzles* '"Closed space" becomes a paradigm for the mystery of being' (209) is a useful entry point into these texts' exploration of the relation between being and space.
8. Enoch Brater was the first to formulate this important question. In his reading of Fizzle 7, Brater asks: 'Who is narrating this story? How has he garnered his information? How has such privileged sighting been achieved? So far as who is viewing whom is

concerned – and from what perspective – the choice of a fixed point cannot be determined' ('Still/Beckett: The Essential and the Incidental' 13).
9. In *Samuel Beckett's New Worlds*, Susan Brienza writes: 'In "Still" [Fizzle 7] the absence of pronouns, especially the expected "I", means that all the discrete body fragments never sum to a being who is undeniably present, and we are left with merely the illusion of a protagonist' (199).
10. On this point, see my essay 'Archives of the End: Embodied History in Samuel Beckett's Plays', in *Samuel Beckett: History, Memory, Archive*.

5

Fables of Posthuman Space: *Company*, *Ill Seen Ill Said*, *Worstward Ho*

A place. Where none. For the body. To be in.

(*Worstward Ho*)

In some crucial ways the so-called second trilogy of *Company*, *Ill Seen Ill Said*, and *Worstward Ho* recapitulates the trajectory of the short prose from *All Strange Away* to *Lessness*. *Company* is a closed space text, par excellence; *Ill Seen Ill Said* moves the subject – now fully spectralised, perhaps even now beyond the category of the posthuman, as such – into a festishised external space, a gravesite; *Worstward Ho*, in some ways Beckett's most difficult text, moves the subject into space that is immediately placed under erasure: 'Say ground. No ground but say ground' (*NO* 90); here the body both is and is not 'The body again. Where none' (*NO* 90). In the second trilogy we move, in other words, from the space of memory, the space of a kind of autobiographical meditation on the possibility of being through remembrance (*Company*), to the space of spectralised mourning (*Ill Seen Ill Said*), to a space that places us beyond even the categories of being, ontology, space, and place. *Worstward Ho*'s intractable difficulty resides in the fact that Beckett here has moved us into a space, the pure space of literature, as Blanchot would call it, where all categories – hermeneutical, ontological, philosophical – collapse. We are asked, as we move through these final texts, to negotiate a relationship to the idea of a fully remaindered subject inhabiting a fully remaindered space: this trilogy reaches the point where mind and world can only be figured as imagined, spectralised traces of themselves: 'Remains of mind then still. Enough still. Somewhose somewhere somehow enough still. No mind and words? Even such words. So enough still' (NO 104). My task here, in my reading of the trajectory offered to us in these three texts, is to begin thinking through the possibility of thinking *beyond* the posthuman. Because the posthuman subject, as I have argued elsewhere, is always haunted by the traces of the human: the term 'post' never fully effaces the nostalgic traces of the human that once was. Even in texts as radically spectralised as *Lessness* or *Fizzles*, there is in place the possibility that the subject is tied in some ways, ontologically or through the complex process of remembrance, to a more fully realised past. The subject in this final trilogy, and the world it inhabits, seems to me to have left even the nostalgia for the human, and its world, behind. And thus ultimately I return to the line from *Texts for Nothing* that is the ground of this entire project – 'what counts is to be in the world' – and now ask: what has happened to the world in these final texts? How are we to understand what Beckett means when he writes: 'No place but the one. None but the one where none. Whence never once in. Somehow in. Beyondless' (NO 92). Does this beyondless 'shade-ridden void' (NO 101) constitute a world? A space? Or have we come, now, to Beckett's terminal vision of the world, a vision that suggests that when the world has vanished, when the very possibility of world has vanished, then we have arrived, finally – but has this been Beckett's dream all along? To inscribe and thereby witness the end of the world? – at the end of the human?

Company

I wish here, in my reading of *Company*, to return to Heidegger's *The Fundamental Concepts of Metaphysics* and his understanding of world, world-formation, and Dasein as being with others. My intention here is to begin thinking carefully about the economy and space of memory in *Company*, to think carefully about what might be said, ultimately, about the world that is offered to us by the imagining or *imagined* subject here. My task is to find a way of understanding what is meant by the phrase used to describe the subject: 'Devised deviser devising it all for company' (NO 33). More precisely, I wish to find a way of understanding what is meant by 'it' here. As a tentative answer I will suggest that a profitable way into this text is to think of the imagined/imagining subject as calling into being, or attempting to call into being, a world. As Heidegger will say, 'Man as man is world-forming'

(*FCM* 285); moreover, as he writes, 'the being-there of Da-sein means *being there with others*' (*FCM* 205; emphasis in original). It is not exactly my intention to read *Company* as an allegory of the ideas of world-forming and being with others. It is, rather, to suggest that Beckett's subject, at once deviser, at once devised, at once, it seems, present in a space of remembering and *presented to* a space of memory, is defined by its aporetic, impossible desire to realise itself as what the text itself calls the 'downright human' (*NO* 19). That is, *Company* is about, in one sense, the attempt to find the space within which a kind of humanity emerges from the catastrophic remains of its own impossibility.[1]

As I say, *Company* is a closed space narrative par excellence. The speaker of the text, who also is, it seems, the 'hearer' of his own disavowed discourse, lies on his back in the dark. As is true for the spaces and places of previous closed space fictions, this space operates on the border between allegory and the material. This is, possibly, a text 'about' the human, reduced to its essential aspect: a fading self, remembering its past; a fading self desperate to assert the reality of a past in order to assert the reality of itself in a present without measure. The speaker speaks in order for the hearer to 'have a past and acknowledge it' (*NO* 24). But there is, equally, the suspicion that the assertion of a history is an illusion. As the speaker says of himself: 'You were once. You were never. Were you ever?' (*NO* 13). The closed, dark, and defined space: more than a metaphor for being, as such, the space speaks beyond the confines of allegory into the material realities of solitude, isolation, and loneliness. And, as always in Beckett's closed space fiction, there is an assertion of the physical, material reality of space, spatiality, and the body. That is to say, the material reality of things is important for Beckett here. Thus we are given the dimensions of the space:

> Imagine closer the place where he lies. Within reason. To its form and dimensions a clue is given by the voice afar. Receding afar or there with abrupt saltation or resuming there after pause. From above and from all sides and levels with equal remoteness at its most remote. At no time from below. So far. Suggesting one lying on the floor of a hemispherical chamber of generous diameter with ear dead centre. How generous? Given faintness of voice at its least faint some sixty feet should suffice or thirty from ear to any given point of encompassing surface. So much for form and dimensions. (*NO* 23)

The imagining voice, and hearer – this devised deviser – will, perhaps, disavow this attempt at measurement (he will suggest that he has 'imagined ill' [*NO* 23] the dimensions and assert only the reality of an 'immeasurable dark' [*NO* 24]); and he will later, as he begins to crawl about attempting to map his space, come to conclude that he inhabits a 'bourneless dark' (*NO* 36), a dark without, that is, limit or boundary, but Beckett is careful to assert that, bourneless or not, this is a material space. The dark is not, as I say, merely a metaphor for being, for being into thrownness. We are again in familiar, if difficult, terrain here in *Company*. This space, in the dark, is not easily read, not easily accommodated to a comfortable ontology. At once allegorical and real, this space, this 'it' the devised deviser devises, is, in a very real sense, a world. And, as always, our questions must be: what kind of world is this? What kind of world-making, to be more precise, allows this world – bourneless, immeasurable – to be?

Company also is about the critical dialectic between the reality of the present state of things, of this conjured world, and what should be called the space of memory. This present state of absolute solitude is marked by a radical disassociation. The subject, in his solitude, imagines himself plural, grammatises himself into the second and third person. He is able, insofar as we are able to imagine agency at work here, to create himself as his own company and, simultaneously, to imagine that he, himself, is in turn created by a subjectivity preceding and exceeding him: devised deviser devising it all for company. Beckett's closed space fictions have always foregrounded themselves as allegories of fiction-making, as, perhaps, world-making (even in Heidegger's sense). Images of conjuration, of isolated selves creating other selves, abound in *All Strange Away*, *Imagination Dead Imagine*, and *Fizzles*, as we have seen. *Company* explicitly thematises the relation between solitude and fiction, explicitly suggests that solitude is a precursor to world-making, or what Heidegger calls 'world-forming' (*FCM* 285).[2] As a fabulist, the narrator/narrated here in *Company* conjures aspects of himself as both consolation for and confirmation of his solitude. Narrative, in other words, is a necessary adjunct to solitude, an inevitable expression of the subject abandoned to itself. But narrative also, agonisingly, confirms the absolute isolation of the present moment. The narrator is described, or describes himself, as 'Devising fragments to temper his nothingness' (*NO* 33). *Temper*, of course, is the perfect word here: it means both to soften and to make strong. The narratives the devised deviser tells operate, perhaps, to ameliorate his loneliness. But they also, inevitably, work only to emphasise, truly, the illusory nature of the imagination, the fancy. The 'fable' (*NO* 46) he tells, as the final words of the narrative make clear, can only be the expression of solitude: 'The fable of one fabling of one with you in the dark. And how better in the end labour lost and silence. And you as you always were. Alone' (*NO* 46).

But what should detain us here is how this 'fable' of isolation plays out rhythmically, oscillating between the space of this bourneless now and the space of memory. We should note that the memories that are presented to us as the text proceeds are for the most part memories of motion, of space, of trajectories. I suggested above that the devised deviser's fiction-making, his fabling, his imaginative capacity, are expressions of a desire for company, but they also are expressions of world-making. I mean by this phrase not simply that he conjures an illusory sense of community; and I also mean by the term world-making more than simply the idea that he is fictionalising his past in order, as he says, to 'have a past and acknowledge it' (*NO* 24). I am using the term world-making in the Heideggerian sense. In his view the human, rather paradoxically, emerges simultaneously with world by the process of world-forming: man does not precede world, but is a precondition for its forming. In a simple way we can perhaps suggest that for Heidegger man and world are self-supporting systems, events, ecologies. There is an intimate connection between man and world:

> For it is not the case that man first exists and then also one day decides amongst other things to form a world. Rather world-formation is something that occurs, and only on this ground can a human being exist in the first place. Man as man is world-forming. This does not mean that the human being running around in the street as it were is world-forming, but that the *Da-sein in* man is world-forming ... The Dasein in man *forms* world: [1.] it brings it forth; [2.] it gives an image or view of the world, it sets it forth; [3.] it constitutes the world, contains and embraces it. (*FCM* 285)

It is not necessarily my argument that Heidegger's notion of Dasein, as that which precedes and exceeds the subject, offers an image of the human as always already merely an expression of a force of the world, rather than a full agent within it. That is, it is not necessarily my purpose here to uncover a latent deconstruction of the human subject's agency in this theory of Dasein and to suggest, for instance, that Heidegger's vision of man is always already one that comes close to a possible posthumanism. Rather, what interests me here is Heidegger's absolute insistence that the relation between world-formation and the human subject is what constitutes the human. To be human is to be a vehicle for the force of Dasein; to be human is to allow oneself to be an expression of Dasein; Dasein, we might say, expresses itself *in* the human *as* world-formation. And what is critical about the event of world-formation, the way in which the human expresses the forces of Dasein, the way, that is, the human comes to be human, as such, is that world-formation is an event where the human emerges in community with others. 'World', Heidegger writes, is the '*manifestness of beings as such as a whole*' (*FCM* 284); 'For the being-there of Da-sein means *being with others*, precisely in the manner of Dasein, i.e., existing with others' (*FCM* 205); 'in accordance with the essence of his being man always already finds that he is with others' (*FCM* 206).

We have analysed this thematic in *Texts for Nothing*, wondering about the ecology of the relation between the posthuman subject and the other. We need again to return to this theme in this late text, if only because Beckett himself chooses to do so. Is it possible to suggest that Heidegger's being-with-others, a condition of being human, is only comprehensible, as such, within the space of world-formation? That is to say: world-formation and the subject's placing of himself within that world with others is an expression of spatiality: space is what allows the subject to be a subject. For Beckett, perhaps, space, both space that is lost and that which is regained through the process of fabling, what I am calling world-formation, is the grounds for the subject. But the intimate dialectic between space that is formed within the fable of imagining and the space the subject now finds himself in – this bourneless, measureless space – does suggest that the subjectivity of the subject, that which is dependent upon space, is only ever present as an oscillation between states of mind and memory that are fictive and imaginary and thus, as Blanchot will show us, grounds not of a fully present humanity but only of its own essential disappearance.

Fables of Posthuman Space 161

In *The Poetics of Space*, Gaston Bachelard offers an idea that could stand as the entry point into any discussion of solitude and space in Beckett: 'as soon as we become motionless, we are elsewhere; we are dreaming in a world that is immense' (184). Indeed it is this relation between motionlessness and being elsewhere that is at the heart of things in *Company*. If, to recall Heidegger once more, the subject is 'spatial' (*BT* 146) and if the spatiality of the subject's being is revealed by its mobilisation of its sense of directionality and de-severance – closing the distance between self and object within space – we may venture the idea that the motionless subject we encounter at the outset of *Company*, the 'one on his back in the dark' (*NO* 3), is not, in Heidegger's ontological reading of things, precisely human. Or, perhaps more fairly, this subject here is deprived of those elements of world that allow for the constitution of its full humanity. To read the subject here at the outset of *Company*, like the subject of *Texts for Nothing*, as poor in world begins perhaps to approach its condition, but not perfectly. We recall that for Heidegger the animal is poor in world, but both has and does not have world. I argued that the subject in *Texts for Nothing* is analogous to the Heideggerian animal, or more exactly, shares its ontological condition, given its essential state of becoming: its condition of being distributed across ontologies – being in both the here and the now – marked it as what Katherine Hayles calls a 'distributed cognition'. And while in *Company* we will trace a dialectic that, as I mention, defines our subject as an oscillation between states of mind and memory, his immobility and his essential solitude mark him as worldless: 'the *worldlessness* of a being can now be defined as its having no access to those beings (*as* beings) amongst which this particular being with this specific manner of being is' (*FCM* 197).

The subject, at the outset of *Company*, thus may, perhaps should, be called worldless. And it is this worldlessness, this essential solitude, that drives the desire for company. This desire is, as mentioned above, initially figured as the creation of a grammatical community: he speaks of himself as an other. But the subject also begins to rehearse, to imagine, to create – these metaphors are all appropriate – what appears to be a past and in so doing accomplishes a kind of world-formation. And while not every memory the subject rehearses instantiates a fantasy of space and movement, we do notice that a great number in fact are expressions of directionality and de-severance. Even as the narrator will conjure figures from his past and by so doing call into being a world of community, this community is grounded on or defined by its relation to spatiality. The narrator's first memory, of walking hand-in-hand with his stern mother, is about a harsh rebuke brought on by a specific questioning of distance and space:

> Looking up at the blue sky and then at your mother's face you break the silence asking her if it is not in reality much more distant that it appears. The sky that is. The blue sky. Receiving no answer you mentally reframe your question and some hundred paces later look up at her face again and ask her if it does not appear much less distant than in reality it is. For some reason you could never fathom this question must have angered her exceedingly. For she shook off your little hand and made you a cutting retort you have never forgotten. (*NO* 6)

I am fascinated by this first memory. The child, more than merely curious about a phenomenon, is, to read this moment through Heidegger, attempting to locate himself within the spatiality of the world. Attempting to ascertain the distance between himself and the sky, the child is, from a fundamental ontological perspective, attempting to locate himself within the world and as a subject (all this, we should note, while walking, while mapping a trajectory on the ground). The mother's rebuke – occurring more than likely because she cannot answer the question – works, in a way, to deny the child's positionality, and the removal of her hand is a clear denial of a primordial community. I am interested in the tension this initial memory sets up in our reading of *Company*. If the text oscillates between a worldless present and the attempt, via memory, to ameliorate that worldlessness by creating a past in which some sense of world is possible, this initial memory is strikingly negative: the narrator's positionality and community are denied.

But I wonder if this initial memory works to highlight what becomes more clearly important to the narrator: his relation with the father, the father whom we meet in the second memory and who is characterised by movement and directionality. And if this first image of the father is marked by his – the father's – desire for movement (he walks as he awaits the birth of his son, the narrator), it works as a precursor to the kind of companionability, of community, his father will lend him. For certainly the memories of imitating his father's laughter is important to the narrator (*NO* 28); as is his memory of his father's encouragement to dive into the ocean (*NO* 12). But what truly is crucial to the narrator in his motionless present, are the memories – and one in particular – of moving through the world with his father's shade at his side and the suggestion that this spectral community formed a crucial part of the subject's trajective relation to his world. The narrator recalls a moment when, accompanied by the ghost of his father, he pauses in his walking to add up the number of steps he has taken in his lifetime:

> You halt with bowed head on the verge of the ditch and convert into yards. On the basis now of two steps per yard. So many since dawn to add to yesterday's. To yesteryear's. To yesteryears'. Days other than today and so akin. The giant tot in miles. In leagues. How often round the earth already. Halted too at your elbow during these computations your father's shade. In his old tramping rags. Finally on side by side from nought anew. (*NO* 9)

This memory returns again a few pages later and given that it is the only memory that is repeated in *Company* we are obliged to register its importance.[3] Critically, when the memory recurs, the narrator deliberately signals that it is subject to creative flourishes. In other words, this is not a memory, or not only a memory: it is a *fable*:

> Nowhere in particular on the way from A to Z. Or say for verisimilitude the Ballyogan Road. That dead old back road. Somewhere on the Ballyogan Road in lieu of nowhere in particular. Where no truck any more. Somewhere on the Ballyogan Road on the way from A to Z. Head sunk totting up the tally on the verge of the ditch. Foothills to left. Croker's Acres ahead. Father's shade to right and a little to the rear. So many times already round the earth. Topcoat once green stiff with age and grime from chin to insteps. Battered once buff block hat and quarter boots still a match. No other garments if any to be seen. Out since break of day and night now falling. Reckoning ended on together from nought anew. (*NO* 16)

This moment is, in my reading, a critical instance of world-building: the narrator, in the bourneless present moment in the dark, recalls, or invents, a space and a time out of the nowhere of history. He conjures both himself and his father (already spectral, now doubly so) in space, as geographically located, but, importantly, perhaps as invented: 'Or say for verisimilitude the Ballyogan Road.' In the assertion of verisimilitude the narrator translates himself from nowhere to somewhere, locating himself in space, mapping the space from 'A to Z' even as he recalls his history. These assertions of place through place names – Croker's Acres, Ballyogan Road – with their implicit conjuring of a real world, speak to a desire for a certainty about the world, even as the fictionality of that world is acknowledged. And of course this assertion of a mapped, knowable world recalls, perfectly and inevitably, the state of the narrator here, now, in the real nowhere of the 'immeasurable dark', the 'bourneless dark'. Given his position in the limitless space of the dark ('bourne' means limit or boundary), we understand absolutely the desire for the world-building of memory, for the fabulist's desire for space and trajectory. The narrative impulse here recalls de Certeau's assertion of the essential function of all narrative. In *The Practice of Everyday Life* de Certeau, in his tracing of the genealogical relation between mapping, narrative, and the trajective impulse (that is to say, walking, as such), asserts that 'every story is a travel story – a spatial practice' (115). Narratives all, in one way or another, map space as they construct the world; any narrative, from the monumental acts of world-building (one thinks of *War and Peace*) to the miniature (one thinks of *Company*), is a way of asserting knowledge about the world. Stories, de Certeau writes, 'traverse and organize places; they select and link them together; they make sentences and itineraries out of them. They are spatial trajectories' (115). More accurately, the narrative functions to create worlds, to authorise knowledge of space and trajectories: 'the story's first function is to authorize, more exactly, to *found*' (123). As it grounds experience in the fundamental authoritative act of world-building – and here the narrative takes on an analogous function to the archive, as Derrida would note – narrative offers the subject a way of being in a knowable, bounded world.

As I say, we understand the narrator's desire to construct a world where the possibility of company and place exist. We understand the impulse even as the narrator himself understands how his own voice, returning to a limited, repeating series of critical narratives, is working to create a past in order to secure a kind of community:

Another trait is repetitiousness. Repeatedly with only minor variants the same bygone. As if willing him by this dint to make it his. To confess, Yes, I remember. Perhaps even to have a voice. To murmur, Yes I remember. What an addition to company that would be! A voice in the first person singular. Murmuring now and then, Yes I remember. (*NO* 10)

But what is the effect of this world-building? Is it not obvious that despite the fiction-making at work here, the narrative voice, even in its plurality, remains alone? This is, of course, the obvious theme of *Company*: as even the final word of the text indicates, the narrator remains utterly alone. But it strikes me that Beckett, by creating his subject explicitly as a fabulist, is offering more than this simple irony. This late text allows itself to be read, I want finally to argue, as a commentary on the monstrous desolation of the act of writing itself, the failure, ultimately, of its attempt at world-building. Blanchot is of some help here in our attempt to read not irony, but the truth of writing. In 'From Dread to Language', Blanchot speaks of the essential solitude of the writer:

> The person who is alone is not the one who experiences the impression of being alone; this monster of desolation needs the presence of another if his desolation is to have a meaning, another who, with his reason intact and his senses preserved, renders momentarily possible the distress that had until then been impotent. (4)[4]

It is here with Blanchot that we can begin to gauge the real desolation at the heart of *Company*. The narrator is not merely creating a world in which a past is possible; he is not merely world-building in order to ameliorate his desolation; he is world-building, creating a past and acknowledging it, creating himself as witness to his own past, in order to confirm his own desolation. By compelling himself to witness his own past – to have the hearer have a past and acknowledge it – the narrator creates a witness to his essential solitude and in so doing confirms its absolute weight. Moreover, as Blanchot reminds us in *The Space of Literature*, the very practice of writing, of creating fables, works only ever to vitiate the subject, to render himself unknown to himself. Blanchot's discussion of the displacement of the first person into the third as the writer enters the discursive moment speaks directly to the fabulist in *Company*:

> When to write is to discover the interminable, the writer who enters this region does not leave himself behind in order to approach the universal. He does not move towards a surer world, a finer or better justified world where everything would be ordered according to the clarity of the impartial light of day. He does not discover the admirable language which speaks honourably for all. What speaks in him is the fact that, in one way or another, he is no longer himself; he isn't anyone any more. The third person substituting for the 'I': such is the solitude that comes to the writer on account of the work. It does not denote objective disinterestedness, creative detachment. It does not glorify consciousness in someone other than myself or the evolution of a human vitality which, in the imaginary space of the work of art, would retain the freedom to say 'I'. The third person is myself become no one, my interlocutor turned alien; it is my no longer being able, where I am, to address myself and the inability of whoever addresses me to say 'I'; it is his not being himself. (28)

The process of world-building, far from calling into being a possibility for being, only displaces the self, threatens the fabulist with a kind of essential vanishing. And it is not, I believe, going too far to suggest that what writing does here, if we follow Blanchot to his logical end, is to instantiate the *end* of the writer, an entry into a condition we might call *discursive posthumanity*: the writer, writing himself into oblivion. For surely this is the condition – being beyond memory, now witnessing one's own essential solitude that is only the grounds of a disappearance – of the speaker as *Company* comes to its end:

> You now on your back in the dark shall not rise to your arse again to clasp your legs in your arms and bow down your head till it can bow down no further. But with face upturned for good labour in vain at your fable. Till finally you hear how words are coming to an end. With every inane word a little nearer to the last. And how the fable too. The fable of one with you in the dark. The fable of one fabling of one with you in the dark. And how better in the end labour lost and silence. And you as you always were. Alone. (*NO* 46)

What fascinates me about this final moment in *Company* is how Beckett forces us to imagine the state of being of the subject here. Having imagined and witnessed his own ultimate isolation – this fable only ever serving as a forceful reminder of his essential solitude – the fabulist finds himself in the originary scene of isolation. Writing – the space of writing – as Blanchot reminds us, only ever serves to displace the self, to confirm his utter isolation, but our subject here, now – 'You *now* on your back' – finds himself, if we can say this, *doubly desolate*. Writing, the process of memory and fabulation, only confirms his isolation; the act of imagination, that lure to company, has failed and thus the subject, whose discourse has vitiated himself, now finds that even that failure, the fable, is vanishing: 'Till finally you hear how words are coming to an end' (*NO* 46). These are his words he is overhearing, and thus he is now compelled to witness the end of the possibility of the fable, the end of the possibility of imagining a world where company, where limits and boundaries confirming the possibility of being, as such, exist. As language loses any force here – his language is 'vain' and 'inane', words both meaning *empty* – and as the fable now comes to an end, the subject is finally and fully beyond memory, beyond the possibility of witnessing, of speaking or imagining. This, in other words, is a solitude beyond the essential solitude of writing. This is a state of being beyond the spectral comfort of a spectral discourse; this, perhaps, is to be beyond the very prop – language – that supports the understanding of oneself as human or even posthuman; this is to be beyond what Blanchot calls the 'imaginary space of the work of art'. This is an essential solitude beyond even the *possibility* of solitude.

Ill Seen Ill Said

I wish in my reading of *Ill Seen Ill Said* to tarry with the idea of what I am calling, after Blanchot, *discursive posthumanism*. In my reading of *Company* I suggested that the fable-making subject, by engaging in the act of imagination, begins to attenuate his presence, his being in the world, begins, that is, to empty himself of himself. Writing, in other words, instantiates the entry into a kind of essential vanishing. This is as much to say that, for Beckett – and perhaps especially the late Beckett, the Beckett who writes with a sense of his own days as creator coming to an end – writing is always already to tarry with the posthuman. Writing always already is to step into imaginative spaces that instantiate the end of subjectivity, as such. To write thus is to enter into what Blanchot calls that state of *subjectivity without any subject*. *Ill Seen Ill Said* I wish to argue, is Beckett's fullest exploration of the relation between narrative, the act of narrating, which here is always already an act of a compromised imagination, and the disappearance of the human, the fullest expression of the idea that writing can only ever be the end of being. But, as we will see, this disappearing act, this entry into this essential vanishing, is deeply compromised: as ever, and here we must recall that guiding line from *Texts for Nothing*, the world still intrudes. If *Ill Seen Ill Said* is a fantasy of the disappearing imagination; if the narrator/witness here figures himself as what Blanchot will call an essential neutrality – spectral, radically exterior to experience, a profound absence – he still seems inevitably to conjure, through what must be now called the perversity of the imagination, a world, though spectral, that is still uncannily, palpably material. The posthuman narrative voice, in other words, always and ever betrays itself even as it attempts to conjure a world beyond the human. If the desire in Beckett is to witness the end of the human, is to enter into a condition of being a step beyond the human, the world always intrudes to claim the human for itself, *as* itself.

Like *Company*, then, *Ill Seen Ill Said* can be read as a meditation on, perhaps an allegory of, the creative act itself. From the second phrase of the text – 'On' – it is clear that the narrator (perhaps in the absence of a knowable narrator we should simply call this the *narrative voice*) is proceeding with some caution, self-consciously allotting details of place and person, self-consciously driving its narrative forward. In some crucial ways *Ill Seen Ill Said* is a narrative that narrates its own process of narration. As the text proceeds and as the narrative voice offers specific details of time, place, and causality – and even as it offers the possibility that one fictional setting may have been better chosen over another ('A moor would have better met the case' (*NO* 52) – the narrative voice repeatedly pauses and admonishes itself: 'The cabin. Its situation. Careful' (*NO* 50); 'How came a cabin in such a place. How came? Careful' (*NO* 50); 'The two zones form a roughly circular whole. As though outlined by a trembling hand. Diameter. Careful'; 'Flowers? Careful' (*NO* 51). Critically, the figure of the woman, she whom the narrative consciousness seems to need in order to *be* a narrative consciousness, requires a ready and alert witness. She seems, curiously, always about to vanish: 'But quick seize her where she is best to be seized. In the pastures far from shelter. She crosses the zone of stones and is there. Clearer and clearer she goes. Quick seeing

Fables of Posthuman Space   169

she goes out less and less' (*NO* 55). This is all to say that this narrative, ostensibly about a woman, perhaps in mourning (certainly she is another figure of an essential solitude), who comes and goes from her cabin and who visits a gravesite, is a self-consciously ordered narrative, is a narrative aware of itself as a narrative. And it is this self-awareness, this self-consciousness, that confers on the narrative its character and its voice. But as we notice, it is impossible to locate this voice, impossible to name it, impossible to speak of it as separate from its actions as narrative voice. Indeed the narrative voice's sole function, as it itself admits, is to narrate the figure of this woman: when she, at one point, disappears from the narrative, the narrative itself ceases; when she reappears, the narrator resumes his labour. The narrative voice, in other words, is always already only in 'wait for her to reappear. In order to resume' (*NO* 56). That is to say, the narrative voice *is* only, comes into being only, as it narrates. And as such, the narrative voice, one I wish, after Blanchot, to call a critical neutrality, is fully dependent on its narrative, and its elusive subject, in order to be. *Ill Seen Ill Said* thus is as much about the being of the narrative voice as it is about the (deeply compromised) being of the figure of the woman, its ostensible subject.

I wish to begin thinking about the relation between the narrative voice and the figure of the woman with a return to Blanchot. As I will attempt to demonstrate, Blanchot's ideas about the peculiar qualities of the narrative voice – its essential neutrality, its effacement of centre and what I previously called positionality – allow us to begin thinking fruitfully about the posthuman qualities of the Beckettian narrative. We recall how in *The Space of Literature* Blanchot suggests that the act of writing works to efface the writing subject to the point where the writer 'is no longer himself; he isn't anyone any more' (28). In *The Step Not Beyond*, Blanchot explicitly figures writing as an act of effacement: 'Writing is not destined to leave traces, but to erase, by traces, all traces, to disappear in the fragmentary space of writing, more definitively than one disappears in the tomb' (50). In *The Infinite Conversation*, Blanchot radicalises his view of the writing subject by essentially effacing him behind the work of the narrative voice. It is as if what becomes important for Blanchot is not any longer the act of writing, but what follows *from* that act. Writing, we might suggest, is only ever a pretext for the coming into being of what he calls the narrative voice, that event of absolute neutrality.⁵ Here Blanchot summarises the characteristics of the narrative voice and its neutrality; note how the narrative voice emerges as an articulation of a particular kind of spatial practice or event:

> The narrative voice that is inside only inasmuch as it is outside, at a distance without there being any distance, cannot be embodied. Although it may well borrow the voice of a judiciously chosen character, or even create the hybrid function of mediator (the voice that ruins all mediation), it is always different from what utters it: it is the indifferent-difference that alters the personal voice. Let us (on a whim) call it spectral, ghostlike. Not that it comes from beyond the grave, or even because it would once and for all represent some essential absence, but because it always tends to absent itself in its bearer and also efface himself as the center: it is thus neutral in the decisive sense that it cannot be central, does not create a center, does not speak from out of a center, but, on the contrary, at the limit, would prevent the work from having one; withdrawing from it the privileged point of interest (even afocal), and also not allowing it to exist as a competed whole, once and forever achieved. (386)

What fascinates me about Blanchot's ideas here is, of course, how they allow us to begin thinking about the narrative voice of especially Beckett's late prose. How perfectly Blanchot's notion of the decentred voice and its disembodiment speaks to the narrative voice of *Ill Seen Ill Said*, a voice that is never identified, never named, never located in history or space; a voice that is, as I suggest, fully dependent upon its subject in order to exist. A narrative voice that comes into being only at the limit of its own decentring discursivity. The narrative voice, 'speaking from nowhere, suspended in the narrative as a whole' (*The Infinite Conversation* 386), is a symptom or affect of the event of writing, writing understood not merely as the act of putting words on paper, the action of what the narrator here calls 'the drivelling scribe' (*NO* 80), but writing understood largely as the act of imagination, of figuration. As the narrator attempts to speak of its world, a world articulating itself as an extended act of witnessing, it produces not only that world but a narrative voice that can only neutralise, can only spectralise, can only exist at a critical limit of its own power. What is, for me, the most important aspect of Blanchot's notion of narrative voice and its neutrality is that it speaks from nowhere and lacks, definitively and a priori, its own proper existence. The narrative voice is neither one thing – the narrative proper – nor another – that which produces the narrative. The narrative voice exists as the limits between narrative and narrator: it is the *space* between.

Blanchot's notion of the spectral and radically displaced quality of the narrative voice, itself a symptom or affect of the act of writing, allows me to suggest that writing, especially the kind of writing that Beckett produces, always already has qualities that may be called posthuman. Writing, if we follow Blanchot, serves not as a transparent expression of an unmediated subjectivity; writing, rather, 'is always different from what utters it'. Writing, inasmuch as it is articulated in its symptom, the narrative voice, and as it serves only to displace and defer the writing subject, instantiates an essential spectrality of the writing subject and its narrative voice. What comes to be crucial for my purposes here, in my overarching concern with Beckett's posthuman spaces, is the way in which this discursive posthumanism – writing as an event of the disappearance of the human – becomes the vehicle for the articulation of subjects within spaces, within worlds. In *Ill Seen Ill Said*, writing, or narrative, is itself at best a differential trace of a mediating subject – call this the narrator of *Ill Seen Ill Said*; call it, perhaps, Samuel Beckett – and is the means by which a representation of the subject in her world occurs. In other words, Beckett here is doubling the posthuman stakes: the posthuman subject emerges only as a symptom of a posthuman discourse. But, and this is crucial, even as the figure of the woman retreats behind differential traces, even as she herself is explicitly figured as a trace or what I will call a symptom of a symptom; that is, even as the figure of the woman seems to be a priori deprived of any possible claims on any kind of ontology, any real claim to a real world, she seems stubbornly to *be*. Even as she emerges as *herself an essential neutrality* – and here I will argue that she is an allegory, or symptom, or objective correlative of the narrative impulse, as such – that neutrality never fully neutralises what Heidegger would call her facticity, her claims on the world. The figure of the woman here, and I will return to these difficult phrases, still has the 'misfortune to be still of this world' (*NO* 50). Further, as the narrative voice struggles with the agony of representation, with, that is, the very attempt to narrate, he wishes the woman 'could be pure figment' (*NO* 58). It is because she is not only pure figment, not only an imaginary being, a symptom of its own narrative voice,[6] but that she persists in this world that must detain and will trouble us. The woman is an irruption of something beyond an effect or affect of language; the woman is something other to the spatialising neutrality of the narrative voice and its narrative; the woman *is* or *exists as* something beyond, perhaps *a step beyond*, the effacement by a posthuman discourse. What she is, what her world is, is exactly our question, and our problem.[7]

If the narrative voice of *Ill Seen Ill Said* is marked as a radical neutrality, what can be said about the positionality – ontologically and spatially – of the main figure in the text, the woman in mourning? At the very least perhaps we can suggest that she now becomes, as a production of a displaced, neutralised, spectral narrative voice, something approaching a symptom of a symptom, an affect of an affect, a further displacement of an already displaced discursivity. As a symptom of a symptom – the narrative voice being, as I argue, the symptom of the act of writing; neutrality, that fact of being displaced and decentred, is the dominant affect of the narrative voice – the figure of the woman must appear to us as a kind of essential fragility, retreating behind the differential traces of the narrative voice that struggles, as we noted above, to call her into being, into narrative: 'But quick seize her where she is best to be seized' (*NO* 55):

> But she can be gone at any time. From one moment of the year to the next suddenly no longer there. No longer anywhere to be seen. Nor by the eye of flesh nor by the other. Then as suddenly there again. Long after. So on. Any other would renounce. Avow, No one. No one more. Any other than this other. In wait for her to reappear. In order to resume. (*NO* 56)

And what marks her own fragility most obviously, and most importantly for us, is her ontological condition which emerges as a critical and uncanny neutrality. By neutrality here I mean to think not necessarily only of how Blanchot employs the term vis-à-vis the narrative voice in *The Infinite Conversation* (decentred, spectral, coming from exteriority and speaking from nowhere). I am, rather, thinking initially of the term itself as designating a state of betweenness. Neuter: neither one thing nor another. Blanchot in fact does turn to this idea in *The Step Not Beyond*: 'The Neuter', he writes, 'derives in the most simple way, from a negation of two terms: neuter, neither one nor the other' (74). The woman, as the narrative voice makes clear, is neutral in several senses of this term. She is, first, a figment of the imagination and not; she is, second, alive and dead, simultaneously. Let me examine this second condition first (although the two conditions are intimately conjoined in the text). As the narrator, at an early stage in the text, grows frustrated with his attempt to conjure the woman, we read, in a passage I will need to revisit:

> Already all confusion. Things and imaginings. As of always. Confusion amounting to nothing. Despite precautions. If only she should be pure figment. Unalloyed. This old dying woman. So dead. In the madhouse of the skull and nowhere else. Where no more precautions to be taken. No precautions possible. Cooped up there with the rest. Hovel and stones. The lot. And the eye. How simple all then. If only all could be pure figment. Neither be nor been nor by any shift to be. Gently gently. On. Careful. (NO 58)

As I say I will return to this anxiety about the woman's materiality, her reality in the world, but for now I need to focus on these phrases: 'the old dying woman. So dead' (NO 58). Here the narrator sounds a critical theme: the woman is both alive (dying) and dead (so dead); she is and is not, simultaneously. Later we will read the following: 'While head included she lies hidden time for a turn in the pastures. No shock were she already dead. As of course she is. But in the meantime more convenient not' (NO 73). This phrase, 'as of course she is', could be read as an indication that what is occurring in the course of *Ill Seen Ill Said* is the process of remembrance, that the woman is dead and this is all a kind of retrospective act of mourning. But this phrase, one that again introduces a metafictional quality to the narrator's discourse – 'but in the meantime more convenient not' – indicates that the woman, in some senses a figure of narrative necessity if only because his status as narrator depends on her, is still alive. But, and here we need to attend to the narrator's real anxiety, the woman is not merely fiction: 'if only she could be pure figment', he tells us. The woman, deeply embedded within a displaced narrative voice, a figure who by rights should be only pure figment, should be only the work of memory and imagination, is not *only* that: she has an element of the real and the imaginary at once. And this, her flickering between the real and the imaginary, the fact that she is radically *neutral*, leads again to another moment of panic, one where the narrator asserts her complete fictionality. But it is an assertion immediately qualified:

> Not possible any longer except as figment. Not endurable. Nothing for it but to close the eye for good and see her. Her and the rest. Close it for good and all and see her to death. Unremittant. In the shack. Over the stones. In the pastures. The haze. At the tomb. And back. And the rest. For good and all. To death. Be shut of it. On to the next. Next figment. Close it for good this filthy eye of flesh. What forbids? Careful. (*NO* 65)

The narrator admits being unable to see her to death. Something forbids her from becoming pure figment and thus an entity to be effaced absolutely. The woman is stubbornly persistent; her ontological persistence, moreover, carries with it not merely her own person, but the world that enfolds her: her shack, the stones, the tomb.

I am fascinated by the compounding ontological and narratological complexities of the status of the woman: she is alive and dead; she is alive because she is a function of the narrative, but she is always already more than mere figment. Neither alive nor dead, neither pure fiction nor pure fact, the woman would at first appear to be the perfect spectre – which of course she is – if not for her dogged persistence in the world, in the now of the world: 'all this in the present tense as had she the misfortune to be still of this world' (*NO* 50). It is this phrase, and we note, again, Beckett's use of the word 'world', with its careful indication of temporality – now – that troubles the idea that all of what is being witnessed here is an act of remembrance. The woman is, and is not, *now*; to call her a spectre is, as I say, accurate, but not: she *is*. To say that she is neutral is perhaps more accurate in that her condition cancels both polarities of life and death: she is neither. As I suggested at the outset of my reading of the late trilogy, Beckett offers a subject, or perhaps this is more accurately an *event* of subjectivity – she is, after all, a performance, a character within an act of witnessing – that confounds our understanding of ontology, perhaps even confounds our reading of the posthuman, which is itself marked by a radical neutrality. In one way, of course, the woman – not only fiction, let us keep in mind – confounds an understanding of the human given her uncanny state of being. If

Heidegger is correct in his argument that the human is defined by its anticipation of its own end, if, that is, the human emerges as an awareness of the death that is to come – where death stands as an absolute inevitability and as such defines the present moment of being ('Death is a way to be', he writes in *Being and Time*) – this woman is not, quite, human. If Blanchot is correct to assert, as he does in 'Literature and the Right to Death' in a gloss on Heidegger, that 'death is man's possibility, his chance . . . death is man's greatest hope, his only hope of being man' (55), then this woman, who exists in a state that cancels death, just as it cancels life, is not, quite, human.

How then are we to think of her? To read her? Perhaps one way is to take the lead from the narrator itself which several times uses the word *trace* to refer either to the woman – her face – or to the vestiges of her appearance in the world, primarily her footprints. Let me just track the references. As the narrator begins to move towards offering a glimpse of the woman's face – and her face, its trace, is crucial as the text concludes – we read:

> Just time to begin to glimpse a fringe of black veil. The face must wait. Just time before the eye cast down. Where nothing to be seen in the grazing rays but snow. And how all about little by little her footprints are effaced. (*NO* 55)

The narrator returns to the image of the footprint, linking it specifically to speculation about the woman's inner thoughts:

> Winter evening in the pastures. The snow has ceased. Her steps so light they barely leave a trace. Have barely left having ceased. Just enough to be still visible. Just enough to be still visible. Adrift the snow. Whither in her head while her feet stray thus? Hither and thither too? Or unswerving to the mirage? And where when she halts? (*NO* 67)

And while these footprints will disappear with the woman – 'Slowly she disappears. Together with the trace of her steps and that of the distant roof' (*NO* 68) – we surely recall the word *trace* as it appears towards the end of the text where the narrator begins to fixate on the woman's face and its stubborn persistence. While the narrator tracks the gradual disappearance of the woman – she is vanishing – her face, which persists as an ineffable remainder, remains: 'The face yet again in the light of the last rays' (*NO* 78);

'Alone the face remains. Of the rest beneath its covering no trace' (*NO* 83). Indeed, the face seems, impossibly, to assert itself in various temporalities: 'Full glare now on the face present throughout the recent future' (*NO* 84); and as the text concludes, the face, as trace, is both there and not there, absent and present:

> Absence supreme good and yet. Illumination then go again and on return no more trace. On earth's face. Of what was never. And if by mishap some left then go again. For good again. So on. Till no more trace. On earth's face. Instead of always the same place. Slaving away forever in the same place. At this and that trace. And what if the eye could not? No more tear itself away from the remains of trace. Of what was never. Quick say it suddenly can and farewell say say farewell. If only to the face. Of her tenacious trace. (*NO* 85–6)

It is clear, if only from this remarkable paragraph, that this word, this idea, of the trace is critical to the narrator's thinking about the woman and her persistence in his world, on what he calls the earth. How are we asked to read and register the resonance of this word? Let us note that for Beckett in *Ill Seen Ill Said*, the trace, the idea of the trace, speaks to the woman's ontology as a spatial and spatially realised subject. When the word first is used in the text, it refers to the woman's footprints, evidence, that is, of her trajectories, her movement, her mapping of her world. These traces, perfectly, disappear just as she does. Her trajective quality thus is marked as spectral, ghostly, and is perfectly suited to the spectral quality of the trace itself. This is perhaps to say that the woman's ontology, her *trajectivity*, her being defined as *neither* subject nor object – and we recall that this is how Virilio defines the traject – emerges as spectral even as she persists in the world, on the earth, now: 'All this in the present as had she the misfortune to be still of this world' (*NO* 50). The woman is spectral; her ontology is spectral; her movement is spectralised as it disappears into the disappearing trace. The word, we now begin to see, is perfectly suited to the woman given that the trace is both noun and verb: she is the trace just as she produces the disappearing trace in her spectralising movement on the earth. This is all to say that the image and idea of the trace is, as Beckett deploys it, unavoidably spatial: it marks the space of her movement, just as it marks the space of her disappearance. Derrida, of course, notes the a-spatialising logic of the trace in his crucial essay 'Differance':

> The trace is not a presence but is rather the simulacrum of a presence that dislocates, displaces, and refers beyond itself. The trace has, properly speaking, no place, for effacement belongs to the very structure of the trace. Effacement must always be able to overtake the trace; otherwise it would not be a trace but an indestructible and monumental substance. (*Speech and Phenomena* 156)

We note how Derrida's definition of the trace echoes Blanchot's notion of the effect of writing or the effect of the neutral narrative voice: both the trace and the neutral are displaced presences; both the trace and the neutral come from nowhere, speak from nowhere. It is of course possible to refer to the narrative voice as itself the trace of writing itself (if not of Beckett, the writer), as the displacement of an authorial presence exterior to the text proper: here the woman becomes, and I return to my previous idea, the symptom of a symptom, the trace of a trace.

What then has Beckett given us here with this woman, her face, her displaced positionality, her 'tenacious trace?' She emerges as a densely spatialised entity, woven into a neutralised, decentred text in which she herself, as trace, withdraws or is withdrawn into a differential web of absence and presence. And this idea, her neutrality, is one we cannot forget: she is absent and present; she is alive and dead; she is on the earth and clearly vanishing from it. *Ill Seen Ill Said* is careful and deliberate in its effacement of categories and boundaries, careful in its elimination of the limits between categories of being: 'Such the confusion now between real and – how say its contrary? No matter. That old tandem ... Real and – how ill say its contrary? The counter-poison' (*NO* 72). Categorical differences between states of being – 'equal liars both' – no longer seem to hold. As the text neutralises differences between states of being, and offers an image of the woman who becomes indefinable, unknowable; as she emerges as the trace, that spatialised state of being beyond presence and location, the woman is so radically displaced as to call into question even the possibility of place, as such, real or imaginary. And what, then, can we say about the subjectivity of the woman who is neutralised, tracked and traced into radical placelessness? How does the idea of being, much less being in the world, obtain here? How does even the idea of the spectre, which, as Derrida reminds us, is always ontopologically linked to place – the spectre is that which returns to a place, as he tells us in *Specters of Marx* – operate if the spectre's place in the world is effaced? If the spectre is one possible version of the Beckettian posthuman, and certainly the varieties of spectrality we have encountered in texts prior to *Ill Said Ill Said* suggest that this is so, we are here, as *Ill Seen Ill Said* concludes and we move into the unsettling spaces of *Worstward Ho*, now perhaps *beyond spectrality*, beyond the logic of the revenant. As the subject becomes trace, the very idea of subjectivity, spectral or otherwise, must recede into what the narrator of *Ill Seen Ill Said* calls the 'haze' of unknowability. Spectrality, in other words, is still tied to a prior state of being, still is a marker of history and place. In *Ill Seen Ill Said*, Beckett's subject – and now this word seems to lose all resonance – as it cannot be cathected to any space or place, recedes into the vanishing point of unknowability. In previous texts, I think here of *Texts for Nothing*, the subject may emerge as positionless, but this precariousness marks the subject as wavering, ecologically, between locations, between the here and there, between being and becoming. In *Ill Seen Ill Said*, there is, it seems, no becoming, no possibility of being any longer on the earth.

This would seem to be a viable reading of *Ill Seen Ill Said*: it tracks the disappearance of the possibility of place and thus of any locus for the subject. The text's deployment of a neutralising narrative voice – a voice that dislocates itself and in turn dislocates the human subject from the figure of the trace – suggests that effacing the subject in some ways is the dominant theme of this text. Without location, without the possibility of space and place, the idea of the human, if we follow Heidegger, vanishes in its turn. But I wonder if this reading, viable as it might be, is rather too simple. Our acknowledgement of the unfolding of the fantasy of the removal of the subject via the removal of spatiality or locatability; our acknowledgement, that is, of the text's figuration of the woman as trace and thus as that which has 'no place' does not fully account for the economy of desire that is clearly operational here in *Ill Seen Ill Said*. Because the narrative is about the desire to cease witnessing, or, properly speaking, to witness the end of this woman, to 'see her to death' (*NO* 65), to speak of her end. We must, if we are to do justice to this economy of desire, return to this grounding fact. But, as I have suggested, this economy brings with it something in excess of itself: the facticity of the woman. She, uncannily, seems to be both of the narrative and able to transcend it; she is an effect of the narrator's discourse and somehow able to supersede it; she is not, that is, only pure figment, to return to that key phrase. *Ill Seen Ill Said* thus maps a particular narrative agony: the agony of a fantasy of disappearance and the knowledge that this fantasy does not, cannot, quite efface the persistence of the never to be lost object. The woman, superseding the neutralising logic of the narrator's own imaginative desire, persists beyond the trace, beyond his desire for her to be the trace, into an impossible space. She is still 'of this world', if only because this world is an effect of the narrator's desire and world-building; she ruptures, and fundamentally so, the equanimity of that world, annuls any possibility of a finality of disappearance because, as a symptom of a symptom, a trace of a trace, she still is an effect of the world within which she is conjured.

Narrative, in other words, always exceeds its own desires, will always, as the narrator says, 'return to the scene of its betrayals' (*NO* 63). The betrayal of language at the heart of *Ill Seen Ill Said* is, finally, that it both effaces and calls into being. As a symptom of the narrative act, as Blanchot says, language serves to efface the subject. In *Ill Seen Ill Said*, the narrator effaces himself in his entry into language, producing a crucial neutral space that is and must be the precondition for any narrative act. It is from here, in this neutral space, that the narrator in turn expresses the desire to witness the woman's vanishing. But that witnessing, any act of discursive witnessing that inevitably begins to look like world-building, must call her into being in order for her to be banished. That is to say, and to follow on from Heidegger, world-building occurs when the subject finds himself with the other. The narrator here, inadvertently perhaps but also inevitably, calls this woman into his world, calls her into being as he instantiates his narrative. This critical dialectic – calling her into the world and sheltering her being within language, as Heidegger might say, and then effacing her, or attempting to see her to death – is what precipitates her becoming the trace, that which is, and is not, still (even *dead still*) in his (narrative) world. The trace, Derrida will argue, is always a sign of radical displacement, but it too is a sign, a space, of that displacement. The trace, in other words, is a space of the persistence of absence, a symptom and sign of the unavoidable act of witnessing and narrating, and thus the sure cause of the narrator's anxiety: his own inability ever to call an end to the act of narrative which inevitably and agonisingly calls worlds into being. *Ill Seen Ill Said*, finally, may allow itself to be read an allegory of an attempt to call an end to narrative, to witness the end of the inevitable creation of worlds within which the subject – narrating and narrated – so long desired to be vanished, always remains, as the remainder, as the trace of its own impossible desire.[8] Perhaps what Beckett discovers, and has known for so long, is that for the subject finally to be vanquished, language itself, *not merely the narrative voice*, must in its turn be annihilated.

Thus we turn to *Worstward Ho*.

Worstward Ho

Worstward Ho is Beckett's terminal vision of the world. The text marks the end of even an attempt to render a world, to represent a viable space within which the subject, imaginary, spectral, or otherwise, could instantiate itself, or be instantiated, as anything other than radically neutralised, groundless, and positionless. *Worstward Ho*, to speak more accurately, is a terminal allegory of the impossibility of world. It unfolds – but such a metaphor suggests a flickering of a narrative agency that betrays the absolute impotence of the imagination and the imagining subject here – at or as the limits of language, limits that speak, in their turn, of the impossibility of tracing more than a hypothetical space for the subject. It is here, in the final substantial prose work of his career, that Beckett perhaps realises a desire expressed forty-six years previously in the 'German Letter' of 1937. Here, in his letter to Axel Kaun, a letter that we may, with some caution (and despite Beckett's own disavowal), take as something of a manifesto, Beckett speaks of the aesthetic desire, thoroughly modernist in its violence, to destroy language, '[t]o bore one hole after another into it, until what lurks behind it – be it something or nothing – begins to seep through' (172); this violence has a goal, the realisation of what he calls 'the literature of the unword' (173). *Worstward Ho* is Beckett's realisation of the literature of the unword. Here there is an attempt – and perhaps it can only ever be an attempt – to offer a remaindered subject within a violently remaindered language. This is a language operating at the limits of sense and grammar, a language of 'worsening words' that do not 'say' or mean, so much as 'ooze' or 'secrete', the mere minimum of any representational economy. My real interest here, in my reading of *Worstward Ho*, is to explore the relation between this remaindered language, its remaindered subjects, and the nonspaces within which it is placed. *Worstward Ho* may only be a radicalised parody of an authorial fantasy. It may, that is, be Beckett's final admission that rendering a subject and its world in language was always to tarry with failure. But even as a terminal allegory of impossibility, even as a parody of the imaginative act, *Worstward Ho* remains, perhaps only as remains, *as* a failure. As a space of failure or disaster *Worstward Ho* still remains as a space, as what Blanchot rather perfectly calls '*Ruin of words. Demise writing*' (*The Writing of the Disaster* 33). I want, in honour of Beckett's own tarrying with failure, to tarry in turn with the space of *Worstward Ho*, to attend to his posthumous vision of the human, his posthuman, terminal vision of the subject, now purely discursive and created out of a radically failing discourse. I want, ultimately, to know if *Worstward Ho* allows us even to speak of place, of world, any longer: 'No place but the one. None but the one where none. Whence never once in. Somehow in. Beyondless' (*NO* 92).

To speak of Beckett's *Worstward Ho* in relation to Blanchot's notion of the disaster, as I wish to do here, is to beg some fundamental questions. It is, for one, to suppose that one is able to stabilise the idea of the disaster, to see it at work within Beckett's text. It is, in other words, to assume that one is able to speak of the disaster, as such. Perhaps we will discover that the disaster, like trauma, like loss itself, is impossible to figure, to represent; perhaps we will discover that only an affect of the disaster remains after the disaster; perhaps, that is, the only way of thinking about *Worstward Ho*, vis-à-vis the disaster, is as an after-effect, an after-*affect*, of the disaster. Beckett thus pulls us into complicated spaces here: to think about affective spaces is to theorise the disaster only from the traces of its absence.

One of the enormous fascinations and frustrations with *The Writing of the Disaster*, as I have observed before, is that Blanchot never defines his key term.[9] Extending beyond the limits of language and yet defined by a ruined language, the disaster, or the experience of the disaster, is beyond comprehension, beyond discourse. The disaster, it seems, is not an event. Or, perhaps, it is an event that has always already taken place. The disaster, thus, is beyond the temporal, yet still impinges upon it:

> There is no reaching the disaster. Out of reach is he whom it threatens, whether from afar or close up, it is impossible to say: the infiniteness of the threat has in some way broken every limit. We are on the edge of disaster without being able to situate it in the future: it is rather always already past, and yet we are on the edge or under the threat, all formulations which would imply the future – that which is yet to come – if the disaster were not that which does not come, that which has put a stop to every arrival. (1)

The disaster reinscribes temporality just as it dismantles the possibility of its experience. In some radical sense, the disaster is only perceivable as an after-effect. The subject, itself effaced by the non-experience of the disaster, itself radically reinscribed and defined by the disaster and thus by an event that cannot be perceived, finds itself in a position of absolute powerlessness and forgetfulness. This position, what Blanchot calls 'passivity', defines the state of being in the after-effects of the disaster: feeling, perhaps, that something has occurred, but being unable to name it, to know it, to interpret it. The disaster annuls the memory of its occurrence even as it threatens to efface the subject who, crucially, bears the marks of the disaster:

> The disaster does not put me into question, but annuls the question, makes it disappear – as if along with the question, 'I' too disappeared in the disaster which never appears. The fact of disappearing is, precisely, not a fact, not an event; it does not happen, not only because there is no 'I' to undergo the experience, but because (and this is exactly what presupposition means), since the disaster always takes place after having taken place, there cannot possibly be any experience of it. (28)

And yet the disaster, even as it effaces itself, even as it retreats before experience, emerges as something like an imminent after-effect. It takes place after having taken place, deforming the subject, as Beckett might say, just as it defines the subject as the bearer of the disaster. Perhaps we could understand the disaster in specifically Beckettian terms and suggest that it *obliges* the subject. In much the same way as Beckett famously defines the obligation of the writer as that of witnessing – expressing – the nothingness that is, Blanchot would understand that the disaster obliges the subject to bear witness to itself in writing that, in some critical way, begins to *become* the disaster.¹⁰ If the disaster, as such, as an event, as a discrete occurrence, cannot be named, cannot be known, cannot be located within history or temporality, the writing of the disaster emerges as the ever-failing attempt to name that unnamable event. Writing, in other words, becomes the space within which the traces of the disaster are archived. But writing, as both Beckett and Blanchot will know, is always already a mis-saying of the event, a mis-saying of the disaster. And as such, as a misrepresentation – and it has to be given that the disaster is beyond knowing – writing the disaster becomes the writing *of* the disaster. These worsening words become disastrous precisely as they attempt to call into being the grounds of a disastrous world. Blanchot puts this idea perfectly:

> The disaster, unexperienced. It is what escapes the very possibility of experience – it is the limit of writing. This must be repeated: the disaster de-scribes. Which does not mean that the disaster, as the force of writing, is excluded from it, is beyond the pale of writing or extratextual. (7)

The disaster de-scribes, provides the spatial limits of what can be said of its own economy. The disaster, beyond experience, still remains within writing, as its limits, as its boundary. In my reading of *Worstward Ho*, I would suggest we locate the disaster at the point where the writing, its very grammar, trembles before its task; as the words worsen, as they acknowledge in their very passivity, in their very weakness, the impossibility of transcribing what they wish to transcribe, the disaster is felt. It is in and at the limit of language, a language critically spatialised, that a failing world disastrously appears as its own impossibility: '*When all is said, what remains to be said is the disaster. Ruin of words, demise writing, faintness faintly murmuring: what remains without remains* (the fragmentary)' (*The Writing of the Disaster* 33). What remains, as remains, is the disaster. *Worstward Ho* is both affect and effect of disaster: it names the terrible effort of trying to realise a world just as it embodies, in its writing, the agonised effects of that effort. The attempt to name a world, to conjure a world, in other words, *is* the disaster and *produces* the space of the disaster as writing. This is the essential, inevitable, and terrible tautology of the disaster.¹¹

One of our first questions about *Worstward Ho*, as we begin to unravel the questions of disaster, world, and writing, is this:

who speaks? Who writes? Whose 'worsening words' are these? We might follow the narrative itself and ask, and answer:

> Whose words? Ask in vain. Or not in vain if say no knowing. No saying. No words for him whose words. Him? One. No words for one whose words. One? It. No words for it whose words. Better worse so. (*NO* 98)

The text's response to the question is that we cannot know: there are no words for the subject – its gender becomes a question – whose own words, we presume, are in turn worsening. And, of course, in a way that must remind us of Beckett's penchant for the neither and the neutral, the subject, first 'him', then 'one', then 'it', becomes the neutral, that decentred subject whose language, as Blanchot reminds us – and Beckett enacts – comes from nowhere. And yet, the words still emerge, still sound here. If their source is unknowable, just as their subject becomes neutralised and thus decentred, the language given to us here in *Worstward Ho* seems only to allow itself to be imagined as ever exteriorised, ever displaced from its source and its subject. The narrative will offer an image of a subject – 'Another. Say another. Head sunk on crippled hands. Vertex vertical. Eyes clenched. Seat of all. Germ of all' (*NO* 91) – and we might be tempted to see this figure as an exteriorised image of the author, the seat of all the language that follows, but we are still vouchsafed an image of this creator from the exterior. If this is the author, he is woven into the very textual fabric of the narrative that he is creating and in turn creates him as an object of its own, now radically vertiginous, language: 'Germ of all. All? If of all of it too. Where if not there it too? There in the sunken head the sunken head' (*NO* 97). This abyssal image of the author – a sunken head within a sunken head – states clearly our difficulty with the very question of who speaks. The voice of *Worstward Ho* is both radically exterior and interior to its subject: it 'says' these figures into the world, into (some kind of) being, but it is, in its turn, said into being: 'Another. Say another' (*NO* 91). This is, perhaps, as much to say that we ask in vain about the source of the language here, as the text itself acknowledges, but we are, despite all that, because of all that, still left with the remains of the text, this demise writing that, while sourceless, is still present.[12]

But present in what sense? Perhaps in the absolute sense that language has an a priori inevitability, in *Worstward Ho*

Fables of Posthuman Space 185

specifically, and in Beckett generally. It is perhaps in vain to ask about the source of words just as it is in vain to deny the secretions, the ooze, of these words which, in my reading, create an inevitable, though radically minimal, world. I deploy this word *world* now with absolute hesitation, offering it as this text does, only as the barest possibility of itself. Perhaps we should be using the Derridean/Heideggerian strategy of deploying the word even as we efface it and place it under erasure: the world crossed out. Because discursively this is how *Worstward Ho* proceeds: by erasure, effacement, assertion, and denial. The world here thus is, first, offered absolutely as a discursive structure; the subjects within this world – equally discursive, perhaps, even now beyond the possibility of the posthuman, as such – exist (but is this the word?) only at the absolute limit of a language fully aware of its impotence. And while the text opens with what we might call the minimum of being – 'on' – offering, perhaps a trace of movement and trajectory, this movement is immediately figured as an effect of discourse – 'Say on' – that cannot be located or defined: 'Somehow on' (*NO* 89). The saying, the creation of narrative, is immediately figured as being said, as the text signals the abyssal logic of a narrative emerging out of the performance of its own grounds. And thus, having acknowledged its absolute discursivity – this is only ever going to be a narrative about narrative; this will only ever manage to be a textual meditation on the limits of textuality, as such – the narrative (and I do not think we can speak exactly of a narrative *voice*) offers the mere minimum of place and subject, of world, as if acknowledging that this, at least, is what constitutes the bones of a story, if only one to be disavowed as it comes into minimal being. This paragraph is crucial:

> Say a body. Where none. No mind. Where none. That at least. A place. Where none. For the body. To be in. Move in. Out of. Back into. No. No out. No back. Only in. Stay in. On in. Still. (*NO* 89)

This is, perhaps, world-making, but world-making at the limits of its own possibility; this is world-making, what Heidegger calls giving an 'image of the world' and setting it forth (*FCM* 285), only to be disavowed. This is offering a world acknowledging that place is where the subject will, again at a minimum, be able to move, to track and trace its place on the earth; but this, now, will be a world where even that minimum of being is denied: 'No. No out. No back. Only in' (*NO* 89). Here then is a world and movement that is offered only to be effaced. Here is a world under erasure. The cancellation still, perhaps, allows the cancelled to be, as spectre, as trace, as a claim that cannot fully disappear, but can never fully claim any real authority. The fifth paragraph of *Worstward Ho* is critical; observe how the narrative contorts itself to move beyond the logic of effacement and assertion/denial, to move beyond even the logic of the neither:

> First the body. No. First the place. No. First both. Now either. Now the other. Sick of the either try the other. Sick of it back sick of the either. So on. Somehow on. Till sick of both. Throw up and go. Where neither. Till sick of there. Throw up and back. The body again. Where none. The place again. Where none. Try again. Fail again. Better again. Or better worse. Fail worse again. Still worse again. Till sick for good. Throw up for good. Go for good. Where neither for good. Good and all. (*NO* 90)

The narrative, figuring itself not as creation but as illness, rejects both body and place – the mere minimum of narrative possibility – and expresses a desire to be in that place of the neutral where neither body nor place is necessary, but rejects even this space of effacement; the paragraph, which figures creation as illness, follows its own discursive logic and returns to the body and place, once rejected, now, again, asserting themselves, if only as an effacement, now twice effaced. And yet, for all that, still present.

And still present in the minimum of place, on the minimum of ground, at what I call the limit of world. In my reading of *Ill Seen Ill Said* I concentrated on the figure of the woman as trace, discursive, spectral or otherwise, of the human: as she becomes spatialised her ontology increasingly becomes unknowable, unlocatable. We will, of course, speak of the subject here in *Worstward Ho* – these shades – but I am equally fascinated by the world here. Specifically, I am wondering if we might be able to speak of this place – which is a void, a groundless ground – as, if not a world, then a trace of world. If Blanchot speaks of the subject without subjectivity, I wonder if we might speak here of a world without worldhood, *world without world*. We arrive at this position, understanding the world without world, via the language which offers the world to us here, a language, sourceless, locationless, positionless: a disastrous language beyond the neutral, a language

Fables of Posthuman Space 187

that neutralises the subject only to neutralise that neutralising. What can be said about the world here thus must be understood to be a condition of the language that offers that world, a language the text itself explicitly theorises. We have seen how the narrative advises against attempting to locate a source for itself; at a critical point further into the text, the narrative pauses once more to offer a meditation on the idea of a language beyond the witnessing subject, a language that may have to accommodate itself to the absolute nothing, a language for when language itself ceases:

> What when words gone? None for what then. But say by way of somehow on somehow with sight to do. With less of sight. Still dim and yet –. No. Nohow so on. Say better worse words gone when nohow on. Still dim and nohow on. All seen and nohow on. What words for what then? None for what then. No words for what when words gone. For what then nohow on. Somehow nohow on. (*NO* 104)

Here is offered an apocalyptic fantasy of the end of language as the end of all things, itself a state of (non-)being that can only function at the limit of possibility: 'Somehow nohow on' (*NO* 104). But we are not (yet) at the point where words are gone. We are at the limit of a language, a language that, we might say, has become a spectre to itself. But even as a spectre this language offers a mere minimum of things, of a world, because, as the text grudgingly admits, there is still the mere minimum of mind at work here. The mind may be locationless and motionless, but it is able, somehow, to produce words. These words, critically, however, do not interpret the world for the mind, the remains of mind, the disastrous mind. These are words the mind does not 'say' but secretes; and as secretions they are at a radical remove from comprehension, from experience. This secretion thus is a perfect instantiation of the disaster: the mind, as remains, is radically removed from the experience of its own experience. Radically passive, made passive by the disaster that is the language for which it now only is a *medium*, the mind stands away from its work. All that follows thus, and it is here that we must begin to talk of the world these secretions produce, must be read as a product of this radical passivity. If this is world-making, the concept of world must be reconfigured:

> Remains of mind then still. Enough still. Somewhose somewhere somehow enough still. No mind and words? Even such words. So enough still. Just enough still to joy. Joy! Just enough still to joy that only they. Only!
>
> Enough still not to know. Not to know what they say. Not to know what it is the words it says say. Says? Secretes. Say better worse secretes. What it is the words it secretes say. What the so-said void. The so-said dim. The so-said shades. To so-said seat and germ of all. Enough to know no knowing. No knowing what it is the words it secretes say. No saying. No saying what it all is they somehow say. (*NO* 104–5)

All that follows here in *Worstward Ho*, the dim, the void, the shades, the image of the author, unfolds in this radical separation of the remains of mind that seem to be its ever-disavowed source. What fascinates me is how we are asked to understand the facticity of this – and again we run up against the limits of our language – world, this space, this discursive ruin of agency. What then is the space the narrative offers? Let us recall, to orient ourselves here, our understanding of what constitutes world, as such. As we learn from Heidegger, world is an expression of being, of Dasein itself. World is intimately connected to a sense of the subject's subjectivity: 'The Dasein in man forms world: [1.] it brings it forth; [2.] it gives an image or view of the world, it sets it forth; [3.] it constitutes the world, contains it and embraces it' (*FCM* 285). As I have argued over the course of this study, world is an expression of Dasein but that sense of world, of worldliness, is known to the subject insofar as the subject finds himself in space, perhaps even as the subject finds himself 'as' space. 'Space is constitutive for the world', as Heidegger tells us in *Being and Time* (135), and the human understands his place in the world as an experience of space, of spatiality, of the closeness of space, its distance. The human emerges as human, again as I have argued, as it learns to orient itself within space and as it maps out its particular coordinates within the givenness of space. The subject is spatial (*BT* 146) and that sense of being as a *being demarcated* can only emerge as the subject comprehends the dimensionality of its own space, the fact that its space is bounded. And thus, for Heidegger, the critical importance of the boundary, that which defines space, as space:

> a space is something that has been made room for, something that is cleared and free, namely, within a boundary... A boundary is not that at which something stops but, as the Greeks recognized, the boundary is that from which something begins its essential unfolding. (*BDT* 332)

Space and the subject unfold at the boundary, at the limit. In *Worstward Ho*, we might suggest that the limit of things is the limit of a language that operates at a bare possibility: the limits of language here, to borrow from Wittgenstein, mean the limits of the subject's world.[13] Yet from within this limit-language an image of a boundary-less space emerges, one that, as seen previously in *Lessness*, makes it difficult to speak of world:

> A place. Where none. A time when try see. Try say. How small. How vast. How if not boundless bounded. Whence the dim. Not now. Know better now. Unknow better now. Know only no out of. No knowing how know only no out of. Into only. Hence another. Another place where none. Whither once whence no return. No. No place but the one. None but the one where none. Whence never once in. Somehow in. Beyondless. Thenceless there. Thitherless there. Thenceless thitherless there. (*NO* 92)

Positing the possibility of a space against which to erase this space of the dim of the void, the narrative ultimately rejects this idea. What is given is only the one place that is 'beyondless': a place of groundless ground, of non-arrival – thenceless – and movement that is not movement. Here the figures of the old man and boy 'Plod on and never recede. Slowly with never a pause plod on and never recede' (*NO* 93). Here the subject plods on in a place that is only ever void, empty and dim.

What is given here thus are shades within a 'shade-ridden void' (*NO* 101); what is given is an image of the world as the effect of a disastrous language, a language ever worsening, which barely supports its own frailty. In one perfect way, the world of *Worstward Ho* is Beckett's realisation of a desire to violate the possibility of language, to have bored holes into language to see what emerges. And at one level, what emerges, what is 'secreted' by this wounding of language, is a place that is no place, a ground which is no ground; a space, beyondless, that cannot be conceptualised as space. And what emerges within this aporia, crucially, is a subjectivity that cannot be called a subject. The narrative prefers the term 'shade' to describe the subject here, but as a secretion of a disavowed, sourceless, locationless language; as a secretion, that is, of a language that is without history, I wonder if this term is even appropriate. The shade, the ghost, as I have argued, is always a reminder, a remainder, of a past, of some trace of a past: the shade, while an absent presence, is always a symptom of history. The figure of the subject here in *Worstward Ho*, always already a figment of a language itself always already disastrous, is not a ghost; it is not even posthuman. The Beckettian posthuman, as I have argued over the course of this study, resembles the spectre. As the figure of the posthuman unfolds over the course of the short texts of the 1950s and 1960s, even as it becomes ungrounded, the subject still carries within it a sense of that loss, of that ungrounding: 'till suddenly I was here, all memory gone' (*Texts for Nothing* 8: 132). The shade here in *Worstward Ho*, silent, neutralised, an effect of a disastrous language, is not linked to history or subjectivity. The shade, like its space, itself is beyondless: there is nothing outside of its formation within a worsening language to offer it a place within history. It is a secretion, more precisely, an effect of a secretion:

> Not to know what it is the words it says say. Says? Secretes. Say better worse secretes. What it is the words it secretes say. What the so-said void. The so-said dim. The so-said shades. The so-said seat and germ of all. Enough to know no knowing. No knowing what it is the words it secretes says. No saying. No saying what it all is they somehow say. (*NO* 104–5)

This is, to return one last time to Heidegger, what one might call a care-less world. What does this mean? Care, for Heidegger, is the being of Dasein: being in the world, he says, is essentially care (*BT* 237). The being of Dasein is care (*BT* 275). Care, as I understand Heidegger to mean, is what Dasein does when it finds itself expressed in the world. Care is the means by which Dasein attaches itself to the world. If the subject, as an expression of Dasein, as a medium of Dasein, finds itself in the world, and orients itself in the world, this orientation – we have used the terms de-severance and directionality to speak of this orientation – is made possible by care: care guides the subject, identifies what is knowable and what must be known about the world. Care is the primordial way for Dasein, and thus the human, to be: 'Care, as a primordial structural totality, lies "before" every factical "attitude" and "situation" of Dasein, and it does so existentially a priori; this means that it always lies *in* them' (*BT* 238). Care, or concern, is the grounds upon which the world emerges for the subject as something to be known, to be radically involved within: 'Being in the world, as concern, is *fascinated* by the world with which it is concerned' (*BT* 88).[14] In *Worstward Ho* we are presented, I would argue, with a world that is care-less, a world – but this is perhaps not even the word – within which the grounding possibility of care does not exist. I mean by this not merely to suggest that a care-less world is one in which the human cannot obtain. Because Beckett, in this late text, does not necessarily make the equation between the loss of care and the loss of the human that easy. It is certainly true that the idea of care, as the primordial expression of Dasein, is hard to locate here, given that the world, and the subjects within this world, are deeply recessed within a language that itself trembles at the limit of possibility. We have, we must recall, been given an idea that this world originates within the head of an author figure itself recessed within an author figure who sets the grounds for this world within the receding, and abyssal, limits of his own disastrous discursivity: 'Germ of all. All? If of all of it too. Where if not there it too? There in the sunken head the sunken head' (*NO* 97). And certainly thus, within this deep recess where language, being, and subject become less than viable, and as they increasingly threaten to vanish into a state beyond the spectral, any idea of care, concern, or solicitude seems to vanish in turn. And as care vanishes, as any link between language and its creation vanishes, worldhood vanishes.[15]

Or seems to. As I say, Beckett does merely offer an image of a post-world world, a posthuman world, a world in which the idea of the human and its world no longer obtain. He does, in fact, offer this, but simultaneously the narrative insists that these figures, these shades, and the void they traverse (without traversal), even as an effect of a worsening and locationless language, are persistent: 'Shades cannot go' (*NO* 11); 'Void cannot go' (*NO* 97). The narrative itself may express a desire for this bare world to vanish, may, in fact, express a desire that everything, including desire, vanishes, but it acknowledges this desire as itself an impossible desire: 'Longing that all go. Dim go. Void go. Longing go. Vain longing that vain longing go' (*NO* 109). And as a text about the desire to witness the end of desire, some vestige of desire must remain, as Blanchot might say, *as remains*, to haunt the text, and the world it calls into being, however half-heartedly. Care, we recall Heidegger telling us, is a primordial structural totality: it precedes and exceeds any particular expression *of* being, any expression *by* being. Care, we might suggest, and the following excerpt from Beckett's text may help us here, precedes its entry into language and thus resists any language's attempt to decompose it, efface it, reduce it to mere trace. Care persists:

> Worse less. By no stretch more. Worse for want of better less. Less best. No. Naught best. Best worse. No. Not best worse. Naught not best worse. Less best worse. No. Least. Least best worse. Least never to be naught. Never to naught be brought. Never by naught be lulled. Unnullable least. Say that best worse. With leastening words say least best worse. For want of worser worst. Unlessenable least best worse.
>
> The twain. The hands. Held holding hands. That almost ring! As when first said on crippled hands the head. Crippled hands! They there then the words. Here now held holding. As when first said. Ununsaid when worse said. Away. Held holding hands! (*NO* 106)

In some ways these two paragraphs present the maximum compression of the major themes of *Worstward Ho*. We see here the manifest struggle with language, as such; we witness here, that is to say, the narrative attempting to find the appropriate language to express this state of being within a language that allows being to emerge at its disastrous limit. An idea is offered – 'less best', 'best worse' – as a way to characterise this state of things only to be denied: 'No'. The narrative reaches a moment of some compromise via the idea of 'least'. This is a text about the least possible and it is the least possible that persists as a kernel of resistance to the desire for absolute oblivion: 'Least never to be naught. Never by naught be brought' (*NO* 106). My sense is that this phrase – never to naught be brought – is a reflection on the language itself as a persistent entity as well as a statement about the uncanny persistence of the subject here in its posthuman, or post-posthuman, form. But it is the phrase in the second excerpted paragraph that should detain us: 'They there then the words.' Beckett has used the phrase before to describe the non-trajective movement of the man and boy: 'And yet say worst perhaps worst of all the old man and child. That shade as last worse seen. Left right left right barefoot unreceding on. *They then the words*' (*NO* 105). I wonder here how Beckett is asking us to read this line, to interpret this idea of the priority of the image over its entry into language. How do we make sense of the idea that somehow, in a text that explicitly suggests that everything is an effect of a locationless language, but still a language, as such, an image has priority over its mediation? And is it possible that this priority extends into the idea that the void and its inhabiting shades 'cannot go' because somehow it and they too have a kind of a priori existence that resists the decomposing effects of a disastrous language?

Perhaps the only way to understand these questions, to understand how a world and its subject exist, and persist, at the limits and frontier of a minimal language, is to return to, and here we must conclude, the idea of the disaster. Perhaps we can say this: for Beckett the true disaster is not the impossibility of expressing the event, nor the realisation that language can only ever approximate its object, can never fully express what it needs to express. Perhaps, for Beckett, the true disaster is that language, even in its disastrous form, can never move past the insistence of the image of the subject, an image that carries with it a world, however minimal, however depleted. The true disaster, in other words, and as the text itself understands, is that shades *cannot* go, the void cannot go, longing cannot go. Something precedes and exceeds language: *this* is the disaster. In the final moment of *Worstward Ho*, a resignation settles over the text, a realisation that despite the 'gnawing to be gone' (*NO* 113), the image remains. Here, as the text comes to its conclusion, Beckett returns to a word that has haunted his oeuvre for decades: 'Nothing'. Here the word speaks to the realisation of the narrative coming to the end of its expressive power, to the very limits of its language and world, and yet, somehow, the image persists. Beckett has said that he has nothing to say, and no power to express; he also says, in his 'Three Dialogues', that there is always already an obligation to express; there is something that must be said despite the impossibility of its saying; there is, in other words, something that precedes and exceeds discourse, its calling into being of a world and a subject. Beckett names it, or the compelling force to express it, 'obligation'. We might suggest, after Blanchot, that what must be said is the remains of the disaster which, here, in *Worstward Ho*, is the disaster; we might, after Heidegger, suggest that what must be expressed, what inevitably is expressed because it prioritises itself as something that *is* prior to everything, is care. Care is what orients the subject in the world; care is what allows Being to emerge in the world; care, in some fundamental way, is the world, and must, therefore, both precede and articulate the understanding of world. Care is the stubborn insistence of something that cannot be effaced or neutralised. Our task here in *Worstward Ho* is to try to negotiate an understanding of the absence of care and its persistence: care *is* and *is not* in this text; the world is and is not; the subject, both absent and present, flickers into being as care's affect phases in and out of possibility.

> Nothing to show a child and yet a child. A man and yet a man. Old and yet old. Nothing but ooze how nothing and yet. One bowed back yet an old man's. The other yet a child's. A small child's.
>
> Somehow again and all in stare again. (*NO* 115)

Somehow again. At the paradoxical bounds of a boundless void – and we must notice how Beckett in the penultimate paragraph of the text, returns insistently to an image of space – there is agonising persistence. If this is not movement, 'Said nohow on', it is still the affect of movement; if this is not space, it is the affect of space; if this is not world – 'in dimmost dim. Vasts apart' – it is an affect of world. This is an impossible, agonising world, but it is always, and still, a world.

Notes

1. In 'The *Company* Beckett Keeps', Enoch Brater argues that *Company* is about the human impulse to narrate despite the text's own determination to 'expose the limits and mechanisms of its own fictivity' (170).
2. In *A Guide to Heidegger's Being and Time*, Magda King argues that Heidegger's notion of world-building or world-forming can also be expressed as *world-imaging* (54).
3. See Daniel Katz's *Saying I No More* for a nuanced reading of the various economies of motion and trajectivity in *Company*; Katz's analysis of what he calls 'the parallelisms Beckett draws between discoursing, waking, thinking, and surviving' (160) is crucial to an understanding of the relation between world(s) and motion.
4. For a superb reading of *Company* and Blanchot (specifically Blanchot's notion of passivity), see chapter 4 of Christopher Langlois' *Samuel Beckett and the Terror of Literature*.

Fables of Posthuman Space   195

5. For an examination of Blanchot's fascination with the idea of neutrality, writing, and Beckett, see my 'Neutral Conditions: Blanchot, Beckett, and The Space of Writing'.
6. On this line, 'if only she could be pure figment', Catharina Wulf writes (assuming that the narrator is male): 'His wish to reduce her to a figment is not sufficient to stop the tale dedicated to her as a trace remains to suspend the final silence' (*The Imperative of Narration* 157).
7. I am interested in Yoshiki Tajiri's characterisation of the woman in *Samuel Beckett and the Prosthetic Body*: 'This is a totally "depthless" portrayal of human movement . . . the reduction to the purely mechanical enhances the impression of the woman's non-human quality' (137).
8. I admire Steven Connor's reading of the ending of *Ill Seen Ill Said*: 'At the end of *Ill Seen Ill Said*, for example, finality is held back momentarily to allow the imminence of the ending to be relished. The text ends by repeating the fact of death in advance, ends by not ending' (*Samuel Beckett: Repetition, Theory and Text* 10). Simon Critchley in *Very Little . . . Almost Nothing* ends his third chapter simply by citing the final words of *Ill Seen Ill Said* and then adding, as gloss, 'No happiness? No? No. Know' (212). Some trace of the human, in other words, remains in this attenuated imperative to know.
9. See my introduction to *Melancholy and the Archive*.
10. In 'Three Dialogues', Beckett argues that he must tarry with 'The expression that there is nothing to express, nothing with which to express, nothing from which to express, no power to express, no desire to express, together with the obligation to express' (139).
11. In her discussion of the opening lines of *Worstward Ho*, Susan Brienza comments on the narrator's use of the word 'on': 'In the next piece, *Worstward Ho*, "on" becomes a chant, a compulsion, a dirge' (*Samuel Beckett's New Worlds* 252). 'Dirge' is the perfect word to characterise the language of the disaster, this ruin of words.
12. Carla Locatelli's reading of *Worstward Ho* as an act of imperilled narration is important: 'I think that *Worstward Ho* constitutes a meditation on the role and structure of the signifier, or, to put it more simply, an investigation of the extent and structure of representation. In order to do so . . . the narrative movement deconstructs designation, and structural repetition corrodes semantic similarity' (*Unwording the World* 226).
13. Wittgenstein, *Tractatus Logico-Philosophicus*, 5.6: '*The limits of my language* mean the limits of my world' (56).
14. Heidegger at times conflates the terms 'care' (*Sorge*) and 'concern' (*Besorgen*): 'In contrast to these colloquial ontical significations, the expression "concern" will be used in this investigation as an

ontological term for an *existentiale*, and will designate the Being of a possible way of Being-in-the-world. This term has been chosen not because Dasein happens to be proximally and to a large extent "practical" and economic, but because the Being of Dasein itself is to be made visible as *care*' (*BT* 83–4).
15. On this question of care, concern, and world, see Irene McMullin's *Time and the Shared World*; McMullin's fascinating reading of Heidegger's care is oriented by the idea that care shows the subject how to 'be' in relation to others.

Conclusion: 'neither'

To and fro in shadow from inner to outershadow

from impenetrable self to impenetrable unself by way of neither

as between two lit refuges whose doors once neared gently close, once turned away from gently part again

beckoned back and forth and turned away

heedless of the way, intent on the one gleam or the other

unheard footfalls only sound

till at last halt for good, absent for good from self and other

then no sound

then gently light unfading on that unheeded neither

unspeakable home[1]

(CSP 258)

In the final sentence of my analysis of *Worstward Ho*, after reading the manifold complexities of being, subjectivity, and language, and after tracing those complexities into and out of the text's representation of spatiality, I was able, at least, and at last, to say this: 'if this is not space, it is the affect of space; if this is not world – "in dimmost dim. Vasts apart" – it is an affect of world. This is an impossible, agonising world, but it is always, and still, a world'. Beckett's second trilogy places particular pressures on our understanding of the subject, presenting it as enmeshed in a spectrality that cancels the viability of its own discursive production even as those productions insist on asserting limits. Even as the subject seems to fade into a space of being beyond subjectivity – this perhaps is the state that Blanchot refers to as 'subjectivity without any subject' – a trace of an affect of the subject, as such, remains: 'Nothing to show a child and yet a child . . . One bowed back and yet a man'. Even if these images in the dim void are only that, only images, the image still carries the potential to be a reminder of what was, even as the lost object – a child, a man, a memory of a past life – fails to achieve a hold on this groundless world. And even as these images fail to cohere, yet insist on bearing on this world *in* that incoherence, the language that transmits, or translates, that failure to cohere similarly marks itself as decentred, groundless, and yet uncannily insistent: 'On. Say one. Be said on'. Even if it is impossible to locate the source of this saying, or being said, even if we cannot posit as knowable the 'seat of all. Germ of all' (*NO* 91), we can still register traces of its disappearance: 'No future in this. Alas yes'. We are given a 'mere minimum. Mere most minimum' (*NO* 91), but it is, alas yes, still a minimum.

The second trilogy, in other words, while pressing the matter of spectrality, being, and space to a point where to speak of the 'human', as such, would make little philosophical sense, seems, at the very least – in the *space* of the very least – to refuse to relinquish the possibility of the forensic trace. We are, in other words, truly in the space of the 'post' in the second trilogy, the space of the 'after', the space that marks the end of the human and space. But in that marking, an affect of the human remains. It is as if perhaps, the second trilogy is a text deeply enmeshed, at a textual as well as philosophical level, in a melancholic admission that the human cannot, will not, ever be fully effaced. Any discursive act, it seems, must come from some source. The discursive act, of speaking or writing, signals, even as it works to efface its source, that as writing, as narrative, there is always already an agency at work, even, perhaps especially, if that agency instantiates itself – or is in its turn instantiated – as a spectrality. In some senses I imagine Beckett's late texts asking a series of questions: how can one write the subject out of writing? How can one record the disappearance of the subject? How does one register the space of that disappearance without reinscribing the subject, if only as a spectre? But for Beckett it is never a question of the 'if only'. The spectre is never a sign of the subject's absence: the spectre is a sign of the presence of the space of the after and, as such, a sign of a world. Language, even a spectralised language, is still the house of being.

I want to conclude this study of Beckett's posthuman spaces by offering a reading of his 1976 text, 'neither'. Specifically, I want to ask this enigmatic text these critical questions posed above: How does one record the disappearance of the subject? How does one register the space of that disappearance without reinscribing the subject? Because, at first glance at least, 'neither' would seem to offer itself as a text which successfully effaces the subject and presents what we may call the *affect* of its disappearance, rather than a registering of its sign or trace. One may be tempted, as I am here at the outset of my reading, to suggest that in 'neither' we have perhaps Beckett's only fully posthuman, that is to say, *subjectless*, text: there is no agent at work here, no traces of bodies, no spectres, no subject. We have, I would suggest, the subjectivity of the subject – that is to say, we have movement, directionality, deseverance, those markers of what Heidegger would have to call the human – but that subjectivity is not located in any subject. And yet, even as the text effaces the subject, even as an affect of subjectivity moves through abstraction – to and fro in shadow from inner to outershadow – metaphors of *knowable* spaces assert themselves with an uncanny insistence: refuges, doors, home. Our task here is to begin to make sense of the relation between this affect of subjectivity, this subjectivity without any subject, and these metaphors which threaten – and I use the word with caution – to ground that affect in a space, perhaps a world, that would consolidate and reconstitute the subject. Our task, in other words, is to test this text to see if we have yet another (complex) admission that a pure inscription of the absent subject is impossible.

Let me begin with a diversion, a digression back into Beckett's past. I want to cite, in full, his short poem 'my way is in the sand flowing'. Written and published in 1948, this short poem offers itself as a striking anticipation of 'neither'; specifically, we should notice the appeal to the space of thresholds and doors, the appeal, indeed, to a state of being beyond what Heidegger would call directionality and what Virilio would call trajectivity:

> my way is in the sand flowing
> between the shingle and the dune
> the summer rain rains on my life
> on me my life harrying fleeing
> to its beginning to its end
>
> my peace is there in the receding mist
> when I may cease from treading these long shifting thresholds
> and live the space of a door
> that opens and shuts
>
> (*Collected Poems* 59)

The poem instantiates itself as a series of appeals to states of being, or points of identification, beyond the speaker's own. It is not, I think, going too far to suggest that the overarching desire here is for the achievement of a state of being beyond the human. It is critical, of course, that what defines his state of being (human) is movement, is directionality, is trajectivity: 'the summer rain rains on my life/on me my life harrying fleeing/to its beginning to its end' (3–5). The speaker's life, his being, is defined by a harried directionality, an enforced movement that defines the shape of its totality, its beginning and its end. The desire here is to be beyond this harried opposition; the desire is, precisely, to find a way that is still framed by movement (movement, it seems, for the Beckettian subject, is impossible to avoid) but a movement beyond the merely human; his way, he suggests, is in the sand flowing; his peace, he says, is there in the receding mist. The desire here is for the speaker to cease, on his own, as his own subject, 'from treading these long shifting thresholds' (7–8). And this expression of a desire for movement beyond his own subject position is not, merely, a desire to locate a point of identification in the natural world: this is not a version of Keats' 'Ode to a Nightingale' with the forlorn subject orienting himself to the natural world.[2] The final figure of non-human movement here is the 'space of a door/that opens and shuts'. It is crucial that this image is an image, again, beyond the human; this is an identification with a space of a threshold (rejected in the line immediately preceding it) that does not 'shift', that is, move its position, but is in constant motion: 'and live the space of a door/that opens and shuts'.

'my way is in the sand flowing' thus figures the subject as projecting himself beyond a kind of enforced movement, a movement that would fix him within the boundaries of a limited being: the beginning and the end of life. It is curious that as the subject disperses himself into other states of being, in the sand flowing, in the receding mist, in the space of a door, he is still inscribed within movement and within a trajectory. Being, in other words, is still defined by motion within space: he is, after all, to 'live the space of a door/that opens and shuts'. 'Living the space', perhaps, is in one sense identical to being in the world; and being in the world, we should always remember, is what 'counts'.

'neither' is also, and obviously, about movement; it too is about a state of being, perhaps, beyond fixity, beyond human location. But unlike 'my way is in the sand flowing', 'neither' has no speaker or subject. If 'neither' is an expression of a desire, that desire is without location, without ground, without source. There is no 'my' and no 'me' in 'neither': there are no pronominal markers of subjectivity or subject (but there are the words 'self' and 'other', to which we will return). There is movement without subject, trajectivity without traject: 'neither' perhaps ultimately is about movement without movement, directionality without direction. Let me recall Heidegger here one final time. Heidegger's assertion that Dasein is spatial, that being in the world is essentially a learning to negotiate the spaces that define and delimit the subject, is grounded on his understanding that the subject, a priori, must learn to read the spaces into which she is thrown. Being is learning to read space. Being is a learning to locate oneself within space, and all that it contains. His terms, de-severance and directionality – closing distances between oneself and points in space; mapping out that distance *as* distance – are, essentially, metaphors for describing the activity of being, the activity of the subject compelled to be in the world:

> *Dasein is essentially de-severance – that is, it is spatial.* It cannot wander about within the current range of its de-severances; it can never do more than change them. Dasein is spatial in that it discovers space circumspectively, so that indeed it constantly comports itself de-severantly towards the entities thus spatially encountered. (*BT* 143)

That is to say, de-severance discloses world (as the encounter between self and other). Movement within space allows the subject to discover its relation to the other which *is* the world (this being Heidegger's assertion of what constitutes world in *The Fundamental Concepts of Metaphysics*).

De-severance, however, assumes a subject, requires a subject for its drive to a cartographic understanding of world to be realised. In other words, for Heidegger, de-severance assumes Dasein, a being-there, a *there* for Being, and a *Being* who is there. In the first lines of 'neither', no subject, no being as such, appears. What precedes all is rhythm, the rhythm of movement: to and fro. And this rhythm moves from within what is not exactly space, but colour, *itself* seemingly spatialised as inner and outer. And as we are invited to balance these spatialisations against the images of the impenetrable self and the impenetrable unself, we may be tempted to read these initial lines as offering to us an image of movement that is the only sign of being within a closed and calcified system of ruin. That is to say, it is not the self, closed to everything ('impenetrable') and it is not the unself, the remainder of that self that is, still, as closed as it precursor ('impenetrable'), that moves: something, *movement itself*, moves between inner and outer shadow, between self and its echoing remainder. But this is movement without agent, without subject. This, moreover, is movement, to and fro, from and to, that cancels even the possibility of what Heidegger would call directionality: movement moves 'by way' – yet another metaphor of trajectivity – 'of neither' self nor unself. The word *neither* here, signalling radically the annihilating economy of the neuter, places movement as such, at this point the only vestige, trace, of the human, within a space of radical unknowability. We have, thus, movement without agent; movement without directionality.

As if to signal an awareness of this radical undecidability, as if the text itself is aware of its own hermeneutical and ontological dilemma, 'neither' offers us, in its third and fourth lines, the first substantial metaphor to, perhaps, explicate this general economy of neutralised being. This condition of agency-less movement is metaphorised, placed within the logic of a simile that attempts to trope what is an unknowable into something at least recognisable. What is being offered here then? This idea of agency-less movement, this trace or cinder of being, this state of being within the mere minimum of being, is likened to the approach to doors that open and shut: 'as between two refuges whose doors once neared gently close,/once turned away from gently part again'. We might here recall the final lines of 'my way is in the sand flowing' where the speaker expresses the desire to 'live the space of a door/that opens and shuts'. Here we are given an image of the refuge, tropes perhaps of self and unself, of inner and outershadow. Now, as we understand that inner and outershadow, impenetrable self and unself, are tropes of home, we may begin to understand that 'neither' is offering an image of radical homelessness, of the radical homelessness of not quite a subject, but the affect of the subject: this is the homelessness not of a being but of the precondition for Being, for Dasein.

I imagine 'neither' as a transcription of the ontology of what we might call a partial subject. I use the term as a way of attempting to come to terms with how the text neutralises all signs and signposts of the human, of even the spectral subject. Neutralised to the point of disappearance, all that remains are absences of the subject that never was. This is not quite a condition of spectrality without spirit; this is a condition of the after without there having been a before. If there is a beckoning, a turning away, there has been no subject to have effected these actions. If there are footfalls, they are 'unheard' and moreover created by no one we can locate. And yet, for all this, we still are given movement, a beckoning without a beckoner, a turning away without one to turn away;[3] footfalls may be unheard (unheard as in ignored, not registered? Unheard as in to cancel what one has heard?) but footfalls remain. We have, as I have said, a mere minimum of an aspect of what constitutes, for Heidegger, the subject: movement. What constitutes the subject, as a totality, is his placement within the world, his ability to map and create that world, his ability to close the distance between self and other. World arises when the self finds himself within the knowable space of the other, within real space of connection and contact. Here, in 'neither' we have only a kind of reflex of movement, movement as reflex, a trace of what would allow a subject to realise his world for himself and his other.

And this movement as reflex, reflex as movement, located in no coherent subject, still is metaphorised by the text, still is, perhaps more accurately, anthropomorphised into a more approximate human being: it is beckoned, it is heedless; it either produces or attends (or fails to attend) to footfalls. This reflex of the affect of the human is, by the economy of metaphor, stitched into an approximate being, an approximation of being, until line 8 when we see what is perhaps a spectral glimmer of an uncanny desire, a desire, preceding and exceeding any knowable subject, that ultimately must neutralise itself: 'till at last halt for good, absent for good from self and other'. It is, of course, the phrase 'self and other' that must detain us here. We first, perhaps, are asked to map this phrase back onto the binary of inner and outer shadow, even the binary of impenetrable self and impenetrable unself; we are tempted, perhaps, to read 'neither', here, as an expression of a desire for the cessation of motion that would instantiate the end of world, as such. Because this is a halting of motion, *for good*, that is, forever. It is the relation between self and other, this minimal dyad, that constitutes the mere minimum of world, as Heidegger tells us. 'neither' may seem as distant from any world-building fiction as is possible, with its radicalised absence of subject, but this image of the self and other, even as it arises to be cancelled (*for good*), still has called into *being the possibility of world having been possible*.

And, of course, our task here is to ask about the minimal world-building narrative time at play here in 'neither'. That is, does the text present an image of an endless cycle of repetition of motion and cessation? Or is this instance, the instance of this 'neither', a discrete instantiation of the final achievement of the cessation of motion and world? This question achieves a kind of maximum pressure in the final lines of the text: 'Till at last halt for good, absent for good from self and other/then no sound/then gently light unfading on that unheeded neither/unspeakable home' ('neither' 8–11). This unspeakable home, this unheeded neither, is a neutral space where being steps past itself, and cancels the possibility of world, as such (no self and no other). The word 'unheeded', echoing as it does the phrase 'heedless of the way', allows us to figure the 'neither' as a space now no longer a space. This unspeakable home, the unheeded neither, is imperceptible, beyond discourse, beyond language, beyond time. The space of the neither, the neutral, the neither one thing nor another, is a space now only comprehensible as metaphor that is, in its turn, unknowable, because beyond language, as such. Because what is an 'unspeakable home'? Moreover, what is, or how does one understand, the image of the unspeakable home, the image that offers itself as a metaphor but a metaphor still material enough (real enough?) to be illuminated, forever, it seems: 'then gently light unfading on that unheeded neither'. That is to say, where are we, where does the reflex of motion stop, here at the final line in 'neither'? Is the cessation itself the achievement of a kind of uncanny homecoming? Has the oscillation of to and fro been the symptom of a kind of homelessness? Does 'neither' end in the space, which is not a space, of perfect nostalgia, a homecoming into non-being, a non-world where motion and space dissolve, endlessly, into mere perfect, and gentle, soundless illumination?

In some crucial ways Beckett is asking us here, in this final phrase – unspeakable home – to think about the metaphoricity of this metaphor of home. By this I simply mean that the line asks to be read as a metaphor for a kind of cessation of movement that is an achievement of a kind of non-being: here unspeakable home comes to stand, and I have argued this before, as a metaphor for a state of non-being that resembles Freud's notion of the uncanny return to nothingness that precedes and exceeds life.[4] Absent now forever – for good – from self and other means that world, as such, is no longer viable, and this is, in another sense of the word, all to the good. On the other hand, this image of the unspeakable home, as I have mentioned, maintains itself – and I use this phrase here carefully: *it* maintains itself: nothing, no subject or object, seems to be accountable for it – in a curious materiality: there is a light, a light that seems not to be easily assimilable to the logic of metaphor (the light seems to be real) that illuminates, unfading (for good?), the space of the unspeakable home. This space, in other words, is both real and imaginative, material and immaterial, simultaneously. And how, I ask finally, are we to attend to such an image? How can we assimilate this image to any horizon of understanding?

Perhaps we cannot. Perhaps what Beckett is offering here is an image of a space beyond subjectivity, beyond objectivity, beyond the logic of a world in which categories of self and other make sense, make sense enough to consolidate the subject, as subject, perhaps against its own wishes or interests. Perhaps this densely, unrelievedly, aporetic image – the unspeakable home – simply (but what a word) is an approximation of a state of being beyond being; perhaps, even, we might think of this impossible image as an approximation of the state of being, even, beyond the posthuman, being beyond the logics of traces, of partial objects, of spectres without spirit.

And yet: *home*. Such a resonant word. A word transposed into metaphor just as, perhaps, it threatens to transpose a free-floating affect of non-locatable, subjectless being into a space that would ground it on a horizon of understanding. Home, the echo and structural culmination of the 'two lit refuges', is, one might say, a metaphor that transcends and supersedes a passage beyond being. *Home still is*. And we should be interested in how Beckett's images of home and refuge are spaces of illumination: light at once confers on the image what I am calling a materiality – these spaces are real enough to be illuminated – and a kind of phenomenological persistence, perhaps insistence. These are metaphors that are *revealed*: as *phainomena*, they are revealed by an agency, a source itself not locatable, but still revealing itself in the showing. The refuge is lit; the home is revealed in its 'light unfading'. And it is in this state of having been revealed that the metaphor becomes something more than metaphor and the image becomes something more than mere image. I am reminded here of Bachelard's analysis of the phenomenology of the images of the house and home in *The Poetics of Space*; his sense that an image of home, metaphors of home, become more than words, more than tropes, as they enter into the space of the imagination, as *the word* in the space of the imagination, is crucial:

> But phenomenology of the imagination cannot be content with a reduction which would make of an image a subordinate means of expression: it demands, on the contrary, that images be lived directly, that they be taken as sudden events in life. When the image is new, the world is new. (47)

I am not, clearly, attempting to posit an organising imagination here in 'neither', nor am I positing, necessarily, a life or even a grounded world. I am interested, rather, in how this text, in its offering of an affect of movement and cessation, in its working out of a trajectory of subjectivity without subject, and as it works, perhaps, to *have offered* a phenomenology of absented subjectivity, transcribes a subjectivity from the margins, from within the economy of an image, a metaphor, that, in its materiality, in its revealed phenomenology, manages, if only barely, if only at a mere minimum, to offer a *possibility* of a world. Because this image of the 'unspeakable home' offered here, revealed here, even in its unknowability, is still revealed, still, in its way, is new. When the image is new, the world is new. And even if this world, this image of a world, has come to us from a neutralised margin, from what Beckett in *Texts for Nothing* calls the 'impossible voice' – a voice from the nowhere, from the neutral, from within the neutral – the world has still come to us, still gently *insists* on its unspeakability.

> What counts is to be in the world, the posture is immaterial, so long as one is on earth.

Notes

1. 'neither' was written for composer Morton Feldman in 1976 and was originally published in the *Journal of Beckett Studies* in 1979.
2. This despite Beckett's use of the word 'cease', which does recall Keats' specific, and perfect, use of the word in his ode to figure a gentle dying to this world: 'to cease upon the midnight with no pain'.

3. I am fascinated by Jeff Malpas' reading of Heidegger's use of the term *Winken* (beckoning) in 'A Dialogue on Language': hermeneutics, Malpas argues, is articulated as a beckoning, a hinting towards an event of revealing ('The Beckoning of Language' 212). What are the implications of a beckoning without a beckoner? A revealing without a revealer?
4. See my reading of Freud's death drive and 'neither' in *Beckett: A Guide for the Perplexed*.

References

Abbott, H. Porter, *Beckett Writing Beckett: The Author in the Autograph* (Ithaca, NY: Cornell University Press, 1996).

Abraham, Nicolas and Maria Torok, '"The Lost Object – Me": Notes on Endocryptic Identification', in Nicholas T. Rand (ed.), *The Shell and the Kernel* (Chicago: University of Chicago Press, 1994), 139–56.

Ackerley, C. J. and S. E. Gontarski (eds), *The Grove Companion to Samuel Beckett* (New York: Grove Press, 2004).

Agamben, Giorgio, *The Open: Man and Animal*, trans. Kevin Attell (Stanford: Stanford University Press, 2004).

Bachelard, Gaston, *The Poetics of Space*, trans. Maria Jolas (Boston: Beacon Press, 1964).

Badmington, Neil, *Alien Chic: Posthumanism and the Other Within* (London: Routledge, 2004).

Bair, Deirdre, *Samuel Beckett: A Biography* (New York: Summit Books, 1990).

Balzano, Wanda, 'Searching for Beckett's Real Worlds in *The Lost Ones*', *Journal of Beckett Studies* 11.1 (2001): 15–37.

Barker, Stephen, '*Qu'est-ce que c'est d'après* in Beckettian Time', in S. E. Gontarski and Anthony Uhlmann (eds), *Beckett after Beckett* (Gainesville: University of Florida Press, 2006), 98–115.

Beckett, Samuel, *Collected Poems* (London: Calder, 1986).

Beckett, Samuel, *The Complete Short Prose: 1929–1989*, ed. S. E. Gontarski (New York: Grove Press, 1995).

Beckett, Samuel, *Endgame* (New York: Grove Press, 1958).

Beckett, Samuel, *Fizzles* (New York: Grove Press, 1976).

Beckett, Samuel, 'German Letter of 1937', in *Disjecta: Miscellaneous Writings and a Dramatic Fragment*, ed. Ruby Cohn (London: John Calder, 1983).

Beckett, Samuel, *Nohow On: Company, Ill Seen Ill Said, Worstward Ho* (New York: Grove Press, 1996).

Beckett, Samuel, 'Three Dialogues', in *Disjecta: Miscellaneous Writings and a Dramatic Fragment*, ed. Ruby Cohn (London: John Calder, 1983).

Beckett, Samuel, *Three Novels: Molloy, Malone Dies, The Unnamable* (New York: Grove Press, 1958).

Bell, L. A. J., 'Between Ethics and Aesthetics: The Residual in Samuel Beckett's Minimalism', *Journal of Beckett Studies* 20.1 (2001): 32–53.

Berlant, Lauren, *Cruel Optimism* (Durham, NC: Duke University Press, 2011).

Blanchot, Maurice, 'From Dread to Language', in *The Gaze of Orpheus and Other Literary Essays*, ed. P. Adams Sitney, trans. Lydia Davis (Barrytown, NY: Station Hill, 1981), 3–20.

Blanchot, Maurice, *The Infinite Conversation*, trans. Susan Hanson (Minneapolis: University of Minnesota Press, 1993).

Blanchot, Maurice, 'Literature and the Right to Death', in *The Gaze of Orpheus and Other Literary Essays*, ed. P. Adams Sitney, trans. Lydia Davis (Barrytown, NY: Station Hill Press, 1981), 21–63.

Blanchot, Maurice, *The Space of Literature*, trans. Ann Smock (Lincoln: University of Nebraska Press, 1982).

Blanchot, Maurice, *The Step Not Beyond*, trans. Lycette Nelson (Albany, NY: State University of New York Press, 1992).

Blanchot, Maurice, *The Writing of the Disaster*, trans. Ann Smock (Lincoln: Nebraska University Press, 1995).

Borg, Ruben, 'Putting the Impossible to Work: Beckettian Afterlife and the Posthuman Future of Humanity', *Journal of Modern Literature* 35.4 (2012): 163–80.

Boulter, Jonathan, 'Archives of the End: Embodied History in Samuel Beckett's Plays', in Sean Kennedy and Katherine Weiss (eds), *Samuel Beckett: History, Memory, Archive* (New York: Palgrave, 2009), 129–49.

Boulter, Jonathan, *Beckett: A Guide for the Perplexed* (London: Continuum, 2008).

Boulter, Jonathan, 'Does Mourning Require a Subject? Samuel Beckett's *Texts for Nothing*', *Modern Fiction Studies* 50.2 (2004): 332–50.

Boulter, Jonathan, *Melancholy and the Archive* (London: Bloomsbury, 2011).

Boulter, Jonathan, 'Neutral Conditions: Blanchot, Beckett and the Space of Writing', in Christopher Langlois (ed.), *Understanding Blanchot, Understanding Modernism* (London: Bloomsbury, 2018), 203–18.

Boxall, Peter, 'Science, Technology, and the Posthuman', in David James (ed.), *The Cambridge Companion to British Fiction Since 1945* (Cambridge: Cambridge University Press, 2015), Online, 127–42.

Boxall, Peter, 'Still Stirrings: Beckett's Prose from *Texts for Nothing* to *Stirrings Still*', in Dirk Van Hulle (ed.), *The New Cambridge Companion to Samuel Beckett* (Cambridge: Cambridge University Press, 2015).

Brater, Enoch, 'The *Company* Beckett Keeps: The Shape of Memory and One Fablist's Decay of Lying', in Morris Beja, S. E. Gontarski and Pierre Astier (eds), *Samuel Beckett: Humanistic Perspectives* (Columbus: Ohio University Press, 1983), 157–71.

Brater, Enoch, *The Drama in the Text: Beckett's Late Fiction* (Oxford: Oxford University Press, 1994).

Brater, Enoch, 'Still/Beckett: The Essential and the Incidental', *Journal of Modern Literature* 6 (1977): 3–16.

Brienza, Susan D., *Samuel Beckett's New Worlds: Style in Metafiction* (Norman: University of Oklahoma Press, 1987).

Bryden, Mary (ed.), *Beckett and Animals* (Cambridge: Cambridge University Press, 2013).

Caruth, Cathy, *Unclaimed Experience* (Baltimore: Johns Hopkins University Press, 1996).

Catanzaro, Mary, 'No Way Out: The Effect of Surveillance in *The Lost Ones*', *Samuel Beckett Today/Aujourd'hui* 25 (2013): 183–96.

Chambers, Iain, *Culture after Humanism: History, Culture, Subjectivity* (London: Routledge, 2001).

Clarke, Bruce, *Posthuman Metamorphoses: Narrative and Systems* (New York: Fordham University Press, 2008).

Connor, Steven, 'Beckett's Atmospheres', in S. E. Gontarski and Anthony Uhlmann (eds), *Beckett after Beckett* (Gainesville: University of Florida Press, 2006), 52–65.

Connor, Steven, 'Making Flies Mean Something', in Mary Bryden (ed.), *Beckett and Animals* (Cambridge: Cambridge University Press, 2013).

Connor, Steven, '"On Such and Such a Day . . . In Such a World": Beckett's Radical Finitude', *Samuel Beckett Today/Aujourd'hui* 19 (2008): 35–50.

Connor, Steven, *Samuel Beckett: Repetition, Theory and Text* (Oxford: Blackwell, 1988).

Critchley, Simon, *Very Little . . . Almost Nothing: Death, Philosophy, Literature* (London: Routledge, 1997).

Davies, Paul, 'Strange Weather: Beckett from the Perspectives of Ecocriticism', in S. E. Gontarski and Anthony Uhlmann (eds), *Beckett after Beckett* (Gainesville: University of Florida Press, 2006), 66–78.

De Certeau, Michel, *The Practice of Everyday Life*, trans. Steven Rendall (Berkeley: University of California Press, 1984).

Deleuze, Gilles and Félix Guattari, *A Thousand Plateaus: Capitalism and Schizophrenia*, trans. Brian Massumi (Minneapolis: University of Minnesota Press, 1987).
Derrida, Jacques, *The Animal That Therefore I Am*, trans. David Wills (New York: Fordham University Press, 2008).
Derrida, Jacques, *Archive Fever*, trans. Eric Prenowitz (Chicago: University of Chicago Press, 1995).
Derrida, Jacques, *The Beast & the Sovereign, Volume II*, trans. Geoffrey Bennington (Chicago: University of Chicago Press, 2011).
Derrida, Jacques, *The Ear of the Other: Otobiography, Transference, Translation*, trans. Peggy Kamuf (Lincoln: University of Nebraska Press, 1985).
Derrida, Jacques, 'Geschlecht II: Heidegger's Hand', in *Deconstruction and Philosophy*, trans. John P. Leavey (Chicago: University of Chicago Press, 1989).
Derrida, Jacques, *Heidegger: The Question of Being and History*, trans. Geoffrey Bennington (Chicago: Chicago University Press, 2013).
Derrida, Jacques, 'Heidegger's Ear', in *Reading Heidegger: Commemoration*, trans. John P. Leavey (Bloomington: Indiana University Press, 1993), 163–218.
Derrida, Jacques, *Of Spirit: Heidegger and the Question*, trans. Geoffrey Bennington (Chicago: Chicago University Press, 1989).
Derrida, Jacques, *Specters of Marx: The State of the Debt, the Work of Mourning, and the New International*, trans. Peggy Kamuf (New York: Routledge, 1994).
Derrida, Jacques, *Speech and Phenomena and Other Essays on Husserl's Theory of Signs*, trans. David B. Allison (Evanston, IL: Northwestern University Press, 1973, 129–60.
Derrida, Jacques and Bernard Stiegler, *Echographies of Television: Filmed Interviews*, trans. Jennifer Bajorek (London: Polity Press, 2002).
Dowd, Garin, 'Figuring Zero in "The Lost Ones"', *Samuel Beckett Today/Aujourd'hui* 9 (2000): 67–80.
Dowd, Garin, 'The Proxemics of "neither"', *Samuel Beckett Today/Aujourd'hui* 24 (2012): 367–77.
Driver, Tom, 'Tom Driver in "Columbia University Forum", 1961', in L. Graver and R. Federman (eds), *Samuel Beckett: The Critical Heritage* (London: Routledge, 1979), 217–24.
Effinger, Elizabeth, 'Beckett's Posthuman: The Ontopology of *The Unnamable*', *Samuel Beckett Today/Aujourd'hui* 23 (2011): 369–81.
Eng, David and David Kazanjian (eds), *Loss: The Politics of Mourning* (Berkeley: University of California Press, 2003).

Freud, Sigmund, 'Beyond the Pleasure Principle', in Ann Richards (ed.), *The Penguin Freud Library, Volume 2* (London: Penguin, 1984), 269–338.
Freud, Sigmund, 'Mourning and Melancholia', in Ann Richards (ed.), *The Penguin Freud Library, Volume 2* (London: Penguin, 1984), 245–68.
Freud, Sigmund, 'Thoughts for the Times on War and Death', in *The Pelican Freud Library, Volume 12*, ed. James Strachey (London: Penguin, 1985), 57–89.
Gadamer, Hans-Georg, *Philosophical Hermeneutics*, trans. David E. Linge (Berkeley: University of California Press, 1977).
Gontarski, Stanley, 'Where Never Before: Beckett's Poetics of Elsewhere', *Samuel Beckett Today/Aujourd'hui* 21 (2009): 135–49.
Haraway, Donna, 'A Cyborg Manifesto: Science, Technology, and Socialist-Feminism in the Late Twentieth Century', in *Simians, Cyborgs, and Women: The Reinvention of Nature* (New York: Routledge, 1991), 149–81.
Haraway, Donna, 'The Human in a Post-Humanist Landscape', in *The Haraway Reader* (London: Routledge, 2004).
Haraway, Donna, *Modest_Witness@Second_Millennium* (New York: Routledge, 1997).
Haraway, Donna, *When Species Meet* (Minneapolis: University of Minnesota Press, 2008).
Harrison, Robert Pogue, *Forests: The Shadow of Civilization* (Chicago: University of Chicago Press, 1992).
Harvey, David, *Cosmopolitanism and the Geographies of Freedom* (New York: Columbia University Press, 2009).
Hayles, N. Katherine, *How We Became Posthuman* (Chicago: University of Chicago Press, 1999).
Heidegger, Martin, 'The Age of the World Picture', trans. Jerome Veith (Bloomington: Indiana University Press, 2009).
Heidegger, Martin, 'Art and Space', trans. Charles Seibert, *Man and World* 6.1 (1973): 3–8.
Heidegger, Martin, *Being and Time*, trans. John Macquarrie and Edward Robinson (New York: Harper, 1962).
Heidegger, Martin, 'Building Dwelling Thinking', in *Martin Heidegger: Basic Writings*, ed. David Farrell Krell (San Francisco: Harper, 1977), 319–39.
Heidegger, Martin, *The Fundamental Concepts of Metaphysics: World, Finitude, Solitude*, trans. William McNeill and Nicholas Walker (Bloomington: Indiana University Press, 1995).

Heidegger, Martin, *Introduction to Metaphysics*, trans. Gregory Fried and Richard Polt (New Haven, CT: Yale University Press, 2000).

Heidegger, Martin, 'Letter on Humanism', in *Martin Heidegger: Basic Writings*, ed. David Farrell Krell (San Francisco: Harper, 1977), 189–242.

Heidegger, Martin, 'The Origin of the Work of Art', in *Martin Heidegger: Basic Writings*, ed. David Farrell Krell (San Francisco: Harper, 1977), 149–87.

Heidegger, Martin, 'The Thing', in *Poetry, Language, Thought*, trans. Albert Hofstadter (New York: HarperCollins, 1971).

Hesla, David, *The Shape of Chaos: An Interpretation of the Art of Samuel Beckett* (Minneapolis: University of Minnesota Press, 1971).

Jones, David Houston, *Samuel Beckett and Testimony* (New York: Palgrave Macmillan, 2011).

Katz, Daniel, *Saying I No More* (Evanston, IL: Northwestern University Press, 1999).

Kendall-Morwick, Karalyn, 'Dogging the Subject: Samuel Beckett, Emmanuel Levinas, and Posthumanist Ethics', *Journal of Modern Literature* 36.3 (2003): 100–19.

Kenner, Hugh, *A Reader's Guide to Samuel Beckett* (London: Thames Press, 1973).

King, Magda, *A Guide to Heidegger's Being and Time* (Albany, NY: State University of New York Press, 2001).

Kochhar-Lindgren, Gray, *TechnoLogics: Ghosts, the Incalculable, and the Suspension of Animation* (Albany, NY: State University of New York Press, 2005).

Krell, David Farrell, *Ecstasy, Catastrophe: Heidegger from Being and Time to the Black Notebooks* (Albany, NY: State University of New York Press, 2015).

LaCapra, Dominick, *Writing History, Writing Trauma* (Baltimore: Johns Hopkins University Press, 2001).

Langlois, Christopher, *Samuel Beckett and the Terror of Literature* (Edinburgh: Edinburgh University Press, 2017).

Latour, Bruno, 'On Actor-Network Theory', *Soziale Welt* 47 (1996): 369–81.

Latour, Bruno, *We Have Never Been Modern*, trans. Catherine Porter (Cambridge, MA: Harvard University Press, 1993).

Laub, Dori and Shoshana Felman, *Testimony: Crises of Witnessing in Literature, Psychoanalysis and History* (London: Routledge, 1991).

Lefebvre, Henri, *The Production of Space*, trans. Donald Nicholson-Smith (Malden, MA: Blackwell Publishing, 1991).

Levinas, Emmanuel, *Otherwise Than Being or Beyond Essence*, trans. Alphonso Lingis (Pittsburgh: Duquesne University Press, 1998).

Levinas, Emmanuel, *Totality and Infinity*, trans. Alphonso Lingis (Pittsburgh: Duquesne University Press, 1969).

Leys, Ruth, *Trauma: A Genealogy* (Chicago: University of Chicago Press, 2000).

Libera, Antoni, '"The Lost Ones": A Myth of Human History and Destiny', in Morris Beja, S. E. Gontarski and Pierre Astier (eds), *Samuel Beckett: Humanistic Perspectives* (Columbus: Ohio State University Press, 1983).

Locatelli, Carla, *Unwording the World: Samuel Beckett's Prose Works after the Nobel Prize* (Philadelphia: University of Pennsylvania Press, 1990).

McLuhan, Marshall, *Understanding Media: The Extensions of Man* (Cambridge, MA: MIT Press, 1996).

McMullin, Irene, *Time and the Shared World: Heidegger on Social Relations* (Evanston, IL: Northwestern University Press, 2013).

Macpherson, C. B., *The Political Theory of Possessive Individualism* (Oxford: Clarendon Press, 1962).

Malpas, Jeff, 'The Beckoning of Language: Heidegger's Hermeneutic Transformation of Language', in Michael Bowler and Ingo Farin (eds), *Hermeneutical Heidegger* (Evanston, IL: Northwestern University Press, 2016), 203–21.

Malpas, Jeff, *Heidegger and the Thinking of Place: Explorations in the Topology of Being* (Cambridge, MA: MIT Press, 2012).

Malpas, Jeff, *Heidegger's Topology: Being, Place, World* (Cambridge, MA: MIT Press, 2006).

Matthews, Steven, 'Bodily Histories: Beckett and the Phenomenological Approach to the Other', in Ulrike Maude and Matthew Feldman (eds), *Beckett and Phenomenology* (London: Continuum, 2009).

Maude, Ulrike, *Beckett, Technology and the Body* (Cambridge: Cambridge University Press, 2009).

Maude, Ulrike, '"Whole Body Like Gone": Beckett and Technology', *Journal of Beckett Studies* 16.1–2 (2007): 150–60.

Merleau-Ponty, Maurice, *Phenomenology of Perception*, trans. Colin Smith (London: Routledge, 1962).

Moody, Alys, 'A Machine for Feeling: Ping's Posthuman Affect', *Journal of Beckett Studies* 26.1 (2017): 87–102.

Mori, Naoya, '"An Animal Inside": Beckett/Leibniz's Stone, Animal, Human and the Unborn', in Mary Bryden (ed.), *Beckett and Animals* (Cambridge: Cambridge University Press, 2013).

Morton, Timothy, *The Ecological Thought* (Cambridge, MA: Harvard University Press, 2012).

Mugerauer, Robert, *Heidegger and Homecoming: The Leitmotif in the Later Writings* (Toronto: University of Toronto Press, 2008).

Nenon, Thomas, '*Umwelt* in Husserl and Heidegger', in Michael Bowler and Ingo Farin (eds), *Hermeneutical Heidegger* (Evanston, IL: Northwestern University Press, 2016), 70–92.

Padrutt, Hanspeter, 'Heidegger and Ecology', in Ladelle McWhorter and Gail Stenstad (eds), *Heidegger and Earth: Essays in Environmental Philosophy* (Toronto: University of Toronto Press, 2009), 17–44.

Perloff, Marjorie, 'In Love with Hiding: Samuel Beckett's War', *The Iowa Review* 35.1 (2005): 76–103.

Perloff, Marjorie, *The Poetics of Indeterminacy: Rimbaud to Cage* (Princeton: Princeton University Press, 1981).

Pyyhtinen, Olli and Sakari Tamminen, 'We Have Never Been Only Human: Foucault and Latour on the Question of the *Anthropos*', *Anthropological Theory* 11.2 (2011): 135–52.

Rabate, Jean-Michel, *Think Pig! Beckett at the Limit of the Human* (New York: Fordham University Press, 2016).

Rabinovitz, Rubin, *Innovation in Samuel Beckett's Fiction* (Urbana: University of Illinois Press, 1992).

Saunders, Paul, 'Samuel Beckett's Trilogy and the Ecology of Negation', *Journal of Beckett Studies* 20.1 (2011): 54–77.

Schwab, Gabriele, *Imaginary Ethnographies: Literature, Culture, and Subjectivity* (New York: Columbia University Press, 2012).

Sharkey, Rodney, 'Beaufret, Beckett, and Heidegger: The Questions of Influence', *Samuel Beckett Today/Aujourd'hui* 22 (2010): 409–22.

Shaw, Joanne, 'The Figure in the Landscape in Jack Yeats and in Samuel Beckett', *Samuel Beckett Today/Aujourd'hui* 25 (2013): 31–43.

Sheehan, Paul, 'Posthuman Bodies', in David Hilman and Ulrike Maude (eds), *The Cambridge Companion to the Body in Literature* (Cambridge: Cambridge University Press, 2015), 245–60.

Sloterdijk, Peter, *Not Saved: Essays after Heidegger*, trans. Ian Alexander Moree and Christopher Turner (Cambridge: Polity Press, 2017).

Smith, Russell, 'Radical Sensibility in "The End"', *Journal of Beckett Studies* 26.1 (2017): 69–86.

Steiner, George, *Martin Heidegger* (Chicago: University of Chicago Press, 1989).

Stiegler, Bernard, *Technics and Time 1*, trans. Richard Beardsworth and George Collins (Stanford: Stanford University Press, 1998).

St. John Butler, Lance, *Samuel Beckett and the Meaning of Being: A Study in Ontological Parable* (London: Macmillan Press, 1984).

Tajiri, Yoshiki, 'Beckett, Coetzee and Animals', in Mary Bryden (ed.), *Beckett and Animals* (Cambridge: Cambridge University Press, 2013).

Tajiri, Yoshiki, *Samuel Beckett and the Prosthetic Body* (New York: Palgrave Macmillan, 2007).

Tonning, Erik, 'Beckett, Modernism and Christianity', in S. E. Gontarski (ed.), *The Edinburgh Companion to Samuel Beckett and the Arts* (Edinburgh: Edinburgh Press, 2014).

Tuan, Yi-Fu, *Space and Place: The Perspective of Experience* (Minneapolis: University of Minnesota Press, 1977).

Virilio, Paul, *Open Sky*, trans. Julie Rose (London: Verso, 1997).

Virilio, Paul, *Politics of the Very Worst*, trans. Michael Cavaliere (New York: Semiotext(e), 1999).

Wall, John, '"L'au-delà du dehors-dedans": Paradox, Space, and Movement in Beckett', *Samuel Beckett Today/Aujourd'hui* 24 (2012): 307–19.

Weisberg, David, *Chronicles of Disorder: Samuel Beckett and the Cultural Politics of the Modern Novel* (Albany, NY: State University of New York Press, 2000).

Weller, Shane, 'Beckett and Late Modernism', in Dirk Van Hulle (ed.), *The New Cambridge Companion to Samuel Beckett* (Cambridge: Cambridge University Press, 2015).

Weller, Shane, 'Phenomenologies of the Nothing: Democritus, Heidegger, Beckett', in Ulrike Maude and Matthew Feldman (eds), *Beckett and Phenomenology* (London: Continuum, 2009), 39–55.

Wills, David, *Prosthesis* (Stanford: Stanford University Press, 1995).

Wittgenstein, Ludwig, *Tractatus Logico-Philosophicus*, trans. D. F. Pears (London: Routledge, 1974).

Wolfe, Cary, *What Is Posthumanism?* (Minneapolis: University of Minnesota Press, 2010).

Wrathall, Mark, *Heidegger and Unconcealment: Truth, Language, and History* (Cambridge: Cambridge University Press, 2011).

Wulf, Catharina, *The Imperative of Narration: Beckett, Bernard, Schopenhauer, Lacan* (Brighton: Sussex University Press, 1997).

Index

References to notes are indicated by n.

A Thousand Plateaus
    (Deleuze and Guattari),
    76, 89
Abraham, Nicolas, 138, 139
absence, 60
Agamben, Giorgio, 17, 120–1
'Age of the World Picture,
    The' (Heidegger), 20, 27,
    30–1
All Strange Away (Beckett), 3,
    4, 20, 96, 98–109
animality, 16, 17, 26, 58–9,
    80–3
anxiety, 41–3, 102, 173–4,
    179–80
archive, 103–4, 105–6

Bachelard, Gaston, 161,
    205–6
Bair, Deirdre, 130–1
bare life, 120–1
Beaufret, Jean, 17, 36n16
Beckett, Samuel, 16–17,
    35n16, 50–1, 130–1
    and language, 180–1
    and narrative, 46–7

being, 63–5, 70–1, 74–6
    and Heidegger, 135–8,
        201
    and 'my way is in the sand
        flowing', 199–200
    see also non-being
Being and Time (Heidegger),
    16, 21, 23–4, 27, 135
    and space, 71–2
'Being Dwelling Thinking'
    (Heidegger), 22
being-there, 11–12
'Beyond the Pleasure
    Principle' (Freud), 132
Blanchot, Maurice, 4, 12–14,
    46, 181–3
    and neutral voice, 151,
        172, 177
    and post-traumatic subject,
        129–30, 133–5
    and writing, 146–7, 165–7,
        169–71
bodies, 6–7, 11, 12
    and *The Calmative*, 46
    and *Imagination Dead
        Imagine*, 108–9

bodies (*cont.*)
  and *The Lost Ones*, 111–12,
    114–15
  and *Texts for Nothing*,
    74, 78
boundaries, 120, 188–9
'Building Dwelling Thinking'
  (Heidegger), 55–7, 118

Calmative, The (Beckett), 2,
  3, 17, 45–55
  and throwness, 38, 39
care *see* concern
catastrophe, 109–10, 117–18;
  see also post-catastrophic
Chambers, Iain, 68
closed space fiction, 96–7;
  see also *All Strange Away*;
  Company; *Imagination
  Dead Imagine*; *Lessness*;
  Lost Ones, The*; *Ping*
community, 43–4, 45,
  164–5
Company (Beckett), 155–67
concern, 24–5, 28–9, 190–1,
  192, 193–4
consciousness, 7, 48
*Cosmopolitanism and the
  Geographies of Freedom*
  (Harvey), 18–19
cyborgs, 5–10, 34n7

darkness, 157–8
Dasein, 12, 23–5, 30
  and being, 136–8, 160,
    188, 201
  and concern, 190–1
  and de-severance, 72–3
  and space, 135
  and world, 56–7, 70

De Certeau, Michel, 164
de-severance, 23–4, 25, 61,
  72–4, 130, 136–7, 201
  and *Company*, 161–2
  and *Fizzles*, 143
death, 33, 46, 47, 173–5
Deleuze, Gilles, 4, 76, 89
Derrida, Jacques, 4, 10–12,
  34n8, 93n10, 100
  and archive, 102, 103–4,
    106, 111
  and mourning, 138–9
  and trace, 176–7, 179
desire, 74, 124–5, 191–2
despair, 125, 126
destruction, 34n2
diagrams, 106
'Differance' (Derrida),
  176–7
directionality, 23, 24, 25, 61,
  72–4, 137–8
  and *Company*, 161–2
  and *Fizzles*, 143, 149
  and 'my way is in the sand
    flowing', 200
disaster, 181–4, 193
disfiguration, 46–7
dispossessed, 17
distributed cognition, 5–6, 7,
  10, 87–8, 90
dreams, 139, 149
dwelling, 55–8, 117–19, 120;
  see also homelessness

Ear of the Other, The
  (Derrida), 138–9
earth, 35n13
ecology, 67, 76–7, 83–5
Emma (character), 101–2,
  106–7

End, The (Beckett), 2, 17, 38–9, 55–65
Endgame (Beckett), 11, 60
exclusion, 43–4, 45, 62–3
Expelled, The (Beckett), 2, 17, 38, 39–45
expulsion, 40–2, 148
eyes, 147–8

fabulation, 159, 160, 163, 165–7
faciality, 115–16, 147–8, 175–6
fantasy, 9–10, 86–7, 179
 and *Fizzles*, 138, 142, 143–6, 147–9
Faux Departs (Beckett), 98, 99–100
Fizzles (Beckett), 3, 4, 12
 and fantasy, 143–6, 147–9
 and post-traumatic subject, 129–30
 and publication, 130–1
 and self, 138, 139–42
 and space, 20, 100, 142–3
 and trajective movement, 19
 and trauma, 131–2, 133, 149–52
Freud, Sigmund, 104, 105, 126n6, 132–3
'From Dread to Language' (Blanchot), 165
Fundamental Concepts of Metaphysics, The (Heidegger), 16, 20, 27–8, 31

gazing, 115–16
Greek subject, 31
Guattari, Félix, 4, 76, 89

Haraway, Donna, 4, 7–9, 10, 34n6–7
Harvey, David, 18–20
haunting, 90, 99, 102–3
Hayles, Katherine, 4–6, 7, 10, 48, 87–8
Heidegger, Martin, 12, 15–17, 20–9
 and animality, 58–9, 80–3, 93n10
 and anxiety, 41–3
 and being, 135–8
 and boundaries, 120, 188–9
 and concern, 190–1, 192
 and Dasein, 135
 and de-severance, 72–3, 130
 and dwelling, 117, 118–19
 and ecology, 83–4
 and humanism, 30–3
 and movement, 201–2
 and place, 100
 and space, 71–2
 and thingness, 50–3
 and thrownness, 38, 39–40
 and world, 55–7, 69–71, 156–7, 159–60
history, 132–3, 152
home, 204–6
homelessness, 17, 29, 37n24
 and *The End*, 55, 57–8, 60–1
 and *The Expelled*, 41, 42, 43–5
How We Became Posthuman (Hayles), 87–8
humanism, 30–3, 160, 161
 and anxiety, 42–3
 and *Ill Seen Ill Said*, 174–5
 and space, 55–6

Ill Seen Ill Said (Beckett), 3, 20, 155–6, 167–80
imagination, 99, 101, 107, 159
Imagination Dead Imagine (Beckett), 3, 4, 11, 96–7, 98–109
Infinite Conversation, The (Blanchot), 169–70, 172

Kaun, Axel, 180
Kenner, Hugh, 9

language, 180–1, 184–5, 187, 189–90, 192–3
lastness, 114–15, 116
Latour, Bruno, 34n4, 97
Lefebvre, Henri, 18, 23
Lessness (Beckett), 3, 4, 11, 12, 96, 97, 116–26
Levinas, Emmanuel, 13, 134
'Literature and the Right to Death' (Blanchot), 146–7
loss, 41, 45, 85–6, 110–14
and *Fizzles*, 150, 151, 152
see also mourning
'Lost Object – Me, The' (Abraham and Torok), 138, 139
Lost Ones, The (Beckett), 3, 4, 96, 97, 109–16
and space, 20
and uncanny container, 11

Malone Dies (Beckett), 68
Malpas, Jeff, 100
man, 30–1
'Manifesto for Cyborgs, A' (Haraway), 7–9
melancholy, 105–6, 107, 145–7, 149, 152

memory, 6, 63–4, 138, 155, 157
and *All Strange Away*, 100–2, 104–6
and *Company*, 159, 161–4
and *Imagination Dead Imagine*, 107–8
and *Ping*, 119–20, 121–1
Merleau-Ponty, Maurice, 22–3, 77–8
motionlessness, 161
mourning, 101–2, 105, 106, 126n6
and *Fizzles*, 138, 139
and *Ill Seen Ill Said*, 155, 173
movement, 124–5, 130, 201–2
and *Fizzles*, 141–2, 144–5, 146, 148–9
and 'neither', 200–1, 203–4
'my way is in the sand flowing' (Beckett), 199–200

narrative, 46–50, 164–5, 169–71
and *Ill Seen Ill Said*, 167–9, 171–4, 178–80
and *Worstward Ho*, 184–7, 192–3
Nazism, 17
'neither' (Beckett), 198–9, 200–1, 202–6
neutral voice, 151, 172–3, 177, 184
non-being, 1, 9, 83, 91, 149–50, 204
now-ness, 49

Index   221

Of Spirit (Derrida), 34n8
'Origin of the Work of Art,
   The' (Heidegger), 28–9,
   51–2

passion, 115
perception, 77–8
*Phenomenology of
   Perception, The* (Merleau-
   Ponty), 77–8
Ping (Beckett), 96, 97,
   116–26
place, 99–100, 105, 164
Poetics of Space, The
   (Bachelard), 161, 205–6
positionlessness, 88–91
post-catastrophic, 2, 12–13,
   30, 97
post-traumatic subject,
   129–30, 139
posthuman, 1–10, 32–3
   and *The Calmative*,
      45–6, 48
   and catastrophe, 12–13
   and *The End*, 60–2
   and Hayles, 87–8
   and Heidegger, 25–6
   and 'neither', 198–9
   and space, 14–15, 17–18,
      109–10
   and spectre, 10–12
   and *Texts for Nothing*,
      67–9, 84–6
poverty of the world, 80, 83,
   85, 161
*Practice of Everyday Life,
   The* (de Certeau), 164
Production of Space, The
   (Lefebvre), 23
prosthesis, 48, 104, 106,
   126n5

reality, 92n8
refuge, 2, 11, 13, 38–9, 40,
   205–6
   and *Lessness*, 117, 122–4,
      125–6
relative space, 18–19
remembrance *see* memory;
   mourning
Robocop (character), 6
Robocop (film), 7
rotunda, 11, 107
ruin, 2, 11, 29, 110, 123,
   130

self, 13, 115–16, 138
   and *Fizzles*, 139–42, 144–6
sepulchral skull, 149
Six Million Dollar Man
   (character), 6
Six Million Dollar Man, The
   (film), 7
solitude, 63, 158–9, 167
space, 4, 9–10, 14–15, 60,
   198
   and *All Strange Away*,
      98–101, 102–3
   and *Company*, 157–8, 161
   and *The End*, 64–5
   and *Fizzles*, 130, 135,
      142–3
   and Harvey, 18–20
   and Heidegger, 15–16,
      21–5, 27, 55–6, 71–2,
      118–19, 188–9
   and *Imagination Dead
      Imagine*, 108
   and *Lessness*, 124–5
   and *The Lost Ones*, 111–12
   and narrative, 46–8
   and 'neither', 204–5
   and *Ping*, 117–18, 119–20

space (*cont.*)
　and posthuman, 17–18,
　　109–10
　and *Worstward Ho*, 155
　see also closed space fiction
Space of Literature, The
　(Blanchot), 165–6, 169
spacetime, 19
Specters of Marx (Derrida),
　10–11, 102
spectres, 10–12, 26, 198
　and *All Strange Away*,
　　102–3, 106
　and *Ill Seen Ill Said*, 174,
　　176, 177–8
Step Not Beyond, The
　(Blanchot), 151, 169
subjectivity without any
　subject, 13–14, 133–5

technology, 97
Texts for Nothing (Beckett),
　3, 4, 6, 9, 38
　and animality, 80–1, 82–3
　and desire, 14
　and homelessness, 17
　and positionlessness, 89–91
　and posthuman, 67–9
　and space, 71
　and time, 84–7
　and the world, 15, 16, 20,
　　26–7, 74–80
'Thing, The' (Heidegger),
　51–3
thingness, 50–3, 54
thrownness, 38–41, 45,
　58, 74
time, 79–80, 84–7, 89, 121–2

Torok, Maria, 138, 139
trace, 175–7, 178–80, 197–8
trajective movement, 19, 61,
　176
trauma, 130, 131–5, 139,
　149–52, 153n5
Tuan, Yi-Fu, 57, 100, 114

uncanny, 11, 25, 42
Unnamable, The (Beckett), 2,
　38, 68–9
unspeakable home, 204–5,
　206

Virilio, Paul, 19, 22, 34n5, 61

Whitehead, Alfred North, 19
world, 56–7, 59, 69–71,
　156–7
world-building, 159–60,
　161–2, 163–5, 166, 179
world, the, 15–16, 20–1,
　26–30
　and *The Calmative*, 50–1,
　　53–4
　and *The Lost Ones*, 113–14
　and 'neither', 203–4
　and poverty, 80, 83, 85
　and *Texts for Nothing*,
　　67–9, 74–80
　and *Worstward Ho*, 185–9
Worstward Ho (Beckett), 3,
　11, 12, 155–6, 180–94
wound, 14, 130, 134
writing *see* narrative
Writing of the Disaster, The
　(Blanchot), 12–14, 133–4,
　181–3

EU representative:
Easy Access System Europe
Mustamäe tee 50, 10621 Tallinn, Estonia
Gpsr.requests@easproject.com

www.ingramcontent.com/pod-product-compliance
Lightning Source LLC
Chambersburg PA
CBHW071449250426
43671CB00043B/2454